MULTICULTURAL LITERATURE FOR CHILDREN AND YOUNG ADULTS

A SELECTED LISTING OF BOOKS BY AND ABOUT PEOPLE OF COLOR

VOLUME TWO:
1991–1996

Ginny Moore Kruse
Kathleen T. Horning
Megan Schliesman

with
Tana Elias

Cooperative Children's Book Center
School of Education
University of Wisconsin–Madison

with
The Friends of the CCBC, Inc.
and
Wisconsin Department of Public Instruction

Cover and interior illustrations by Michael Bryant from the book *Bein' With You This Way* by W. Nikola-Lisa. Used by permission of Lee & Low Books and Michael Bryant. Copyright © 1994 by Michael Bryant.

Poem "All the Colors of the Race" by Arnold Adoff from the book *All the Colors of the Race* by Arnold Adoff. Used by permission of Lothrop, Lee & Shepard Books, a division of William Morrow and Company, Inc. Copyright © 1982 by Arnold Adoff.

First edition, first printing

0–931641–07–1

This publication is available from: **1)** Publication Sales, Wisconsin Department of Public Instruction, P.O. Box 7841, Madison, Wisconsin 53707–7841 USA (1–800–243–8782); and **2)** The Friends of the CCBC, Inc., P.O. Box 5288, Madison, Wisconsin 53705–0288 USA.

Funding for this publication, in part, has been provided through the Library Services and Construction Act, administered by the Wisconsin Department of Public Instruction, Division for Libraries and Community Learning. Other funding and support for this publication were provided by the Cooperative Children's Book Center of the School of Education of the University of Wisconsin–Madison and by the Friends of the CCBC, Inc.

Cooperative Children's Book Center
4290 Helen C. White Hall
600 N. Park St.
Madison, WI 53706
Phone: (608) 263–3720
Fax: (608) 262–4933
ccbcinfo@mail.soemadison.wisc.edu
http://www.soemadison.wisc.edu/ccbc/

All the colors of the race

All the colors of the race
are
      in my face, and just behind my face:
                behind my eyes:
    inside my head.

And inside my head, I give my self a place
    at the end of a long
           line   forming
              it self into a
                circle.

And I am holding out my hands.

—Arnold Adoff

CONTENTS

PREFACE

Selecting the Books

This annotated bibliography represents a careful selection of children's and young adult books with multicultural themes and topics which were published in the United States and Canada between 1991 and 1996. Most of these books first appeared in the *CCBC Choices* annotated bibliographies of recommended books published annually between 1991 and 1996. The books in these listings were evaluated, selected, and annotated by Kathleen T. Horning, Ginny Moore Kruse, Merri V. Lindgren (1991–1992), and Megan Schliesman (1993–1996).

Despite the seemingly wide range of books represented here, these titles are not all of the books with multicultural themes and topics published during this time. These books are those published between 1991 and 1996 that the CCBC recommends: high quality children's and young adult literature innovative in style, accurate in content, important in theme, and/or unusual in insight.

Creating the Publication

This second volume of *Multicultural Literature for Children and Young Adults* represents a continuation of the publication *Multicultural Literature for Children and Young Adults: A Selected Listing of Books by and about People of Color, Volume One: 1980–1990* (CCBC/DPI, 1991). The first volume grew out of a mutual commitment to multicultural literature on the part of the staff at the Cooperative Children's Book Center; the Friends of the CCBC, Inc.; former University of Wisconsin–Madison Chancellor Donna E. Shalala; former UW–Madison School of Education Dean John Palmer; and former State Superintendent of the Wisconsin Department of Public Instruction Herbert J. Grover. Barbara A. Bitters and Leslyn Shires of the Wisconsin Department of Public Instruction (DPI) were also instrumental in the publication of Volume One. The second volume is one expression of ongoing partnership and mutual commitment to multicultural literature. We particularly appreciate the leadership and support of Dean W. Charles Read of the UW–Madison School of Education; Larry Nix of the DPI Division for Libraries and Community Learning; and The Friends of the CCBC, Inc. We also deeply appreciate the ongoing support of our work as expressed in many ways by Dianne M. Hopkins, formerly of DPI and now a faculty member of the UW–Madison School of Library and Information Studies.

Volume Two follows the overall format of the first volume, with books arranged in 16 sections by theme or genre. Three appendices follow the annotated sections, providing further information about the books and book creators included in this publication, as well as a list of recommended resources about multicultural literature. This volume contains an index that provides full subject access to the recommended books, in addition to the authors and titles. Every effort has been made to use diacritical markings where applicable throughout the publication.

Finding the Books To Share with Children and Teenagers

Each book in this volume is cited in the specific edition or editions available when it was first published, usually a hardcover trade or library edition, as well as in its paperback edition if one was available as of April, 1997. A few of the titles are now out of print but may be republished in the same format or a different one in the near future.

Because prices as well as editions can and do change, price information is not included. The international standard book number (ISBN) is listed for each available edition of the book.

Individuals wanting to borrow any of these books from a public library, school library media center, academic children's literature collection, or through interlibrary loan will find the bibliographic information provided in this volume of use when making such a request.

Anyone wanting to buy one or more of these books for an agency or institution will be able to place an order with a book distributor using the bibliographic citation information presented here. Anyone wanting to buy a book for personal use or for a gift can inquire at a local bookstore. Even if a particular book is not in stock, a bookstore should be able to order it as long as it is still in print. Most libraries and bookstores have access to up-to-date information from either *Books in Print* or *Children's Books in Print* (R.R. Bowker), in which current edition information and prices are listed.

The Cooperative Children's Book Center does not loan or sell these books.

Addresses are provided for small publishers so that individuals interested in obtaining a small press book can easily contact the publisher and arrange to place an order directly, or inquire at a bookstore. If ordering from the publisher directly, plan on sending a check with the order. For bookstores, libraries, or schools wanting to secure books from small publishers via a book distributor, contact each publisher to inquire about distributor information. Include a self-addressed, stamped envelope along with any inquiry mailed directly to a small publisher.

Out-of-state residents wanting to obtain a copy of future editions of the annual publication *CCBC Choices* are urged to inquire early in the calendar year by mailing an inquiry and self-addressed stamped envelope to: Publications, Friends of the CCBC, Inc., P.O. Box 5288, Madison, WI 53705–0288, USA.

Additional copies of this publication are also available from the Friends of the CCBC, Inc., and from Publication Sales, Wisconsin Department of Public Instruction, P.O. Box 7841, Madison, Wisconsin 53707–7841, USA (1–800–243–8782).

Acknowledgments

We are indebted to the many colleagues who served as content specialists in evaluating one or more of the books in this volume and from whom we continue to gain insight. They include Susan Matoba Adler, Janice Beaudin, Alan Caldwell, Cathy Caldwell, Peggy Choy, Sandi Cornelius, Dorothy Davids, Frances de Usabel, Ruth Gudinas, Linda Kreft, Amy Ling, Caroline Majak, Fumiko Saito, and William L. Van Deburg.

We appreciate colleagues and friends from across the nation who continue to teach and challenge us with regard to multicultural literature. Our teachers, mentors, and guides on this subject are too numerous to name in entirety, but they include Mary Jo Aman, Rudine Sims Bishop, Pauletta B. Bracy, Malore Brown, Naomi Caldwell-Wood, Barbara Jones Clark, Eliza T. Dresang, Patricia Enciso, Carolyn Garnes, Graciela Italiano, Oralia Garza Cortes, Violet J. Harris, Julie Kline, Doris Seale, Beverly Slapin, Henrietta M. Smith, and Junko Yokota.

We are ever mindful of the earlier groundbreaking work of Mrs. Augusta Baker and Mrs. Barbara Rollock, formerly of New York Public Library, and Mrs. Charlemae Hill Rollins, of the Chicago Public Library. Their commitment to finding and writing about books that accurately reflected African-American life and history began at a time when the need for such books, though no less great than it is today, had not begun to enter the general consciousness of either the mainstream publishing industry or the nation as a whole. Today we continue to be inspired by this level of dedication to meeting the needs of all children and families.

We thank members of the CCBC student staff during 1991–1997; our University of Wisconsin–Madison colleagues, especially those in the School of Education and the School of Library and Information Studies; the members of the CCBC Advisory Board throughout the past six years; and the Friends of the CCBC, Inc., for what each individual and group contributed to the Cooperative Children's Book Center and/or to the creation and publication of Volume Two.

The assistance and support of publishers both large and small throughout the history of the Cooperative Children's Book Center has been vital to all who use this unique book examination center and research library for adults. The books provided to the CCBC for review and examination year after year make many dynamic dimensions of CCBC information service possible. Publisher interest in this bibliography is encouraging to us. We hope the visibility given here to specific excellent books will further encourage the publication of interesting, authentic, and accurate books for children and young adults containing what author Walter Dean Myers has termed "cultural substance."

We especially thank the people who write and illustrate books for the young. It is a privilege to discover and work with their books. We hope our understanding of their literary and artistic works conveys some of the vitality they express to the children and teenagers in whose service we all stand and hope to be effective.

Ginny Moore Kruse, Kathleen T. Horning and Megan Schliesman
May, 1997

INTRODUCTION

This publication grew out of the CCBC's longstanding commitment to promoting excellence and equity in literature for the young. During the 1980s, that commitment led to a growing awareness of the need for books that reflect and represent the lives of all children and culminated in the publication of *Multicultural Literature for Children and Young Adults: A Selected Listing of Books by and about People of Color, Volume One: 1980–1990* (CCBC/DPI, 1991). Many changes have taken place in the field of children's and young adult literature since the publication of Volume One. In our professional lives as readers and critics, we continue to learn from colleagues who share our interest in and concern for children growing up in our diverse society. We understand that issues of race and ethnicity are complex and multi-faceted. There are no easy answers and sometimes even the questions are difficult to voice. We strive to keep the lines of communication open, to be active as listeners as well as speakers.

Whenever we talk and listen to others on the subject of multicultural literature, questions about terminology and definitions nearly always arise. Even the use of the term *multicultural* is sometimes called into question. How do we define it? For our purposes, we use the term *multicultural literature* to refer to books by and about people of color: Africans, Afro-Caribbeans and African Americans; American Indians; Asians, Asian Pacific Peoples and Asian Americans; and Latinos. Inasmuch as possible, we use terms that have been chosen and/or are in general use by the people themselves, though we recognize there is not always agreement among individuals or within a group.

In the area of multicultural literature for children and young adults we have seen encouraging signs of growth in the first half of this decade. The most noticeable overall change is the increased visibility multicultural literature is receiving. Due to the demand from parents, teachers, librarians, and others concerned with children's books that mirror the diversity in our society at large, publishers and booksellers have placed multicultural literature front and center. On the one hand, it is good to see multicultural literature being promoted to the general public. On the other, this gives many people the impression that multicultural literature accounts for a larger proportion of children's books currently being published than it actually does. In reality, according to statistics kept at the Cooperative Children's Book Center, books by or about people of color amount to only 6 percent of the current overall whole. It is important to note that this percentage refers to books both **by or about** people of color, meaning, for example, that it includes books written about American Indians by non-Indians and books written by Asian Americans that have nothing obvious to do with specifics of Asian-American history, culture, or fictional characters. The statistics we are reporting here have been calculated without regard to quality, accuracy, authenticity, or authority. They simply document the small number of books being published in the United States for children and teenagers that are created by authors who are not white, as well as those created by white authors who choose to write about people of other racial backgrounds.

In Volume One of this publication, we paid a great deal of attention to books that we described as "inclusive," meaning that the paintings and photographs used to illustrate books and the choices made in poetry anthologies and collective biographies represented people from a range of ethnic and racial backgrounds. It seemed to us that these choices were the result of conscious efforts on the part of the authors, illustrators, and/or editors, who recognized that diversity enriches everyone. Over the years we have come to greatly appreciate the works of book creators such as George Ancona, Pat Cummings, Ruth Gordon, Sheila Hamanaka, Shirley Hughes, Susan Kuklin, Nancy Larrick, Naomi Shihab Nye, Vera B. Williams, and many others who make diversity such a natural part of the books they create for children and teenagers. We are happy to acknowledge that this sort of inclusiveness has become the norm in youth literature of all types, particularly picture books, poetry anthologies, and books of information.

One of the most encouraging signs we have seen in the 1990s is that, more and more, people of color are telling their own stories. A prime example of this is Lerner's ongoing series about contemporary Native children called "We Are Still Here." Not only do these books focus on individual Native children who are allowed to tell about an important aspect of their own lives, they also are written by Native peoples, most often from the same tribe as the child in the book. In addition, the books in this series are edited by two American Indian editors, specifically engaged by Lerner for this project. In addition to the "We Are Still Here" series, we have seen several other Native writers and artists join Joseph Bruchac in the children's book field, including Murv Jacob, Lenore and Polly Keeshig-Tobias, George Littlechild, Sandra de Coteau Orie, Ferguson Plain,

Erwin Printup, Jr., Gayle Ross, and Leo Yerxa. About half of these writers and artists have had their books published, at least initially, by small, independent presses, who remain strongest when it comes to authentic Native literature for youth. Native literature for children and young adults has also been greatly enriched over the past several years by the work of two Native writers who are well known as adult authors, Michael Dorris and Paula Gunn Allen, both of who became involved in one way or another with books for young people in the 1990s.

Within the context of authentic multicultural literature, we have seen the biggest growth in the area of Latino literature. At the beginning of this decade, it was almost possible to count these books on the fingers of one hand; however, in 1992 there was an enormous change in that we saw a sudden leap in numbers, seemingly overnight. Outstanding Latino writers and artists have quickly moved to the forefront of the children's book world since then, including Omar Casteñeda, David Diaz, Lucía González, Susan Guevara, Carmen Lomas Garza, Victor Martinez, Francisco X. Mora, Pat Mora, Judith Ortiz Cofer, and Enrique O. Sánchez. They join the ranks of well-established writers and artists such as Alma Flor Ada, George Ancona, Lyll Becerra de Jenkins, Robert Casilla, Lulu Delacre, Nicholasa Mohr, and Gary Soto, many of who were newcomers to youth literature when we published the first volume of *Multicultural Literature for Children and Young Adults*. Along with the flowering of Latino literature for children and teenagers, we are seeing an increasing number of bilingual (Spanish/English) and Spanish language books being published in the United States. In the first few years of this decade we have also seen the establishment of two awards for excellence in Latino literature for youth: The Américas Award (administered by the Center for Latin American Studies Programs of the University of Wisconsin–Milwaukee) and The Pura Belpré Award (administered by the American Library Association through REFORMA and the Association of Library Services to Children).

There has not been comparable growth, unfortunately, in literature for children and young adults by and about Asians, Asian Pacific Peoples and Asian Americans. This continues to be the most under-represented racial group in children's and young adult literature in the United States. Although the number of books by or about Asians, Asian Pacific Peoples and Asian Americans has increased slightly, most fall into the category of folklore, history, or historical fiction. Picture books featuring contemporary Asian-American children are the rarest type of multicultural literature available. Still, we are pleased to see that several Asian-American writers and artists have entered the field in the past several years, including Haemi Balgassi, Ina Chang, Karen Chinn, Sook Nyul Choi, Yumi Heo, Dom Lee, Huy Vuon Lee, Marie G. Lee, Ken Mochizuki, Kyoko Mori, Chris K. Sontpiet, and Clara Yen. They and others join Laurence Yep's long-term commitment to writing for the young. We hope to see a flowering of Asian-American children's literature by the close of the 20th century.

In Volume One we noted that the overall number of books created by African and African-American authors and artists dropped in the first half of the 1980s, after a decade of growth throughout the 1970s. By the mid–1980s, we began to see a reversal and the number of books by and about Africans and African Americans began to increase, rising from 18 books in 1985 and again in 1986 to 51 books by 1990. Book creators established during the 1970s, such as Ashley Bryan, Lucille Clifton, Pat Cummings, Tom Feelings, Eloise Greenfield, Virginia Hamilton, Julius Lester, Walter Dean Myers, Jerry Pinkney, and Mildred Taylor, were joined by many newcomers to the field. Book creators entering the field during the last few years of the 1980s included Candy Dawson Boyd, Floyd Cooper, Jan Spivey Gilchrist, Cheryl and Wade Hudson, Angela Johnson, Brian Pinkney, Glennette Tilley Turner, Rita Williams-Garcia, and Jacqueline Woodson. This trend continued into the 1990s with the first published works of Michael Bryant, Nina Crews, Christopher Paul Curtis, Sharon Draper, Angela Shelf Medearis, Andrea Davis Pinkney, and James Ransome among many others. In addition, established authors and artists for adults such as Maya Angelou, Jacob Lawrence, and Faith Ringgold have turned their considerable talents toward creating books for young people in the 1990s.

In compiling the second volume of *Multicultural Literature for Children and Young Adults* we carefully considered books that were written or illustrated by people of color; we also looked carefully at books written or illustrated by individuals whose racial backgrounds are outside those of the experiences depicted in their books. We paid careful attention to issues of accuracy and authenticity, often seeking the opinions of content specialists when we were unsure about a certain historical or cultural matter, as well as listening to colleagues who pointed out significant features or cultural values that we, as outsiders, would otherwise have missed.

Our commitment to equity and excellence in literature for the young is sustained by the knowledge that it is essential for children of all races and ethnicities to find books in which they will see a wide variety of accurate portrayals of their own diverse cultures, histories, and everyday lives.

BOOKS FOR BABIES AND TODDLERS

Bang, Molly. *Yellow Ball.* Morrow, 1991. 24 pages. (0–688–06314–4) (lib. bdg. 0–688–06315–2) (pbk. 0–14–054828–9; Puffin, 1993)

Three beach-goers interrupt a game of catch to build a sand castle on a busy sandy stretch. Two individuals are African American, one being toddler-sized. The third person involved is a white female. Their ages and roles are as open to interpretation as the rest of the events in this stunning book bearing large ideas and few words: "Catch . . . Throw . . . Uh-oh . . ." Although the people in the book don't notice, young readers will see the big yellow ball as it is carried away on the tide and begins a long journey out to sea. Bang's dazzling full-color pastel paintings tell most of the story as they trace the progress of the ball, over dolphins and under sea gulls, beyond a bridge and through a night storm, before it is washed ashore on a different beach and into the open arms of another brown-skinned child. (Ages 1–3)

Bunting, Eve. *Flower Garden.* Illustrated by Kathryn Hewitt. Harcourt Brace, 1994. 32 pages. (0–15–228776–0)

A pleasant, lilting text describes the shopping expedition of a brown-skinned toddler and her dad who are planning a special surprise for mom's birthday. The shifting perspectives of the brightly colored gouache paintings add to the sense of anticipation felt by all involved in the preparations for a celebration. (Ages 2–4)

Burton, Marilee Robin. *My Best Shoes.* Illustrated by James E. Ransome. Tambourine, 1994. 28 pages. (0–688–11757–0) (lib. bdg. 0–688–11756–2)

A multi-racial cast of children participates in a rhyming romp through the days of the week, with each child citing his or her favorite pair of shoes to wear on a particular day for a particular purpose: tap shoes for dance class on Tuesday, old shoes for a trip to a farm on Thursday, sandals for a Saturday at the beach, and so on. The story concludes with a surprise: a tribute to the very best pair of shoes of all, according to children: bare feet! (Ages 2–5)

Fleming, Denise. *In the Small, Small Pond.* Henry Holt, 1993. 32 pages. (0–8050–2264–3)

"In the small, small pond / wiggle, jiggle, tadpoles wriggle / waddle, wade, geese parade . . ." There's a lot of activity in and around the small pond, beginning with a child of Asian heritage at water's edge who's trying to catch a frog. Each page follows the pattern of offering two deliciously onomatopoeic words followed by a single critter's corresponding activity. The words truly become part of the visual story as well, as large typeface playfully bounces around the page, echoing the activity it describes. Larger-than-life paintings, filled with color and energy and humor, extend and enhance the sense of life and wonder in an underwater world. (Ages 18 months–3 years)

Fleming, Denise. *In the Tall, Tall Grass.* Henry Holt, 1991. 32 pages. (0–8050–1635-X) (pbk. 0–8050–3941–4, 1993)

As a small child of Asian heritage inspects the busy world "in the tall, tall grass," she observes "crunch, munch, caterpillars lunch / dart, dip, hummingbirds sip" and a host of other insects, birds, reptiles, and rodents going about their business. Bold, brightly colored illustrations and a tight, well-chosen text of few words make this an ideal read-aloud. (Ages 2–5)

Greenfield, Eloise. *Big Friend, Little Friend.* Illustrated by Jan Spivey Gilchrist. Black Butterfly/Writers and Readers (Box 461, Village Station, New York, NY 10014), 1991. 10 pages. (0–86316–204–5)

Greenfield, Eloise. *Daddy and I . . .* Illustrated by Jan Spivey Gilchrist. Black Butterfly/Writers and Readers, 1991. 10 pages. (0–86316–206–1)

Greenfield, Eloise. *I Make Music.* Illustrated by Jan Spivey Gilchrist. Black Butterfly/Writers and Readers, 1991. 10 pages. (0–86316–205–3)

Greenfield, Eloise. *My Doll, Keisha.* Illustrated by Jan Spivey Gilchrist. Black Butterfly/Writers and Readers, 1991. 10 pages. (0–86316–203–7, out of print)

Four board books feature day-to-day activities of young African-American children, described in brief, first-person narratives. *Big Friend, Little Friend* compares and contrasts the ways in which a small boy plays and interacts with a friend who is older than he and a friend who is younger. *Daddy and I . . .* recounts the many things a young boy and his dad do together. In *I Make Music* a little girl describes a variety of ways she makes music, from playing a toy xylophone to tapping her leg. Another little girl talks about playing with her doll and with her friend David in *My Doll, Keshia.* Simple, patterned texts, child-centered concerns, and clear, boldly colored illustrations make these books appealing to the youngest listeners. (Ages 1–3)

Greenfield, Eloise. *On My Horse.* Illustrated by Jan Spivey Gilchrist. (Let's Read Aloud) HarperFestival, 1995. (0–694–00583–5)

A young African-American boy enjoys his weekly ride at the horse park, pretending to be riding alone ". . . My horse and I are free, / we see a wide, wide grassy space. / We race . . . I laugh loud. / On my horse / I laugh." Happy moments of freedom, of imagination, and of accomplishment for a child are celebrated in this joyful, short book with durable pages intended to be turned by many small hands and read by newly independent young readers. (Ages 2–7)

Greenfield, Eloise. *Sweet Baby Coming.* Illustrated by Jan Spivey Gilchrist. HarperFestival/HarperCollins, 1994. 12 pages. (0–694–00578–9)

An African-American family looks forward to the arrival of a new baby in this board book written from the point of view of their young daughter who appears to be about two years old. Greenfield's simple verses capture the sense of excitement, curiosity and, yes, a bit of trepidation on the part of the soon-to-be older sister. (Ages 6 months–2 years)

Greenfield, Monica. *The Baby.* Illustrated by Jan Spivey Gilchrist. HarperFestival/HarperCollins, 1994. 12 pages. (0–694–00577–0)

A straightforward account of a baby's repertoire ("The baby kicks / cries / sleeps / eats / yawns / stretches / eats again . . .") is accompanied by engaging watercolor illustrations of an African-American mother and child. (Ages 6 months–2 years)

Heo, Yumi. *One Afternoon.* Orchard, 1994. 32 pages. (0–531–06845–5) (lib. bdg. 0–531–08695–X)

Minho accompanies his mother on her errands through noisy city streets ("honk / honk / denga / denga") as she stops at the laundromat ("tump-thud / tump-thud"), the beauty parlor ("snip / snip / snip"), the ice cream store ("reeeeeeee"), the pet store ("wuf /wuf / tweedle / wuf"), the shoe repair store ("whurra / whurra"), and the supermarket ("kaching! / clink / clink") before returning to a comparatively quiet home ("plink!"). Yumi Heo's mixed-media illustrations use collage and oil painting to capture the hubbub of an urban routine, experienced through the eyes (and ears) of a small child. While this Korean-American artist's style is uniquely modern, Heo's text is comfortably traditional and child-centered, reminiscent of Margaret Wise Brown. (Ages 2–4)

Hudson, Cheryl Willis. *Animal Sounds for Baby.* Illustrated by George Ford. (What a Baby Board Books) Cartwheel/Scholastic, 1995. 10 pages. (0–590–48029–4)

Hudson, Cheryl Willis. *Let's Count Baby.* Illustrated by George Ford. (What a Baby Board Books) Cartwheel/Scholastic, 1995. 10 pages. (0–590–48028–6)

In *Let's Count Baby* a little girl points out familiar objects in her bedroom, including a teddy bear, toy trucks, stars on a mobile, and building blocks, as she counts from one to ten. A visit to a farm inspires a little boy to make sounds for the familiar animals he sees: cow, cat, chicken, horse, etc., in *Animal Sounds for Baby*. Both books are written with a short rhyming text which will please the smallest listeners and encourage them to participate in the story. (Ages 9 months–2 years)

Hudson, Cheryl Willis. *Good Morning Baby.* Illustrated by George Ford. Cartwheel/Scholastic, 1992. 10 pages. (0–590–45918–7, 1997)

Hudson, Cheryl Willis. *Good Night Baby.* Illustrated by George Ford. Cartwheel/Scholastic, 1992. 10 pages. (0–590–45761–6)

A pair of board books featuring African-American toddlers frame the day with gentle rhyming texts that describe typical activities at the beginning of the day (getting dressed, eating breakfast) and at bedtime (taking a bath, reading a story). A girl and her father are pictured in the full-color illustrations in *Good Morning Baby* and a boy and his mother are shown in *Good Night Baby*. (Ages 9 months–2 years)

Hutchins, Pat. *My Best Friend.* U.S. edition: Greenwillow, 1993. 32 pages. (0–688–11486–5) (lib. bdg. 0–688–11485–7)

The young child narrator admires her best friend for all the things she can do well—run fast, climb high, jump far, and even eat spaghetti with a fork. But when this impressive individual accepts an invitation to a sleep-over, she surprises her host by seeing monsters where there are only curtains blowing in the breeze. Brightly colored, stylized illustrations depict the best friend who-can-do-no-wrong as being just a little bit older than her young devotee, making the story's resolution all the more satisfying for young readers. Both of the young friends are Black. (Ages 2–4)

Hutchins, Pat. *Titch and Daisy.* Greenwillow, 1996. 32 pages. (0–688–13960–4) (lib. bdg. 0–688–13959–0)

Titch is reluctant about attending a friend's birthday party on his own until his mother assures him that his best friend Daisy will be there. When he gets to the party, however, he can't join in any of the fun because Daisy's not there after all. Ah, but she is! Young readers will be quick to pick her out hiding on every page because, like Titch, she's a bit shy herself. Daisy is a brown-skinned child. Titch is white. Children at the party are from diverse racial backgrounds. (Ages 2–4)

Johnson, Angela. *Joshua by the Sea.* Illustrated by Rhonda Mitchell. Orchard, 1994. 10 pages. (0–531–06846–3)

A small but self-confident African-American boy recounts the events of a quiet day at the seaside. Within the confines of a small, square board book, artist Rhonda Mitchell remarkably manages to capture the immensity of the ocean and Joshua's sense of wonder in its presence. (Ages 2–4)

Johnson, Angela. *Joshua's Night Whispers.* Illustrated by Rhonda Mitchell. Orchard, 1994. 10 pages. (0–531–06847–1)

The same small boy featured in *Joshua by the Sea* is a little less confident at bedtime, when the wind brings night whispers into his bedroom. But self-reliant Joshua knows just what to do: go down the hallway to find Daddy so that they can listen to the night whispers together. (Ages 2–4)

Lee, Hector Viveros. *I Had a Hippopotamus.* Lee & Low (95 Madison Ave., New York, NY 10016), 1996. 32 pages. (1–880000–28–8)

A box of *galletas* (animal crackers) inspires numerous acts of creative generosity on the part of one small boy who imagines all the animals as living creatures that he gives as gifts to friends and family. Hector Viveros Lee's stylized paintings provide exactly the right blend of fantasy and reality. Although the story is universal in its patterned playfulness, small details throughout mark the characters and setting as distinctively Latino. (Ages 2–5)

Narahashi, Keiko. *Is That Josie?* Margaret K. McElderry, 1994. 27 pages. (0–689–50606–6)

From the time she awakens in the morning to the time she goes to bed at night, a small Asian-American girl imagines all the everyday activities of an ordinary human girl to be the comparable everyday actions of various animals: Josie's thumping down the stairs becomes a kangaroo hopping, for example, and her evening bathing becomes a dolphin diving. Watercolor paintings show an energetic child accompanied by the pictures she has inside her head. (Ages 2–4)

Reid, Rob. *Wave Goodbye.* Illustrated by Lorraine Williams. Lee & Low (95 Madison Ave, New York, NY 10016), 1996. 24 pages. (1–880000–30–X)

Reid, a librarian, traditionally ends his storytimes with a humorous rhyme that encourages children to wave goodbye from the tips of their toes to the ends of the hairs on their head. Over the years, he has gotten many requests for a written version of his famous farewell—now we are lucky to have it in a picture book version, illustrated with brightly colored paintings showing a diverse group of children waving goodbye at a birthday party. Young listeners will enjoy demonstrating their own methods for waving their elbows, eyes, ears, knees, and hair when you read this one aloud. (Ages 2–5)

Roe, Eileen. *Con Mi Hermano = With My Brother.* Illustrated by Robert Casilla. Bradbury, 1991. 32 pages. (0–02–777373–6) (pbk. 0–689–71855–1; Aladdin, 1994)

A preschool-aged Latino boy describes all the things he admires about his teenaged brother who rides a bus to school, has a paper route, and plays on a baseball team. The younger brother looks forward to a time when he'll be big enough to do all those things, too, but in the meantime he enjoys the time he and his big brother spend together wrestling, playing catch, and reading stories. The simple patterned text, in English and Spanish, is accompanied by realistic full-page watercolor paintings. (Ages 3–6)

Scott, Ann Herbert. *Hi.* Illustrated by Glo Coalson. Philomel, 1994. 32 pages. (0–399–21964–1)

Waiting in line with her mother at the post office, little Margarita greets every stranger who passes by, only to be ignored. By the time she reaches the front of the line, she has become so dejected that she doesn't even hazard a smile at the postal clerk, so she is pleasantly surprised when the postal clerk greets her first! Glo Coalson's watercolor paintings aptly capture a Latina toddler's many moods, expressed through body postures and facial expressions. (Ages 2–4)

CONCEPT BOOKS

Greenfield, Eloise. *Aaron and Gayla's Counting Book.* Illustrated by Jan Spivey Gilchrist. Black Butterfly/Writers and Readers (Box 461, Village Station, New York, NY 10014), 1993. 24 pages. (0–86316–209–6) (pbk. 0–86316–214–2, 1993)

Two young African-American children don shiny raincoats and boots and venture out into a wet spring day in this activity book that invites children to count from one to twenty. Among the things Aaron and Gayla encounter on their walk to their neighborhood park are "Seven people walking fast . . . Nine puddles to splash in . . . Ten wet tulips . . ." and "Nineteen children looking at the sky." A counting poem at the end of the book celebrates the joy of splashing through a rainstorm, and the skill of counting from one all the way to twenty! Another book of note is *Aaron and Gayla's Alphabet Book* (Black Butterfly/Writers and Readers, 1992), by the same author and illustrator. Eloise Greenfield's simple text is perfectly matched by Jan Spivey Gilchrist's clean-lined, colorful art. (Ages 3–5)

Grimes, Nikki. *C Is for City.* Illustrated by Pat Cummings. Lothrop, Lee & Shepard, 1995. 40 pages. (0–688–11808–9) (lib. bdg. 0–688–11809–7)

Rhyming verses for each letter of the alphabet celebrate the sights and sounds of a lively Manhattan neighborhood with residents of diverse racial backgrounds. Pat Cummings's shimmering color illustrations extend the text even further by adding several objects for children to identify in each picture. At the end of the book, she has provided an alphabetical key which lists the illustrated objects corresponding to each letter, right down to the names of typefaces she has used (**A**irkraft, **B**enguiat, **C**ooper Black, etc.), which also go in corresponding alpabetical order. (Ages 3–6)

Martin, Mary Jane. *From Anne to Zach.* Illustrated by Michael Grejniec. Boyds Mills, 1996. 40 pages. (1–56397–573–4)

"A my name is Anne / B my name is Barry / C my name's Carlota / And my dog is hairy. Very! . . ." So begins a rhyming romp through the alphabet with active, mostly brown-skinned children telling their names. Every third child adds a little something extra for good measure. Zach's claim to fame is that he can write the entire alphabet so that the book concludes with a satisfying reprise of the famous 26. (Ages 3–6)

Miller, Margaret. *Now I'm Big.* Greenwillow, 1996. 32 pages. (lib. bdg. 0–688–14078–5)

Clear, attractive color photographs show six ethnically diverse kindergartners as they are today and as they each were as babies to contrast the things they have each learned to do by themselves: riding bikes, getting dressed, drinking from a glass, cleaning up after themselves, etc. (Ages 4–6)

Serfozo, Mary. *What's What? A Guessing Game.* Illustrated by Keiko Narahashi. Margaret K. McElderry, 1996. 32 pages. (0–689–80653–1)

Two African-American children ask—and answer—a series of questions about opposites: What's hard/soft, cold/warm, wet/dry, long/short, light/dark, before posing the real puzzler: What is all these things at once? The surprising answer provides this delightfully original concept book with a satisfying, child-like conclusion. (Ages 2–5)

Spinelli, Eileen. *If You Want to Find Golden.* Illustrated by Stacey Schuett. Albert Whitman, 1994. 32 pages. (lib. bdg. 0–8075–3585–0)

Expertly composed acrylic and pastel paintings illustrate an imaginative color concept book in which a brown-skinned young boy and his mother look for objects of particular hues in the busy streets of their diversely populated urban neighborhood. From the bright blue mailbox to the steely gray pigeons, mother and son find every color of the rainbow because they know exactly where to look. (Ages 3–5)

Tapahonso, Luci and Eleanor Schick. *Navajo ABC: A Diné Alphabet.* Illustrated by Eleanor Schick. Simon & Schuster, 1995. 32 pages. (0–689–80316–8)

A singular alphabet book ties each letter of the alphabet to an item, object or relationship important in the Diné, or Navajo, culture. Most letters of the alphabet are represented by an English-language word, such as **G**randma and **T**urquoise, but some are represented by a Diné word, such as **H**ooghan (home) and **K**éyah (land). A glossary at the back of the book provides the corresponding Diné or English word for each representation and briefly explains the significance of each in the Diné culture. The full-page illustrations rendered in colored pencil are washed with Southwest light. A Foreword provides brief information about the Diné people and language. (Ages 4–8)

PICTURE BOOKS

Adoff, Arnold. *Hard to Be Six.* Illustrated by Cheryl Hanna. Lothrop, Lee & Shepard, 1991. 32 pages. (lib. bdg. 0–688–09013–3)

"Hard to be six / when your sister is ten. / There are things she can do that / must wait until then: when i am / seven or eight, nine or ten. / Hard to be six until then . . ." Adoff's poems about the ups and downs of a typical six-year-old who can't wait to grow up are marvelously illustrated with full-color paintings which show the six-year-old and his sister as biracial children with a white father and an African-American mother. (Ages 4–6)

Albert, Burton. *Where Does the Trail Lead?* Illustrated by Brian Pinkney. Simon & Schuster, 1991. 32 pages. (0–671–73409–1) (pbk. 0–671–79617–8, 1993)

A short, lyrical text traces the steps of an African-American boy on Summer Island as he follows a rustic trail along the beach until he reaches his family at a seaside picnic. Brian Pinkney's scratchboard illustrations are colored with aqua, green, brown, and purple oil pastels, providing the perfect ambience for the quiet story of a solitary journey. (Ages 4–7)

Allen, Judy. *Eagle.* Illustrated by Tudor Humphries. U.S. edition: Candlewick, 1994. 24 pages. (1–56402–143–2) (pbk. 1–56402–952–2, 1996)

In spite of his teacher's assurances, young Miguel worries that he'll be attacked by an eagle when he and his class make a field trip to the Philippine rainforest near their school. His obsessive fear nearly ruins the trip for Miguel and just about everyone else, until a chance encounter with a real eagle absolves the boy of his worries. Softly colored realistic paintings skillfully capture the drama of Miguel's story, as well as the majesty of the rain forest. (Ages 4–8)

Ashley, Bernard. *Cleversticks.* Illustrated by Derek Brazell. Crown, 1991. 32 pages. (pbk. 0–517–88332–5; 1995)

Ling Sung is discouraged about school after his first day. He can't tie his shoes or write his name, and although he can button his own coat, it's uneven. However, after Ling Sung skillfully uses the handles of two paintbrushes to chopstick broken cookie pieces into his mouth, the other children want to find out how to do this, too. A diversely populated nursery school and a loving Chinese-American family are the settings for a brightly colored picture story about self-esteem. (Ages 3–5)

Barber, Barbara E. *Allie's Basketball Dream.* Illustrated by Darryl Ligasan. Lee & Low (95 Madison Ave., New York, NY 10016), 1996. 32 pages. (1–880000–38–5)

When Dad gives her a basketball, Allie heads for the playground thrilled at the thought of shooting baskets. But her plan—and her dream of becoming a professional basketball player—is frustrated by the attitude of her playground companions, who think a girl's time is better spent on other things. The fact that she's not good at making baskets is pretty discouraging too. But this young African-American girl is spirited and stubborn enough to endure the teasing and her own self-doubt, and when she makes her first basket, the joy she feels makes it all worthwhile. A simple story illustrated with bright, slightly surreal dreamlike images. (Ages 6–9)

Barber, Barbara E. *Saturday at The New You.* Illustrated by Anna Rich. Lee & Low (95 Madison Ave., New York, NY 10016), 1994. 32 pages. (1–880000–06–7) (pbk. 1–880000–43–1, 1996)

Every Saturday, Shauna looks forward to going to work with her mother who owns her own beauty parlor called The New You. She likes to help her mother get the shop ready to open, and she helps out throughout the day by performing tasks such as taking magazines to the customers sitting under the big hairdryers and sorting hair rollers for her mother. Although Saturdays are always busy, Shauna finds time to play, too, as she combs and braids her dolls' hair, pretending they are her customers. Most of all, she enjoys the social life of The New You, where their regular customers include neighbors, friends and even red-headed Ms. Escobar, the popular teacher Shauna hopes to have when she enters third grade herself. In addition to being an appealing story about the adult work world, *Saturday at The New You* also celebrates the strength of the African-American community and the hard-working women at its core. (Ages 4–8)

Barbot, Daniel. *A Bicycle for Rosaura.* Translated from the Spanish. Illustrated by Morella Fuenmayor. (A Cranky Nell Book) U.S. edition: Kane/Miller, 1991. 24 pages. (0–916291–34–0) (pbk. 0–916291–51–0, 1994)

A delightful picture book from Venezuela details the predicament of Señora Amelia when her handsome hen Rosaura asks for a bicycle for her birthday. An indulgent pet owner, Señora Amelia searches high and low but is simply unable to find a shop that caters to athletically inclined chickens. Happily, an inventive street peddlar is equal to the task of building a custom-made two-wheeler. Much of the humor of this fast-paced story comes from Morella Fuenmayor's softly colored realistic illustrations which give an air of eerie possibility to the absurd. (Ages 3–6)

Belton, Sandra. *May'naise Sandwiches & Sunshine Tea.* Illustrated by Gail Gordon Carter. Four Winds, 1994. 32 pages. (0–02–709035–3)

Belton's child narrator remembers her grandmother's stories, especially the one about her friendship with Bettie Jean and the fun they had with imaginary play. One family was working class and the other was not. Belton handles an important theme seldom approached in books for the young in a picture book story featuring African-American characters. (Ages 5–8)

Best, Cari. *Taxi! Taxi!* Illustrated by Dale Gottlieb. Little, Brown, 1994. 32 pages. (0–316–09259–2)

Tina, a school-aged daughter of divorced parents, looks forward to the Sunday afternoons she spends with her *papi*, driver of the most yellow taxi in New York City. Each Sunday, Tina and Papi drive to the country to tend their flower and vegetable garden and to enjoy quiet times in each other's company. Spanish words and phrases are sprinkled throughout this realistic picture of life in a bilingual, divorced family. Boldly colored pastel paintings enhance the spirited account of a loving relationship between a father and daughter. (Ages 4–8)

Blanco, Alberto. *Angel's Kite = La Estrella de Angel.* Illustrated by Rodolfo Morales. English translation by Dan Bellm. Children's Book Press (246 First St., Suite 101, San Francisco, CA 94105), 1994. 32 pages. (0–89239–121–9)

An enchanting picture book featuring lively, colorful collage art and an engaging, original story about Angel, a young man who consoles himself over the disappearance of the church bell in his Mexican town by making beautiful kites. His "comets" and "stars," as the kites are called, cheer everyone but Angel himself, until he creates one particular kite that is not only beautiful, but magical as well. Originally written in Spanish, the text is presented in both English and Spanish. The singular illustrations are alive with detail created from items that the artist in every child will recognize: string, foil stars, tissue paper, fabric, and other art box treasures. (Ages 4–7)

Chocolate, Debbi. *On the Day I Was Born.* Illustrated by Melodye Rosales. Scholastic, 1995. 32 pages. (0–590–47609–2)

A contemporary African-American family welcomes its newest member with a combination of ancient African traditions, such as holding the baby up to the heavens and presenting him with a *kofia* and *kente* cloth, and modern American practices. Boldly colored realistic gouache paintings illustrate the celebratory moods of a loving extended family. (Ages 3–5)

Choi, Sook Nyul. *Halmoni and the Picnic.* Illustrated by Karen M. Dugan. Houghton Mifflin, 1993. 32 pages. (0–395–61626–3)

Yunmi's Korean grandmother has lived with her U.S. family in New York City for two months but is still reluctant to use English words when she sees Yunmi's school friends, even though she was a teacher in Korea. Rather than proving to be the embarrassing situation Yumni expects, a school picnic provides Yunmi and her classmates with an opportunity to encourage this very smart, exceedingly gracious woman to enjoy herself in a social setting. The picnic features Halmoni's *kimbap*, which she has made as a treat for them all, as well as a chance for her to turn the jump rope. The children find out that it is polite to call her Halmoni (grandmother) but rude to address an elder by her name. A contemporary story specifies ways to understand how someone new to a language might feel. Korean language words are used in context within this cheerful 10^1/4 x 7^1/2" picture story illustrated in full color. (Ages 5–8)

Cisneros, Sandra. *Hairs = Pelitos.* Illustrated by Terry Ybáñez. Apple Soup/Alfred A. Knopf, 1994. 32 pages. (0–679–86171–8) (lib. bdg. 0–679–96171–2)

A young Latina lyrically describes the hair of every member of her family, as each is distinctively unique. She especially delights in her mama's hair which has ". . . the warm smell of bread before you bake it / . . . the smell when she makes room for you on her side of the bed . . . ." This eloquently spare celebration of differences within one close-knit, loving family first appeared as a short chapter in Cisneros's adult novella, *House On Mango Street* (Arte Público, 1983; Vintage, 1991). For this picture book edition the text is printed in Spanish and English and the striking illustrations playfully extend the theme of individuality. (Ages 3–7)

Crews, Donald. *Bigmama's.* Greenwillow, 1991. 32 pages. (0–688–09950–5) (lib. bdg. 0–688–09951–3) (pbk. 0–685–64817–6)

When Donald Crews was a child growing up in the 1940s, he and his family made annual trips to spend the summer on his grandmother's farm near Cottondale, Florida. In this autobiographical reminiscence aimed at the young children who are the primary audience for Crews's popular picture books, such as *Freight Train* (Greenwillow, 1978), *Truck* (Greenwillow, 1980), and *School Bus* (Greenwillow, 1984), the author focuses on their arrival day when he and his siblings checked out every detail of the house, barn, and yard, just to make sure nothing had changed since their last visit. Although the details are specific to Donald Crews's own family, the experience of spending a summer "down home" was common to many African-American families living up north. (Ages 3–6)

Crews, Donald. *Shortcut.* Greenwillow, 1992. 32 pages. (0–688–06436–1) (pbk. 0–688–13576–5, 1996)

In a companion book to *Bigmama's* (Greenwillow, 1991), Donald Crews recounts a dramatic event remembered from a childhood summer on Bigmama's farm. As darkness falls one night seven children decide to take a dangerous shortcut home along the train tracks to save time. When a distant whistle signals the approach of an oncoming train, the children try to outrun it but are finally forced to slide down the steep slope at the side of the tracks to avoid catastrophe. Five wordless double-page spreads of the passing train cars underscore the terror and the relief of the children who are humbled by their close brush with disaster: "We walked home without a word. . . . We didn't tell anyone. We didn't talk about what happened for a very long time." (Ages 6–9)

Crews, Nina. *I'll Catch the Moon.* Greenwillow, 1996. 32 pages. (0–688–14134–X) (lib. bdg. 0–688–14135–8)

Collages made from a combination of black-and-white and color photographs illustrate a dreamlike story about a young brown-skinned girl who builds a ladder to the moon so she can play in outer space. Crews's mixed-media approach allows for an unusual juxtaposition of reality and fantasy in this exuberant, child-like romp. (Ages 3–5)

Cummings, Pat. *Clean Your Room, Harvey Moon!* Bradbury, 1991. 32 pages. (0–02–725511–5) (pbk. 0–689–71798–9; Aladdin, 1994)

The Voice of Doom that Harvey Moon hears when he's settled down to watch Saturday morning cartoons is that of his mother, reminding him to clean his room. A humorous, rhyming text lists the ordinary and the extraordinary items poor Harvey, who is Black, has to find a place for while the colorful, angular illustrations amusingly depict the child's archetypal problem bedroom. (Ages 3–6)

Cummings, Pat. *Carousel.* Bradbury, 1994. 32 pages. (lib bdg. 0–02–725512–3)

Disappointed when her father doesn't make it home in time for her birthday party, Alex storms off to her room in a temper, too angry to appreciate the delicate little carousel he gave her as a gift. When she awakens in the middle of the night, it is to the sight of the last of the carousel animals hopping out her bedroom window. Eager to round them all up before her father returns in the morning, Alex chases after them on an incredible night in which the animals of the carousel have all come alive. Pat Cummings's magical fantasy story is grounded in the life of a very realistic young African-American girl and her family. The delightful full-color illustrations in colored pencil, watercolor, and gouache lend additional mystery and magic to the fantasy scenes. (Ages 4–7)

Derby, Sally. *My Steps.* Illustrated by Adjoa J. Burrowes. Lee & Low (95 Madison Ave., New York, NY 10016), 1996. 32 pages. (1–880000–40–7)

An African-American girl describes all the fun she has year round (but especially in summer) playing on the front steps of her house in a busy urban neighborhood with her friends Essie and Nicholas. Two elements work particularly well to bring the book to life: the realistic voice of the child narrator and the bright cut-paper collages used to illustrate the story. The collages give both texture and dimension to the illustrations, making every scene look like a real front stoop. (Ages 3–6)

Dorros, Arthur. *Abuela.* Illustrated by Elisa Kleven. Dutton, 1991. 40 pages. (0–525–44750–4) (pbk. 0–14–056226–5; Puffin, 1997)

Rosalma and her Spanish-speaking *abuela* (grandmother) spend the day together in a city park where the two of them share an imaginary flight over the city. All of Abuela's comments and observations are made in Spanish, while either the context or Rosalma's translations into English make her statements clear for non-Spanish speakers. Elisa Kleven's vibrant mixed-media collages add colorful whimsy to this visual and verbal delight. (Ages 4–7)

Flournoy, Valerie. *Tanya's Reunion.* Illustrated by Jerry Pinkney. Dial, 1995. 40 pages. (0–8037–1605–2)

When Grandma and Tanya travel to the old farm where Tanya's mother grew up, Tanya does not immediately warm up to the place about which she's always heard, though Grandma feels immediately at home. A sequel to the popular *Patchwork Quilt* (Dutton, 1985) offers the reassuring tone of Flournoy's narrative and carefully rendered illustrations of Jerry Pinkney to expand a story of the same loving, multi-generational African-American family. Eventually, the night sounds of the farm tell Tanya that all is well, and it is. (Ages 5–8)

Garland, Sarah. *Billy and Belle.* U.S. edition: Reinhardt/Viking, 1992. 32 pages. (0–670–84396–2, out of print)

School-aged Billy must take his preschool-aged sister Belle to class with him while Dad takes Mum to the hospital for the birth of a new baby. It's an exciting and extraordinary day for both of them—not just because they're getting a new brother or sister but because it's pet day at school. Even with last minute notice, Belle manages to muster up a pet of her own to take to school: a spider! The full-color illustrations set in a comic-strip format are filled with amusing details of a bustling home life and a refreshingly disorderly school. Billy and Belle (and baby Adam) are biracial: their mother is white and their dad is Black. (Ages 3–6)

Gilchrist, Jan Spivey. *Indigo and Moonlight Gold.* Black Butterfly/Writers and Readers (Box 461, Village Station, New York, NY 10014), 1993. 32 pages. (0–86316–210–X)

Standing on her front porch gazing at the nighttime sky, Autrie wishes she could freeze time. Not only could she keep the stars forever, but Mama would always be watching over her from the window, bathed in night's colors of indigo and moonlight gold. Yet Autrie knows that night turns to day, warm breezes grow cold, and "Mama's don't sit and watch forever." The prospect of change doesn't frighten her, however, because Mama's love has helped her grow strong. Gilchrist's luminous oil paintings lend a quality of mystery to this African-American mother and daughter's special bond. (Ages 5–8)

Greenfield, Eloise. *First Pink Light.* Illustrated by Jan Spivey Gilchrist. Revised edition: Black Butterfly/Writers & Readers (Box 461, Village Station, New York, NY 10014), 1991. 32 pages. (0–86316–207–X) (pbk. 0–86316–212–6)

Preschooler Tyree anxiously awaits the return of his father, who has been away from home for a month taking care of Tyree's grandmother. Even though his mother tells him his daddy won't be home until daybreak, Tyree is adamant about staying up so he can hide in a cardboard box underneath the dining room table to surprise his daddy. After some marvelously realistic negotiating, mother agrees to let Tyree sit in a rocking chair at the living room window, watching for the "first pink light" of dawn. As determined and excited as little Tyree is, he just can't stay awake much later than his usual bedtime and soon he is fast asleep, only to be awakened hours later by a hug from his daddy. First published in 1976, Greenfield's humorous yet poignant story featuring an African-American family unfolds entirely through Tyree's believable actions and reactions, achieving a depth of character and drama rarely seen in realistic stories about and for preschoolers. Through facial expressions and postures, Gilchrist's full-color gouache and pastel paintings skillfully capture the many moods of a four-year-old at bedtime. As a read-aloud selection either one-on-one or for groups of preschoolers, this will delight the grown-ups as well as the children. (Ages 3–5)

Greenfield, Eloise. *William and the Good Old Days.* Illustrated by Jan Spivey Gilchrist. HarperCollins, 1993. 32 pages. (lib. bdg. 0–06–021094–X)

A young African-American boy remembers his grandmother's lively, active leadership when she owned the neighborhood restaurant Mama's Kitchen. He recalls how people loved her, how he loved seeing her there in the restaurant, how she would fix sweet potatoes and greens and on Saturday a barbecue for everyone. Everything has changed for him—and for her, too, he realizes—now that she is in a wheelchair. A realistic first-person narrative sensitively illustrated in full color explores expressions of grief in ways that very young children can understand. (Ages 3–7)

Guback, Georgia. *Luka's Quilt.* Greenwillow, 1994. 32 pages. (0–688–12154–3) (lib. bdg. 0–688–12155–1)

The traditional Hawaiian quilt Luka's *tutu* (grandmother) makes for her looks nothing like the elaborate, brightly colored quilt Luka had pictured in her head, and she cannot hide her disappointment when Tutu presents it to her. When the two attend a Lei Day celebration, Luka's nontraditional approach to lei-making gives Tutu an idea about enhancing the quilt to suit both generations. Charming cut-paper collages reveal a surprising amount of cultural detail through the folk-art-style illustrations. (Ages 4–8)

Guy, Rosa. *Billy the Great.* Illustrated by Caroline Binch. U.S. edition: Delacorte, 1992. 32 pages. (0–385–30666–0) (pbk. 0–440–40920–9)

From the time he was a baby, Billy's parents have had big plans for his future. When Billy was six, ten-year-old Rod moved in next door. Billy's parents think Rod plays too rough and they are wary of Rod's dad because he's a truck driver with broad shoulders and tattoos on his arms. But Billy thinks Rod is wonderful! After all, Rod always treats him like a big kid and taught him how to do a handstand after just three tries. An appealing picture story deals with the issue of class prejudice in a urban British neighborhood. Binch's marvelous watercolor paintings of Billy (who is Black) from babyhood through young childhood capture the childlike energy and openness that make him truly great. (Ages 4–8)

Haggerty, Mary Elizabeth. *A Crack in the Wall.* Illustrated by Rubén De Anda. Lee & Low (95 Madison Ave., New York, NY 10016), 1993. 32 pages. (1–880000–03–2)

Until Carlos's mom finds another job, she can only afford a small dingy apartment for the two of them to live in. Carlos tries to brighten it up, first by painting leaves on a crack in the wall to make it look like a tree branch, then by placing shining stars made out of gum wrappers on the branch. But each day his mom returns from her job hunt so exhausted that she never notices Carlos's handiwork. A realistic story about one child's attempts to cheer up a discouraged parent in a time of stress has a completely unpredictable surprise ending. Carlos and his mother are Latino. (Ages 4–8)

Hamanaka, Sheila. *Be Bop-A-Do-Walk!* Simon & Schuster, 1995. 36 pages. (0–689–80288–9)

Emi and her friend Martha join Emi's father on a long walk to Central Park. It is an unparalleled adventure for the two young girls—they even pack peanut-butter and jelly sandwiches for the journey. Emi's first-person narrative describes the many and diverse people and places they pass along the way, from the Jewish delicatessen and Italian bakery in their own neighborhood to the Empire State Building (where King Kong resides) and jazz clubs on Fifty-Second Street. In Central Park, they ride the carousel and play with paper boats which Emi's father has folded. Emi, who is Japanese American, and Martha, who is African American, embrace the day's events with the enthusiasm and wonder of children who find pleasure in the simplest acts. A delightful picture story that celebrates the diversity of the city is enhanced by Hamanaka's full-color illustrations that span each two-page spread. (Ages 5–8)

Haseley, Dennis. *Crosby.* Illustrated by Jonathan Green. Harcourt Brace, 1996. 32 pages. (0–15–200829–2)

Crosby prefers to sit in back of the classroom, never answering or asking questions. At home he keeps old things he finds, rather than use new ones his mama gives him. "What he keeps, mostly, is to himself." Crosby gives every impression he doesn't care about anything. He is a singular child, but not a disturbed one. One day Crosby makes a red kite from scraps and finds it possible to share the wonder of flying it with a younger child who is also playing alone. The boys experience the kind of freedom caused by looking around and opening up—to the wind, to life. "All that afternoon, in all that blue, the red kite hangs like the sky's necktie." An unusual picture story about loneliness, material value, and imagination is filled with vivid colors and strong emotions due in large part to the powerful impact of Green's oil paintings, in which Crosby is depicted as a singular Black child. (Ages 7–11)

Hayashi, Akiko. *Aki and the Fox.* U.S. edition: Doubleday, 1991. 40 pages. (0–385–41948–1)

Kon the stuffed fox has been Aki's constant companion since she was a baby and now that Aki's almost old enough to go to school, poor Kon is getting pretty ragged. When a seam splits on Kon's arm, Aki decides that it's time for a trip to Grandma's house for a repair job, so the two set out on a journey by train. An appealing adventure combines realistic details of life in contemporary urban Japan with a whimsical world in which a stuffed animal not only talks, he assumes the role of adult caregiver. (Ages 3–6)

Heo, Yumi. *Father's Rubber Shoes.* Orchard, 1995. 32 pages. (0–531–06873–0) (lib. bdg. 0–531–08723–9)

Yungsu has difficulty adjusting to life in the United States after his family moves from Korea. Since they were all happy in Korea, he can't understand why they left. When his father tells him a story from his own childhood, it helps him to understand a parent's desire to provide a better life for the next generation. Yumi Heo combines oil paintings, pencil drawings, and collage to create her distinctive art style. Her innovative use of color and perspective reflects Yungsu's moods throughout the book. (Ages 4–8)

Herrera, Juan Felipe. *Calling the Doves = El Canto de las Palomas.* Illustrated by Elly Simmons. Children's Book Press (246 First St., Suite 101, San Francisco, CA 94105), 1995. 32 pages. (0–89239–132–4)

In lyrical bilingual prose (Spanish/English) Chicano poet Juan Felipe Herrera recalls his childhood growing up in a family of migrant farmworkers. "The road changed with the seasons," he observes, but some things stayed the same: his mother's love of poetry and music and his father's ability to whistle a tune that would attract doves. Color pencil and acrylic paintings express the warmth and security felt by a child growing up in a loving household. (Ages 4–8)

Hort, Lenny. *How Many Stars in the Sky?* Illustrated by James E. Ransome. Tambourine, 1991. 32 pages. (0–688–10103–8) (lib. bdg. 0–688–10104–6) (pbk. 0–688–15218–X, 1997)

An African-American boy is kept awake at night by a question that nags at him: just how many stars are there up in the sky? Pajama-clad, he situates himself in his own backyard and sets out to count them, but there are too many stars and they keep moving, besides. Finally he and his dad get into their pickup truck and head for the country, where they can get the best view of the stars. The deep blue, green, and brown hues of James Ransome's richly textured oil paintings aptly depict a nighttime suburban neighborhood as well as city and rural scenes. (Ages 3–7)

Howard, Elizabeth Fitzgerald. *Aunt Flossie's Hats (and Crab Cakes Later).* Illustrated by James Ransome. Clarion, 1991. 32 pages. (0–395–54682–6) (pbk. 0–395–72078–8), 1995. (pbk. 0–395–72077–X, 1995)

Susan and her sister Sarah love to visit their Great Aunt Flossie's house each Sunday afternoon because Aunt Flossie lives in "a house crowded full of stuff and things." The sisters are particularly intrigued with Aunt Flossie's collection of hats—she has saved every hat she has ever owned and each one reminds her of a story from her past. James Ransome's elegant oil paintings move easily from the present to the past as he illustrates Aunt Flossie's stories, as well as the context in which she is telling them. A skillful use of dialogue aptly portrays a strong intergenerational relationship in an African-American family. (Ages 4–9)

Howard, Elizabeth Fitzgerald. *Mac & Marie & the Train Toss Surprise.* Illustrations by Gail Gordon Carter. Four Winds, 1993. 32 pages. (0–02–744640–9)

Anticipation builds on a warm summer night long ago as Mac and Marie wait eagerly for the Florida train to rumble by the Big House, where they live near Baltimore, as it makes its way north. Uncle Clem works on the train and has promised to toss them a surprise as it passes. Big brother Mac isn't as fidgety as Marie, but even he has a hard time waiting. As the two children pass the time, Mac dreams of the day when he, too, will work on the railroad as a fireman or an engineer, travelling across the land. Skillfully paced text measures the waiting time perfectly, slowly building to the moment when the train finally approaches, and marking its passing in a rush of words that leaves the reader breathless. When Mac and Marie open Uncle Clem's package gift, it serves as a solid reminder to Mac of the places he will someday see. Lovely colored pencil and water color illustrations by Carter illuminate the beauty and mystery of this midsummer night and echo the warmth of the African-American family relationships depicted in the text. (Ages 5–8)

Howard, Elizabeth Fitzgerald. *Papa Tells Chita a Story.* Illustrated by Floyd Cooper. Simon & Schuster, 1995. 32 pages. (0–02–744623–9)

A character first introduced in *Chita's Christmas Tree* (Bradbury, 1989) is back and this time it's her father who's the center of attention as he tells Chita stories of his life as a soldier in the Spanish American War. It seems the more often Papa tells the tale, the taller it gets. The audience soon realizes, along with Chita, that Papa is engaging in impossible acts as he battles a snake and an alligator and spends the night in an eagle's nest. Floyd Cooper's soft-edged gold-tone paintings create just the right mood for this story about an early 20th century middle class African-American family. (Ages 4–7)

Howard, Elizabeth Fitzgerald. *What's in Aunt Mary's Room?* Illustrated by Cedric Lucas. Clarion, 1996. 32 pages. (0–395–69845–6)

The characters who first appeared in *Aunt Flossie's Hats (and Crab Cakes Later)* (Clarion, 1991) are back in an equally charming story about the relationship between two African-American sisters and their great-great aunt. Here Susan and Sarah help Aunt Flossie open up a long-locked (and somewhat mysterious) room that had once belonged to their Aunt Mary to look for an old family Bible so the girls can add their own names to the family tree. Elizabeth Fitzgerald Howard builds suspense through the girls' natural curiosity about what's in the room. Cedric Lucas's soft pastel illustrations complement the author's tone by getting across a sense of family intimacy in an original picture story exploring African-American heritage. (Ages 4–7)

Hru, Dakari. *The Magic Moonberry Jump Ropes.* Illustrated by E.B. Lewis. Dial, 1996. 32 pages. (0–8037–1754–7) (lib. bdg. 0–8037–1755–5)

Sisters Erica and April want to jump Double Dutch but they can't get any of their friends to join them and their little sister Carmen is too small to twirl the ropes. When Uncle Zambezi returns from Tanzania, he brings them some magic moonberry ropes, claiming the ropes will grant them a wish. Of course the girls wish for a third jumper and, of course, their wish comes true when a new family moves in next door. But are the ropes really magic? Dakari Hru's gentle, humorous tale of the endless days of summer and the seriousness of child's play is aptly illustrated with E.B. Lewis's sun-dappled watercolor paintings. Jump in! (Ages 4–7)

Hudson, Wade. *Jamal's Busy Day.* Illustrated by George Ford. Just Us Books (356 Glenwood Ave., 3d Floor, East Orange, NJ 07017), 1991. 24 pages. (0–940975–21–1) (pbk. 0–940975–24–6)

Jamal's parents work hard all day; his dad as an architect, his mom as an accountant. Like them, Jamal works hard, too, because school is his "job." Readers follow Jamal through a typical day as he works with numbers, does research, attends meetings, helps out his supervisor, etc.—all activities described in terms his parents use for their work—while the illustrations show him in a familiar elementary school setting. The clever interplay between text and pictures distinguishes the second title in a series created to enhance the self-esteem of African-American children. (Ages 4–6)

Hughes, Shirley. *Wheels.* (A Tale of Trotter Street) U.S. edition: Lothrop, Lee & Shepard, 1991. 24 pages. (0–688–09880–0, out of print)

Trotter Street is full of Spring motion and locomotion. Sanjit Lal has roller skates; Barney a skateboard; and Mae's baby sister a stroller. Carlos deals gamely with the disappointment of receiving perfectly fine birthday presents but no bike like Billy's. Mum had warned Carlos in advance about this, but he was completely unprepared for his brother Marco's handmade surprise. This gift and a subsequent neighborhood non-bicycle race exhibit the small moments of high drama at which Hughes excels. Hughes's full-color artwork harmonizes wonderfully with the diverse, down-to-earth fictional Trotter Street community she's populated with appealing folks living their daily lives. An outstanding addition to a great series. (Ages 3–8)

Hunes, Susan Miho. *The Last Dragon.* Illustrated by Chris K. Soentpiet. Clarion, 1995. 32 pages. (0–395–67020–9)

While spending the summer with his great aunt in Chinatown, Peter Chang develops a fascination for a faded old dragon that has been collecting dust in a shop window for years. After he convinces his great aunt to buy it for him, Peter spends the ensuing weeks enlisting the help of community elders who know enough about the old traditions that they can help him repair the crest, the body, the tail, and the head. Each person who helps Peter out contributes not only time and materials, but also wisdom and, like the dragon, the value of the whole is greater than the sum of its parts. Chris K. Soentpiet's realistic watercolor paintings provide a great deal of cultural detail through his depiction of street scenes, various shop interiors, and everyday domestic life. (Ages 4–8)

Igus, Toyomi. *The Two Mrs. Gibsons.* Illustrated by Daryl Wells. Children's Book Press (246 First St., Suite 101, San Francisco, CA 94105), 1996. 32 pages. (0–89239–135–9) (lib. bdg. 0–516–20001–1)

The two Mrs. Gibsons don't seem to have much in common—one is tall, has dark skin and was born in Tennessee and the other is short, light-skinned and was born in Japan. The narrator of this story describes the two by pointing out all their differences but, in the end, they have one important thing in common: ". . . they both loved my daddy and they both loved me." This lyrical and unusually direct story of an interracial (Japanese/African American) family focuses on the child's joyful acceptance of differences. (Ages 3–7)

Johnson, Angela. *The Leaving Morning.*
Illustrated by David Soman. Orchard, 1992.
32 pages. (pbk. 0–531–07072–7, 1997)

"The leaving happened on a soupy, misty morning . . ." begins the account by a young African-American boy of the day the moving van came to help his family move from a city apartment to a new home. Although his narration focuses on the neighborhood he's leaving and the difficulty of leaving friends and family ("We said good-bye to the cousins all day long."), Johnson's text carries a subtle undercurrent of excitement and anticipation. The boy's changing moods are aptly depicted in Soman's watercolor illustrations, which also realistically show the older sister looking wistful and tentative while the parents seem to glow with happiness and confidence. (Ages 3–6)

Johnson, Angela. *One of Three.* Illustrated by
David Soman. Orchard, 1991. 32 pages.
(0–531–05955–3) (pbk. 0–531–07061–1,
1995)

The youngest of three daughters in an African-American family describes the day-to-day activities she shares with her two older sisters as "one of three." On occasions when her older sisters leave her behind, saying she's too little to come along, she feels left out and lonely, until Mama and Daddy find some things for her to do at home with them. Then she's one of three again—"a different kind of three, and that's fine, too . . . ." Once again, Angela Johnson demonstrates her remarkable skill at telling a good story that's just right for preschool listeners. David Soman's watercolor paintings capture the energy and emotions of three distinctive sisters. (Ages 3–5)

Lauture, Denizé. *Running the Road to ABC.*
Illustrated by Reynold Ruffins. Simon &
Schuster, 1996. 32 pages. (0–689–80507–1)

Based on memories of his own childhood, Haitian poet Denizé Lauture writes a lyrical story in which six young children arise before dawn and embark on their daily journey to school. "They go barefoot. Their feet remember the way in the dark." The children run on narrow trails, "by the slopes of coffee trees and the meadows of corn plants, . . ." to the main road as the sky is lightening. "They run and run" through the village, past merchants and bread sellers, "only the horse tamers keep up with them . . . on roads of white turf and roads of red clay they run. On roads of rocks and roads of mud they run." As the day comes into its own, the children arrive at their small school, where they eagerly await "one more letter and one more sound, one more sound and one more word and one more line, one more line and one more page . . ." Children will be enriched by Lauture's beautiful prose and fascinated by the lengths that some other children go to in order to attend school. Reynold Ruffins's colorful gouache illustrations feature beautifully rendered skyscapes of the awakening day, and lush, colorful depictions of rural and village life. (Ages 5–8)

Lee, Huy Voun. *At the Beach.* Henry Holt,
1994. 24 pages. (0–8050–2768–8)

There's no better place for Xiao Ming to practice his Chinese character writing than in the sand at the beach, where real people and objects mirror the images of the characters he's writing. Cut-paper collages work beautifully to convey abstract symbols through simple, concrete images, from "big" (a man stretched out on the beach) to "good" (mother and child together). (Ages 6–10)

McKissack, Patricia C. *A Million Fish . . .
More or Less.* Illustrated by Dena Schutzer.
Alfred A. Knopf, 1992. 32 pages.
(0–679–80692–X) (lib. bdg. 0–679–90692–4)
(pbk. 0–679–88086–0; Random House, 1996)

Inspired by the tall tales of Papa-Daddy and Elder Abbajon, young Hugh Thomas recounts a whopper of a fish tale of his own after a day of fishing on the Bayou Clapateaux. On his way home after having caught a million fish, he loses half of them to a wily alligator, half of the remaining lot to a band of pirate raccoons, and several thousands more to a flock of attacking crows before running into his neighbor's greedy cat. A well-paced, wildly funny story that features an African-American child in the Louisiana bayou is whimsically illustrated with boldly colored oil paintings. (Ages 4–7)

Miller, William. *Zora Hurston and the
Chinaberry Tree.* Illustrated by Cornelius Van
Wright and Ying-Hwa Hu. Lee & Low
(95 Madison Ave., New York, NY 10016),
1994. 32 pages. (1–880000–14–8)

A picture-book account of the childhood of African-American writer Zora Neale Hurston focuses on the influence of her mother, who told Zora all the world belonged to her, contrary to the messages she got from her father and society at large. When her mother died, young Zora, who liked climbing trees, wearing pants, and listening to old men spin their stories at the town store or around a nighttime camp fire, promised herself that she would live up to her mother's expectations. Miller has chosen small, significant details to give a sense of Zora's intellect and personality through his spare account of her childhood. Somber pencil and watercolor paintings provide the perfect match for the text and depict Zora as a strong, active girl, even when she appears in the background as an observer. (Ages 6–9)

Mills, Claudia. *A Visit to Amy-Claire.*
Illustrated by Sheila Hamanaka. Macmillan,
1992. 32 pages. (0–02–766991–2)

Five-year-old Rachel can't wait to get to her seven-year-old cousin's house. She is anxious to repeat all the fun she remembers having with her the previous summer—taking bubble baths, swinging on a tire swing, and playing school. But once she and her family get to Amy-Claire's house, Rachel is in for a major disappointment because all Amy-Claire wants to do is play with Rachel's two-year-old sister, Jessie. Hamanaka's bold, sun-dappled oil paintings depict Amy-Claire as Asian American while her cousins are biracial (Asian/white) in a realistic story about imaginary play and shifting family relationships. (Ages 4–7)

Mohr, Nicholasa. *The Song of el Coqui and Other Tales of Puerto Rico.* Illustrated by Antonio Martorell. Viking, 1995. 40 pages. (0–670–85837–4) (0–670–86296–7)

Three original folktales that acknowledge the rich, distinct cultures on the island of Puerto Rico comprise a collection distinguished by Nicholasa Mohr's skillful storytelling and Antonio Martorell's breathtaking full-color illustrations. "The Song of El Coqui" is a creation story based on beliefs of the Taino, the indigenous people of the island. The story of "La Guinea, the Stowaway Hen" represents Africans who were brought to Puerto Rico as slaves and became a vibrant part of the culture. "La Mula, the Cimarron Mule" is woven from experience under the conquering Spaniards. An author's note provides the framework for these three stories that collectively embody the rich culture of contemporary Puerto Rican life and the spirit of the Caribbean. (Ages 9–12)

Myers, Walter Dean. *The Story of the Three Kingdoms.* Illustrated by Ashley Bryan. HarperCollins, 1995. 32 pages. (0–06–024286–8) (lib. bdg. 0–06–024287–6) (pbk. 0–06–443475–3)

An original story with many mythic themes tells of a time when The People came to earth and tried to assert themselves over Elephant, Shark, and Hawk, who ruled the Kingdoms of the Earth, Water, and Sky respectively. Although The People, depicted as Black, were able to outwit the rulers of each of the Three Kingdoms, they realized they did so through the power of story, the same power that made it possible for them to be the caretakers of the Kingdoms. This 12$\frac{1}{4}$ x 7$\frac{1}{4}$" volume is handsomely illustrated by Ashley Bryan's luminous abstract paintings which complement the story's mythic qualities. (Ages 4–8)

Nikola-Lisa, W. *Bein' with You This Way.* Illustrated by Michael Bryant. Lee & Low (95 Madison Ave., New York, NY 10016), 1994. 32 pages. (1–880000–05–9) (pbk. 1–880000–26–1, 1995)

A rhyming, patterned text celebrates human diversity with an otherwise straightforward series of observations about physical differences. Energetic watercolor and colored pencil illustrations show children of various colors and sizes at play in a busy city park. A book that will engage young children offers a realistic and positive picture of who we are. (Ages 3–6)

Nodar, Carmen Santiago. *Abuelita's Paradise.* Illustrated by Diane Paterson. Albert Whitman, 1992. 32 pages. (0–8075–0129–8) (0–685–66422–8; Varsity, 1993)

After her *abuelita* (grandmother) dies, Marita cuddles up in the rocking chair and faded blanket Abuelita has left to her. As she rocks, she remember stories her grandmother told her about her childhood in Puerto Rico, a time and place which seemed like a paradise to her. Brightly colored watercolor illustrations skillfully blend the present, recent past, and distant past into a visual continuum of family traditions. (Ages 4–7)

Olaleye, Isaac. *Bitter Bananas.* Illustrated by Ed Young. Boyds Mills, 1994. 32 pages. (1–56397–039–2) (pbk. 0–14–055710–5; Puffin, 1996)

Set in the heart of an African rain forest, this original story by a Nigerian writer has many folkloric qualities. Young Yusef gathers palm sap to sell at the market but notices with dismay that someone has been raiding his stores. When he discovers that the thieves are a family of baboons, he devises a scheme to discourage them from stealing from him. Frequent repetition of the phrases "Oh no! Oh no!" and "Oh yes! Oh yes!" to signal a bad or good turn of events, along with a generous use of onomatopoeia, makes this a great read-aloud. Ed Young's stunning artwork features his pastel and watercolor paintings, employed with a cut-paper technique that layers images to give a three-dimensional sense of the dense rain forest. (Ages 4–8)

Oppenheim, Shulamith Levey. *Fireflies for Nathan.* Illustrated by John Ward. Tambourine, 1994. 28 pages. (lib. bdg. 0–688–12148–9) (pbk. 0–14–055782–2; Puffin, 1996)

An African-American child staying with his grandparents in their rural home enjoys hearing stories about what his father was like when he was his age. Six-year-old Nathan especially likes hearing about his daddy's fondness for fireflies because he shares his dad's enthusiasm, so much so that the day seems to drag and Nathan can hardly wait for it to get dark. Once it does, the night seems almost magical to Nathan as he watches for the tiny flashes of lightning, just like his daddy used to do. John Ward's engaging acrylic paintings make it clear that the grandparents are as delighted with the simple pleasures of a summer evening as Nathan himself is, as they are no doubt recalling similar times a generation earlier. (Ages 3–7)

Peterson, Jeanne Whitehouse. *My Mama Sings.* Illustrated by Sandra Speidel. HaperCollins, 1994. 32 pages. (0–06–023859–3)

A poetic text describes the loving relationship between a young African-American boy and his single-parent mother, and the special role that music plays in their lives. When the mother loses her job, she comes home too sad to sing, and in his need for reassurance the little boy imagines his own song to make his mother happy again. Sandra Speidel's warm, colorful paintings fill many of the two-page spreads. In some instances, this creates a difficulty in reading the words from a distance, but it will not detract from sharing this lyrically written picture book one-on-one. (Ages 4–7)

Pilkey, Dav. *The Paperboy.* Orchard, 1996. 32 pages. (0–531–09506–1) (lib. bdg. 0–531–08856–1)

On the opening wordless double-page spreads we see a truck leaving the loading dock of the *Morning Star Gazette* and traveling through residential streets to the house where the paperboy, a Black child, is just getting out of bed. The moon and stars shine brightly in the pitch black sky as the paperboy and his dog go through their early morning rituals of preparing for their route: moving quietly through the house, eating breakfast, and folding newspapers in the garage. The understated, poetic text brilliantly captures the rhythm of routine as Pilkey highlights small but evocative details, such as the snap of green rubber bands and the awkwardness of riding a bicycle while carrying a red cloth bag filled with newspapers. As the paperboy and his dog make their rounds through the dark, familiar streets, the early morning sky gradually lightens. It is streaked with bright orange and pink hues by the time all the newspapers are delivered, and the paperboy must pull down his window shade to shut out the light when he returns to his own warm bed. Pilkey's expressive acrylic paintings playfully use light and dark contrasts to provide a delicious sense of being awake and active in a sleeping world. His paintings carry this mood right through to the story's satisfying conclusion in which we find the paperboy asleep and dreaming in the wide-awake world. (Ages 3–7)

Pinkney, Brian. *Max Found Two Sticks.* Simon & Schuster, 1994. 32 pages. (0–671–78776–4) (pbk. 0–689–81593–X; Aladdin, 1997)

On a day when Max doesn't feel like talking to anyone, he sits brooding on the front steps of his apartment building until he notices two sticks on the ground. They make perfect drumsticks, and as people in Max's African-American neighborhood pass by and say hello, Max responds by beating a rhythm with his sticks on something left behind by the previous passerby. Primary and secondary colors brighten Pinkney's sweeping scratchboard illustrations which are filled with rhythmic motions. (Ages 3–7)

Pinkney, Gloria Jean. *Back Home.* Illustrated by Jerry Pinkney. Dial, 1992. 40 pages. (0–8037–1168–9) (lib. bdg. 0–8037–1169–7)

Eight-year-old Ernestine travels south by train for a mid–20th century summer visit with relatives in rural North Carolina. Except for Cousin Jack's teasing, she immediately feels at home in her mother's childhood environs. Ernestine tries to overlook Jack's condescending attitude while exploring the farm, learning about its animals, visiting a family cemetery, and seeing the house where she herself was born. Period details support the text and can also be found in household objects, clothing, and vehicles so faithfully pictured in Pinkney's luminous illustrations created with pencil, colored pencils, and watercolor. Heritage, memory, renewal, and family ties are linked in a strong vignette about an African-American family's warm welcome to their city relative. (Ages 4–8)

Pinkney, Gloria Jean. *The Sunday Outing.* Illustrated by Jerry Pinkney. Dial, 1994. 32 pages. (0–8037–1198–0) (lib. bdg. 0–8037–1199–9)

A prequel to *Back Home* (Dial, 1992), *Sunday Outing* shows the days and steps leading up to Ernestine's visit to her relatives' rural southern home. Both stories, set in the mid 20th century, provide a view of one middle-class African-American family's means of keeping in touch and passing down family traditions to their children. The Pinkneys depict Ernestine's close relationship with her Aunt Odessa through their mutual interest in trains and adventure. A wise elder, Aunt Odessa knows exactly how to encourage Ernestine's budding sense of independence and assure that the child will be able to make the long train trip back home by herself. (Ages 5–8)

Plain, Ferguson. *Little White Cabin.* Pemmican Publications (1635 Burrows Ave., #2, Winnipeg, Manitoba, Canada R2X OT1), 1992. 24 pages. (pbk. 0–921827–26–1, out of print)

Waaboozoons is an Ojibway boy who passes by a little white cabin nearly every day when he's out walking. Some days he sees an elder known as Ol' Danny sitting on the cabin's front porch and when Waaboozoons sees him, the boy always calls out *"Aniish naa?"* (How are You?). He gets used to the fact that Ol' Danny never responds to his greeting. Much to the boy's surprise, however, one day the old man answers him and from that day on the two become good friends, with Ol' Danny teaching Waaboozoons much about the old ways. A quiet picture story, illustrated in distinctive dark-blue-and-white paintings by a self-taught Ojibway artist, shows the importance of respect for elders in the Native American value system. (Ages 5–8)

Reiser, Lynn. *Margaret and Margarita = Margarita y Margaret.* Greenwillow, 1993. 32 pages. (0–688–12239–6) (lib. bdg. 0–688–12240–X) (pbk. 0–688–14734–8; Morrow, 1996)

Margaret, who speaks English, and Margarita, who speaks Spanish, meet on a trip to the park with their mothers. The language barrier immediately distances the adults (Margaret's mother buries her nose in a book while Margarita's mother concentrates on her knitting), but the two little girls, who at first peer shyly at one another from behind their mother's skirts, soon are chattering away. The openness of young children is warmly depicted in this simple bilingual text. Each mother-daughter pair speaks the same or similar phrases in their own language on facing pages as Margaret and Margarita experience the joy of newfound friendship. The English words are in blue, and the Spanish words are in red. By the end of the book, most of the dialogue is red and blue intermingled as the children excitedly speak a mix of both languages. Whimsical watercolor illustrations add to the celebratory tone. (Ages 3–6)

Ringgold, Faith. *Aunt Harriet's Underground Railroad in the Sky.* Crown, 1992. 32 pages. (0–517–58767–X) (lib. bdg. 0–517–58768–8) (pbk. 0–517–88543–3, 1995)

Cassie Lighfoot, the eight-year-old who shared the glories of flying with little brother Be Be in *Tar Beach* (Crown, 1991), is at it again. This time she and Be take a dream journey to the past, where they travel through history on the Underground Railroad with Harriet Tubman herself. Details about the harsh realities of slavery and the dangers fugitives faced are balanced (but never trivialized) by Ringgold's stunning oil paintings which show Cassie's childlike, whimsical interpretations of Aunt Harriet's oral account of history: she pictures the Underground Railroad, for example, as a real train and Harriet Tubman dressed in a conductor's hat and apron. A two-page note at the book's end offers biographical information about Harriet Tubman as well as a list of resources. (Ages 6–11)

Ringgold, Faith. *Tar Beach.* Crown, 1991. 32 pages. (0–517–58030–6) (lib. bdg. 0–517–58031–4) (pbk. 0–517–88544–1; Random House, 1996)

Eight-year-old Cassie Lightfoot and her baby brother Be Be lie stretched out on a mattress on the rooftop of their Harlem apartment while her parents play cards with their next door neighbors. During that magical time that comes between wakefulness and sleep, the adult conversation blends into Cassie's daydream as she envisions herself flying high above the city, claiming that she owns it all and can change anything to make life come out the way she wants it to be. Ringgold's boldly imaginative acrylic paintings brilliantly capture the power of a child's soaring imagination on the twilight edge of dreams. Set in 1939, and based on Ringgold's story quilt of the same name, *Tar Beach* succeeds as an appealing story for children illustrated with fine art, as an astute societal commentary, and as a new variation on a traditional African-American liberation motif. (Ages 5–11)

Rochelle, Belinda. *When Jo Louis Won the Title.* Illustrated by Larry Johnson. Houghton Mifflin, 1994. 32 pages. (0–395–66614–7) (pbk. 0–395–81657–2, 1996)

Jo Louis is so tired of people making fun of her name that she dreads her first day in a new school. But her grandpa manages to raise her spirits by telling her the story behind her name, a story that begins when he was a young man and had just arrived in Harlem on the day of the fighter Joe Louis's great victory. Artist Larry Johnson is so skillful with a paintbrush that he manages to pull feeling and drama from the stance of a listening child, and he aptly characterizes the African-American grandfather and granddaughter with expressions of great mutual affection and respect. (Ages 5–8)

Schaefer, Carole Lexa. *The Squiggle.* Illustrated by Pierr Morgan. Crown, 1996. 32 pages. (0–517–70047–6) (lib. bdg. 0–517–70048–4)

On an outing with her daycare group, a Chinese-American girl finds a piece of red string on the ground and launches into a series of imaginative scenarios. The "squiggle" becomes a dragon, a wall, a tightrope, fireworks, a thundercloud, and a pool. Her exuberance soon spreads to the entire group of children who easily join in the fun in this playful tribute to the imagination. (Ages 3–6)

Schertle, Alice. *Down the Road.* Illustrated by E.B. Lewis. Browndeer/Harcourt Brace, 1995. 40 pages. (0–15–276622–7)

Hetty's first solo errand is to walk down the country road to the store to buy a dozen eggs and carry them safely back home. Solemn with responsibility, Hetty walks very carefully both ways and almost makes it home without breaking a single egg until she happens on an apple tree bearing ripe delicious fruit. An enchanting story of a contemporary African-American rural family is well matched with E. B. Lewis's sun-dappled watercolor illustrations which brilliantly capture the determination of a young girl out to prove herself. (Ages 4–7)

Scott, Ann Herbert. *On Mother's Lap.* Illustrated by Glo Coalson. Revised edition: Clarion, 1992. 32 pages. (0–395–58920–7) (pbk. 0–395–62976–4)

A newly illustrated edition of a picture book first published in 1972 features an Iñupiaq toddler learning to share his mother's attentions with a baby sister. Family bonds and homey security are depicted in both the text and full-color illustrations. The realistic, childlike conflict, reassuring resolution, and patterned text make this a favorite read-aloud for young preschoolers. (Ages 2–4)

Shea, Pegi Deitz. *New Moon.* Illustrated by Cathryn Falwell. Boyds Mills, 1996. 32 pages. (1–56397–410–X)

A down-to-earth picture book shows a home in which a toddler delights in learning a new word, considers a fresh idea, and experiences a dependable wonder of the universe when her sibling shows her *la luna*, the full moon in the sky, and then helps stem her disappointment when the moon can't be seen again for a period of time. The fictional narrator can be either a brother or sister, unless readers pay attention to the book's flap copy suggesting the older child is a brother. The family is probably Latino. Rereadings prove the warm sibling relationship within this low-key story to be as, or even more, important than a child's gender or the family's culture. The illustrations were created in cut paper collage. An outstanding book for both emergent and newly independent readers. (Ages 4–7)

Smalls-Hector, Irene. *Jonathan and His Mommy.* Illustrated by Michael Hays. Little, Brown, 1992. 32 pages. (0–316–79870–3) (pbk. 0–316–79880–0, 1994)

An imaginative "walk" across their neighborhood is hardly a walk for a young African-American boy and his mother because it involves them hopping, running, zig-zagging, itsy-bitsy baby stepping, and much more. They match their talk to their walk, which is exactly what children who see and hear this cheerful, lively story will want to do—get right up and try it! (Ages 2–5)

Soto, Gary. *Chato's Kitchen.* Illustrated by Susan Guevara. Putnam, 1995. 32 pages. (0–399–22658–3)

Chato and his best friend Novio Boy are streetwise cool cats from "East Los" who are thrilled when a family of mice move in next door. When Chato invites his new neighbors over for dinner, they innocently accept, not realizing that their host plans to serve them as the main course. Gary Soto skillfully integrates Spanish into the text of this wry cat-and-mouse tale. While surprising plot twists and amusing turns of phrase will delight monolingual English-speaking readers, there will be double the fun for those who understand Spanish as well, as Soto plays with both languages simultaneously. Equally playful is artist Susan Guevara, who fills her illustrations with cultural references: a calendar page open to May 5 (Cinco de Mayo); an elegant birds' wedding taking place in mailbox; and tiny letters on a banana label reading *sangre de Honduras*. Small visual details such as these add an extra layer of meaning for observant readers without detracting from the overall fun of the story. Guevara's style suits the broad humor perfectly, as she is especially gifted at expressing subtleties of character through controlled exaggeration. *Delicioso!* (Ages 4–8)

Spohn, David. *Home Field.* Lothrop, Lee & Shepard, 1993. 32 pages. (0–688–11173–4, out of print)

Bare spots in the grass serve as bases, maple trees behind home plate provide a backstop, and barn swallows are like fans in bleachers when young Matt and his dad get in a quick game of baseball before early morning farm chores. With his dad coaching, Matt's perfecting his stance and his hitting this summer. His real growth can probably be attributed to the fact that dad makes time for a little one-on-one baseball before the hectic pace of daily life takes over. David Spohn's understated, gentle story of a father and son relationship in a rural interracial (African American/white) family is itself a little solace in a busy world. (Ages 3–7)

Spohn, David. *Nate's Treasure.* Lothrop, Lee & Shephard, 1991. 32 pages. (0–688–10091–0, out of print)

When a skunk dies after a fight with Bruno, the family dog, Dad takes the body out into a far field. The passing of the seasons brings autumn brush fires, winter snows, and finally spring sunshine and growth to the field where Nate ventures in the warmer weather and discovers the skunk has become a skeleton. The bones are a treasure that Nate keeps in an old leather pouch on his bike all summer long. Now, Nate sometimes still takes the bones out to look at them, but they usually stay in the old pouch, next to the socks in his drawer. A gentle, observant book about change features an interracial family: Nate is African American, Dad is white. (Ages 3–7)

Straight, Susan. *Bear E. Bear.* Illustrated by Marisabina Russo. Hyperion, 1995. 32 pages. (1–56282–527–5, out of print)

Gaila's little sister accidentally dropped her favorite stuffed bear in a mud puddle and now Gaila is waiting patiently while Bear E. Bear goes through a wash and rinse cycle in the washing machine and then bounces around in the dryer. While she waits, Gaila remembers several past experiences with Bear E. Bear—the time Grandma sewed his nose back on, the time another child made fun of him, and the time he got jelly in his hair. A young child's devotion to a special toy is realistically depicted in this warm picture story which features an interracial (African American/white) family. (Ages 3–5)

Stroud, Bettye. *Down Home at Miss Dessa's.* Illustrated by Felicia Marshall. Lee & Low (95 Madison Ave., New York, NY 10016), 1996. 32 pages. (1–880000–39–3)

After Miss Dessa falls down, an older sister and a younger sister find they must shift roles and keep an eye on the old woman who used to keep an eye on them. A quiet intergenerational story set in the U.S. South during the 1940s overflows with mutual respect in this glimpse of rural African-American neighborliness. (Ages 5–8)

Sun, Chyng Feng. *Mama Bear.* Illustrated by Lolly Robinson. Houghton Mifflin, 1994. 32 pages. (0–395–63412–1, out of print)

From the moment she first saw it in the toy shop window, Mei-Mei has desperately wanted the huge stuffed bear, even though she knows her mama doesn't earn enough money in her job at the neighborhood Chinese restaurant to buy such extravagant luxuries. Mei-Mei manages to earn some money of her own with occasional odd jobs around the restaurant but she still can't save enough to buy "the softest, warmest bear in the whole world." Luckily, Mei-Mei's mama is soft and warm and gives great bear hugs, and that is the most important thing of all. The warm, quiet tone of the refreshingly realistic story is echoed in the softly colored illustrations that accompany it. (Ages 4–8)

Thomassie, Tynia. *Mimi's Tutu.* Illustrated by Jan Spivey Gilchrist. Scholastic, 1996. 32 pages. (0–590–44020–9)

As the first daughter born into her extended African-American family in many years, little Mimi is lavished with attention from all her female elders. More than anything, Mimi likes to observe her family's tradition of African dance by attending classes with her mother and by wearing the beautiful *lapa* (African tutu) made by Gramma M'bewe. Boldly colored pastel and watercolor paintings deftly capture a young child's enthusiasm for dance, movement, and participating in the social and cultural world of grown-ups. (Ages 3–5)

Torres, Leyla. *Saturday Sancocho.*
Farrar Straus Giroux, 1995. 32 pages.
(0–374–36418–4)

Maria Lili can't imagine how her grandmother is going to turn one dozen eggs into mouthwatering chicken sancocho for supper, but Mama Ana just smiles as she and Maria Lili head off for the Saturday market. There, her resourceful grandmother barters and trades the eggs for plantains, vegetables, and other ingredients they need to make their traditional Saturday meal. Full-color illustrations span across each two page spread of this delightful story set in South America that includes the author's own recipe for Mama Ana's Chicken Sancocho. (Ages 5–8)

Walter, Mildred Pitts. *Darkness.* Illustrated by Marcia Jameson. Simon & Schuster, 1995. 24 pages. (0–689–80305–2)

Many small children who are afraid of the dark will find reassurance in this evocative story that reminds us of all the good things darkness brings us: our shadows and cool shade, soothing rain from dark clouds, dreamtime, and the bright stars that can only be seen at night. The comforting, poetic text is nicely interpreted by Marcia Jameson's abstract acrylic paintings which contrast deep shades of blue and purple with occasional touches of orange and gold to express the beauty of darkness. (Ages 3–7)

EASY FICTION

Ada, Alma Flor. *My Name Is María Isabel.* Illustrated by K. Dyble Thompson. Atheneum, 1993. 57 pages. (0–689–31517–1) (pbk. 0–689–80217–X; Aladdin, 1995)

"We already have two Marías in this class. Why don't we call you Mary instead?" So begins the first day at a new school for nine-year-old María Isabel Salazar Lopez, who is proud of her real name and the Puerto Rican family heritage it represents. María Isabel can't get used to the strange new name Mary Lopez, but she is shy and doesn't know how to tell her teacher. If that weren't enough, her mother gets a job and is no longer at home when María Isabel finishes school each day. María Isabel's struggle to adapt to changes, and to find her voice, is at the center of this inviting story exploring important issues of identity and understanding. (Ages 8–10)

Altman, Linda Jacobs. *Amelia's Road.* Illustrated by Enrique O. Sánchez. Lee & Low (95 Madison Ave., New York, NY 10016), 1993. 32 pages. (1–880000–04–0) (pbk. 1–880000–27–X, 1995)

A young child living in a Mexican migrant family hates "the road," which to her symbolizes another round of backbreaking work, degradation, and insecurity. More than anything else she would like to feel a sense of belonging in one place, but it is unlikely that will ever happen. Then she discovers the "accidental road," an overgrown path that leads to a place no one else frequents, and she claims it for her own. A poignant yet realistic story of a plucky young girl who comes up with her own solution to a problem is stunningly illustrated with full-color acrylic paintings. (Ages 7–9)

Brenner, Barbara and Julia Takaya. *Chibi: A True Story from Japan.* Illustrated by June Otani. Clarion, 1996. 63 pages. (0–395–69623–2)

An inviting design and engaging story distinguish this chapter book in which a mother duck hatches and raises her ducklings in the midst of a Tokyo business park. Based on a true story, the author was one of the thousands of Tokyo residents who waited and watched each day for the moment the mother duck would lead her ducklings across a busy, congested roadway to the pond on the other side. Mr. Sato, a news photographer sent to cover the story, names the smallest duckling Chibi, which means tiny in Japanese. The ducks make a safe journey, but when a typhoon strikes Mr. Sato and others go for days not knowing the fate of Chibi or his family. Full-color illustrations in water color and ink on each double-page spread are a charming accompaniment to a warm, dramatic, satisfying story for young readers. (Ages 7–10)

Castañeda, Omar S. *Abuela's Weave.*
Illustrated by Enrique O. Sánchez. Lee & Low
(95 Madison Ave., New York, NY 10016),
1993. 32 pages. (1–880000–00–8)
(pbk. 1–880000–20–2, 1995)

When it comes to weaving, young Esperanza couldn't have a better teacher than her grandmother, a Mayan elder who is well known for her beautiful tapestries in the rural area of
Guatemala where they live. But when it comes to taking the weavings into town to sell in
the market, her grandmother insists on staying behind. She is afraid that the birthmark on
her face will discourage customers from buying their work, and she is especially anxious for
the elaborate weaving she and Esperanza worked on together to get the attention it
deserves. Abuela's reluctance to enter the marketplace makes Esperanza feel self-conscious
about the items she has for sale, until she sees customers walking past the commercial stalls
to look at her weavings. Brightly colored, distinctive illustrations by a talented new artist
add to the overall appeal. Authentic cultural details enrich both the text and the pictures in
this unusual story of a child's first steps toward pride and self-sufficiency. (Ages 6–9)

DeGross, Monalisa. *Donavan's Word Jar.*
Illustrated by Cheryl Hanna. HarperCollins,
1994. 71 pages. (0–06–020190–8) (lib. bdg.
0–06–020191–6)

Third-grader Donavan Allen collects words like other kids collect trading cards. When
his word jar becomes filled to the brim with the slips of paper on which the words he's
collected and memorized are written, Donavan has a problem. What should he do with
all of them? Donavan's search for the perfect solution is at the center of this story featuring his loving, supportive African-American family. A perfect read-aloud! (Ages 7–10)

Hamilton, Virginia. *The All Jahdu
Storybook.* Illustrated by Barry Moser.
Harcourt Brace Jovanovich, 1991. 108 pages.
(0–15–239498–2)

Jahdu, the magical trickster hero created by Virginia Hamilton over 20 years ago, is
rooted in African and American folklore, mixed with some story elements borrowed
from European folk literature as well. The result is a collection of wholly original new
tales that feel ancient. This anthology of Jahdu tales combines 11 stories from three previous Jahdu collections and introduces four brand new tales, all beautifully illustrated in
one elegant volume. (Ages 7–11)

Hamilton, Virginia. *Drylongso.* Illustrated by
Jerry Pinkney. Harcourt Brace Jovanovich,
1992. 54 pages. (0–15–224241–4)

Growing up on a farm in the drought-stricken Midwest of the 1970s, Lindy can barely
remember a time when mud and cloudbursts were ordinary features of her landscape.
She is sustained by her gentle, loving parents who patiently answer Lindy's questions
about life in easier times past. But even her parents' stories haven't prepared her for the
day of the windstorm when a strange young man named Drylongso literally blows into
their lives. Full-page, full-color pastel and watercolor paintings appear on nearly every
double-page spread of this powerful story about hope, hard work, and gifted African-American people who can make something out of nothing. (Ages 7–11)

Hru, Dakari. *Joshua's Masai Mask.*
Illustrated by Anna Rich. Lee & Low
(95 Madison Ave., New York, NY 10016),
1993. 32 pages. (1–880000–02–4)
(pbk. 1–880000–32–6, 1996)

Joshua loves to play the *kalimba*, an instrument tied to his African heritage, and his family enthusiastically encourages him to perform with it in the school talent contest, but
the thought has him mortified—the kids in school will laugh! Even when Uncle Zambezi gives Joshua a Masai mask to wear in the show, Joshua can't help wishing he could
rap like popular Kareem Cooper. But when the power of the mask allows Joshua to experience other people's lives firsthand, he develops a new appreciation for his own, especially when he and his *kalimba* save the show. Brightly colored full-page illustrations
provide a vivid backdrop for the text. (Ages 5–8)

Picó, Fernando. *The Red Comb.* Illustrated by
María Antonia Ordóñez. Translation and
adaptation by Argentina Palacios. U.S. edition:
BridgeWater, 1994. 48 pages.
(0–8167–3539–5) (pbk. 0–8167–3540–9;
Troll, 1995)

Because Pedro Calderón has received rewards for capturing runaway slaves, considered
"lawbreakers," he is envied by other young men in his Puerto Rican village. "Black folks
should help black folks, not hurt them," counsels Old Rosa Bultrón. Ultimately Rosa
tricks Pedro and saves a runaway girl. The author is a history professor in Puerto Rico.
The Cuban-born artist, whose illustrations appear in full color in this 8^{1}/2 x 9^{1}/4" book,
has lived in Puerto Rico since 1961. (Ages 7–11)

Pomerantz, Charlotte. *The Outside Dog.*
Illustrated by Jennifer Plecas. (An I Can Read
Book) HarperCollins, 1993. 64 pages.
(0–06–024782–7) (lib. bdg. 0–06–024783–5)
(pbk. 0–06–444187–3, 1995)

Marisol wants a dog, but grandfather says no. "They have fleas and ticks and who knows
what." But when a skinny brown dog with perky ears and a bright nose wanders into
their yard, she is quick to point out that this dog has no fleas. It's only a matter of time
before she's talked grandfather into feeding the dog, then letting her buy him a collar,
and, of course, she has to give him a name. This beginning reader set in Puerto Rico
integrates simple Spanish words into the easy text as it tells the story of a young girl, her
soft-hearted grandfather, and a little brown dog named Pancho. (Ages 4–7)

Russell, Ching Yeung. *First Apple.* Illustrated
by Christopher Zhong-Yuan Zhang. Boyds
Mills, 1994. 127 pages. (1–56397–206–9)
(pbk. 0–14–03723–5; Puffin, 1996)

An easy-to-follow story set in China during the late 1940s involves nine-year-old Ying,
an energetic girl whose constant activities bring almost daily mishaps. Ying's determination to get an apple for her grandmother requires her to do boring chores, and she gets
into one scrape after another. The idea that there are children as well as adults who have
only read about but never tasted "sweet and crunchy" apples will intrigue many U.S.
readers. The fast-paced plot includes cultural details that do not get in the way of the
sparkling dialogue. (Ages 6–9)

Soto, Gary. *The Skirt.* Illustrated by Eric Velasquez. Delacorte, 1992. 74 pages. (0–385–30665–2) (pbk. 0–440–40924–1; Dell, 1994)

Miata Ramirez is devastated when she discovers she's left her *folklórico* skirt—her mother's skirt from Mexico—on the school bus. It's Friday afternoon and Miata's supposed to wear the skirt at Sunday afternoon's folk dance. Unable to admit that she's forgotten the skirt, Miata convinces a friend to join her in a Saturday afternoon secret expedition to the fence-enclosed lot where the buses are parked. Of course, nothing turns out quite as planned in this easy-to-read short novel printed in clear, large typeface. (Ages 8–11)

Stolz, Mary. *Go Fish.* Illustrated by Pat Cummings. HarperCollins, 1991. 73 pages. (lib. bdg. 0–06–025822–5) (pbk. 0–06–440466–8, 1993)

Thomas and Grandfather share a passion for thinking about fishing, catching fish, cooking fish, eating fish, and playing the "Go Fish" card game. And, of course, Grandfather always has a story to tell when Thomas fishes around for a reason to stay up just a little bit longer. Both Stolz's story and Cummings's drawings depict a strong and tender intergenerational relationship in an African-American family. An easy chapter book with black-and-white illustrations on every page continues the story of eight-year-old Thomas and his grandfather, who were introduced in the picture book *Storm in the Night* (Harper, 1988). (Ages 5–9)

Williams, Vera B. *Scooter.* Greenwillow, 1993. 147 pages. (0–688–09376–0) (lib. bdg. 0–688–09377–9)

Elana Rose Rosen and her mother moved to an apartment on the 8th floor of 514 Melon Hill Avenue, and, according to Elana, she loved it from the first minute. Not so, says her mom, but that doesn't matter because as soon as her scooter was unpacked, Elana was out on the sidewalk practicing jumps. A minor accident proves to be one way to get acquainted, and Elana does—with other kids like Jimmy Beck, Eduard from 4K, Adrienne whose parents own the store, and Vinh and Siobhan and Beryl, who wears lipstick already. She becomes friends with Petey, the child who brought home Elana's scooter after the accident, the child who always wears a hat, which is OK, but doesn't talk, which isn't. Elana also gets to know some of the adults in her building: Benny Portelli the super, Mom's longtime friend Celia, and Mrs. Grenier, the most trying of the grown-ups. Elana can also be trying, and even stages a major pages-long absolutely authentic tantrum following a misunderstanding with her mother. In addition to scooter tricks, Elana creates personal acrostics, makes vegetable soup and even allows Mrs. Grenier to show her how to make a good fat pom-pom. Elana, her mother and the diverse community in which they live are marvelously characterized. On every page in the 29 brief chapters, Williams's black and red artwork provides exciting visual dimensions, from inventive wordplay to a soup recipe to a few scooter tire tracks. This highly original novel involves the **S**ecurity provided by a **C**ommunity, seems **O**ld-fashioned in comforting ways, **O**ffers a **T**riumphant main character, is **E**motionally honest and **R**olls along fast while exploring matters of immediacy to children. (Ages 4–7 for listening and 8–11 for reading and doing)

FICTION FOR CHILDREN

Anzaldúa, Gloria. *Prietita and the Ghost Woman = Prietita y la Llorona.* Illustrated by Christina Gonzalez. Children's Book Press (246 First St., Suite 101, San Francisco, CA 94105), 1996. 32 pages. (0–89239–136–7)

La curandera (traditional healer) needs a rue plant to make a remedy so that she can cure Prietita's sick mother and Prietita wants to do everything she can to help, even if it means trespassing on the land owned by King Ranch where rue is said to grow freely. When she sneaks under the barbed wire fence, not only does she risk being shot at by guards, she also risks running into *la Llorona*, the legendary ghost woman who is said to steal children. This short bilingual story features a courageous Latina girl as its heroine. She uses her wits and knowledge of her Mexican cultural heritage to find what she needs to help her *mami*. (Ages 7–10)

Boyd, Candy Dawson. *Chevrolet Saturdays.* Macmillan, 1993. 176 pages. (lib. bdg. 0–02–711765–0) (pbk. 0–14–036859–0; Puffin, 1995)

Joey Davis, certain that he belongs in the gifted and talented program at his school, has difficulty getting along with his teacher when he starts fifth grade. To make matters even worse, his mother's remarriage has destroyed Joey's dream of his divorced parents ever reconciling their differences. Joey is determined to make his new stepfather pay the price, even though the latter is trying hard to be Joey's friend by including the boy in his work routine every Saturday. Joey knows Mr. Johnson will never take his father's place and gradually realizes that Mr. Johnson knows it, too. The complexities of adjusting to changes in family life are skillfully and realistically woven into a fast-paced novel starring a true-to-life African-American boy who is at once exasperating and vulnerable. (Ages 9–12)

Bruchac, Joseph. *Children of the Longhouse.* Dial, 1996. 150 pages. (0–8037–1793–8) (lib. bdg. 0–8037–1794–6)

A finely detailed novel from storyteller Joseph Bruchac tells of a 14th century Mohawk village and a brother and sister who live there. Twins Ohkwa'ri and Otsi:stia are 11 winters old; still children but gaining a deeper understanding of the ways of their people each day. When he was younger, Ohkwa'ri admired the older boy known as Grabber for his skill and strength, but now his eyes are wiser. When Ohkwa'ri overhears Grabber and some other young men planning a raid on the Anen:taks, with whom the Mohawk peacefully trade, he tells Otsi:stia, whose good judgment he can always rely on. As a result Grabber and his friends are punished, and Ohkwa'ri has made an enemy. A fast and furious game of *Tekwaarathon* (now known as lacrosse) through woods and across a meadow lends added tension and excitement to the climax of this story that pays homage to the Great League of Peace of the Iroquois Nations. An author's afterword discusses the Mohawk Nation and the Iroquois League of Peace. (Ages 9–12)

Case, Dianne. *92 Queens Road.* U.S. edition: Farrar, Straus and Giroux, 1995. 164 pages. (0–374–35518–5)

Cape Town, South Africa. One day at the beach, Kathy crosses a border she never knew existed when she approaches white children to play. She is made to feel like something dirty because of the color of her skin. Sheltered in her working class neighborhood, among family and friends whose quarrels are as intense as their joy, Kathy was innocent of the pain of racism until that moment. Now when her light-skinned cousins ignore her on the street she understands why. When her Uncle Reg says, "This is not our country" she wonders "Where do we belong?" Set in the 1960s, Case's autobiograhical novel is a child-centered exposé on the injustices of Apartheid and its impact on the identity of one young girl. (Ages 9–11)

Curtis, Christopher Paul. *The Watsons Go to Birmingham—1963.* Delacorte, 1995. 210 pages. (0–385–32175–9)

In an impressive literary debut, Christopher Paul Curtis recounts events in the life of ten-year-old Kenny Watson, the middle child in a middle-class African-American family living in Flint, Michigan, in 1963. A smart, sensitive boy, Kenny refers to his family as the "Weird Watsons," because each member stands out as an individual when Kenny just wants to blend in with the crowd. Much of their family life revolves around 13-year-old Byron who is a self-confident, sarcastic, rebellious adolescent. When Dad and Momma decide that Byron needs to spend some time down home with relatives in Birmingham, the whole family goes along to deliver Byron into Grandma's hands. During their brief stay in Birmingham, tragedy strikes when a bomb explodes at Grandma Sands' church one Sunday morning, killing four little girls, an experience that deeply affects Kenny. On a symbolic level this funny, provocative novel mirrors events in the life of our nation in 1963, a year when the United States, like Kenny, lost its innocence as hope turned to cynicism. (Ages 10–14)

Davis, Ossie. *Just Like Martin.* Simon & Schuster, 1992. 215 pages. (0–671–73202–1) (pbk. 0–14–037095–1; Puffin, 1995)

The year is 1963, and 14-year-old Isaac wants to go to the March on Washington. Reverend Dr. Martin Luther King, Jr.'s preaching and teaching about nonviolence inspired Isaac and other African-American youth from church to become active in this dimension of the struggle for equality. Reverend Cable has confidence in Isaac's leadership, but for some reason Isaac's daddy doesn't, even though the men are longtime friends who also went together to Korea to fight in the war. Family and community tensions build, especially after a bombing of the church building causes tragic deaths in this Alabama community. Effective dialogue develops characterizations and moves the plot that tells about the church involvement of some of the courageous African-American youth in the Civil Rights Movement. (Ages 11–14)

Dorris, Michael. *Guests.* Hyperion, 1994. 119 pages. (0–7868–0047-X) (lib. bdg. 0–7868–2036–5) (pbk. 0–7868–1108–0, 1996)

A novel offering young readers the opportunity to consider the life and perspective of an American Indian child at the time of the first European settlement in North America features Moss, a young boy who is unhappy that his father has asked outsiders to share his village's harvest meal. "Someday, you'll understand," his father tells him, but to Moss that answer is only another way in which he is treated as a child. Impatient to grow up and unhappy at the change in tradition, Moss ventures alone into the forest, thinking he will have his "away-time," the time when a boy seeks out solitude in the hopes of returning with his adult identity and new understanding. But in the forest Moss finds Trouble, a girl from his village whose desire to go against tradition makes her as restless and unhappy in her own way as he is in his. (Ages 9–11)

Greenfield, Eloise. *Koya Delaney and the Good Girl Blues.* Scholastic, 1992. 124 pages. (0–590–43300–8) (pbk. 0–590–43299–0, 1995)

Koya loves to laugh, and she'll do anything to make those around her laugh too. Her abundant sense of humor and dedication to diffusing potentially difficult situations is often appreciated by her friends and family, but at times Koya is so intent on producing good feelings that she denies her own occasional, but inevitable, emotions of anger and unhappiness. When her cousin, a pop music star, comes to town for a concert, Koya is thrilled at the opportunity to attend the event, but a conflict between her sister and best friend threatens to create a situation that even Koya cannot prevent. A fast-paced novel for young readers, Koya's story skillfully combines light-hearted scenes of popular music and double-dutch competitions with the struggle of learning to deal with one's positive and negative feelings. (Ages 8–11)

Hamilton, Virginia. *Plain City.* Scholastic, 1993. 194 pages. (0–590–47364–6) (pbk. 0–590–47365–4, 1995)

Twelve-year-old Buhlaire is completely mystified about her family's immediate past, a subject her mother, aunts, and uncles never discuss. Who was her father, she wonders, and why did he leave them? When Buhlaire finds out that he's living right in the same town as she is, she sets out to find him, certain that he may hold the key that will unlock the mystery of her past. Hamilton's carefully crafted novel about a young biracial girl's search for identity is filled with imagery of frozen landscapes, winter storms, and a sudden spring thaw, all of which symbolize Buhlaire's emotional state during her quest for truth. (Ages 11–14)

Myers, Walter Dean. *Mop, Moondance, and the Nagasaki Knights.* Delacorte, 1992. 150 pages. (pbk. 0–440–40914–4; Dell, 1994)

Can T.J., Moondance, Mop, and the rest of their championship baseball team find victory again? The Elk's competition is stiff as they face a tournament with visiting teams from Japan, Mexico, and France. It doesn't help that a new member of the Elks seems to be having some problems of his own, while another local team and its coach are promoting a nationalistic "win at all costs" attitude that the Elks don't agree with. Homelessness, chauvinistic attitudes, and lots of baseball combine in this easy-to-read sequel to *Me, Mop, and the Moondance Kid* (Delacorte, 1988). (Ages 8–11)

Smothers, Ethel Footman. *Down in the Piney Woods.* Alfred A. Knopf, 1992. 151 pages. (0–679–80360–2) (lib. bdg. 0–679–90360–7) (pbk. 0–679–84714–6, 1994)

Based on the author's own childhood experiences in rural Georgia, this story of an extended African-American family exudes a strong regional voice. Ten-year-old Annie Rye is less than pleased when her Mama announces that Annie Rye's three half-sisters are coming to live with Annie Rye and her younger brother and sister. The animosity Annie Rye feels is strongly shared by one of her newly arrived sisters, and they, along with their other siblings and parents, must work out a way to live together as a family. The sibling rivalry is convincingly presented in a family novel containing both humor and sober reality. (Ages 9–12)

Soto, Gary. *Taking Sides.* Harcourt Brace Jovanovich, 1991. 138 pages. (0–15–284076–1) (pbk. 0–15–284077–2, 1992)

When 14-year-old Lincoln Mendoza moves with his mother from a working-class Latino community to a white suburban neighborhood, his main concern is that he make the basketball team at his new junior high. Once he does, life gets even more complicated as he tries to come to terms with his feelings about playing on the new team against his old junior high school. An appealing, fast-paced novel about divided loyalties and ethnic identity has many moments of humor and poignancy in addition to a credible, down-to-earth teen protagonist. (Ages 9–14)

Stolz, Mary. *Coco Grimes.* HarperCollins, 1994. 89 pages. (0–06–024232–9) (lib. bdg. 0–06–024233–7) (pbk. 0–06–440512–5, 1996)

Thomas, who has just turned 11, is eager to go to Miami to meet Coco Grimes, a man who once played baseball in the Negro Leagues. But Grandfather's old pickup truck is too unreliable to make the trip across Florida. Thomas's disappointment turns to excitement when Grandfather is able to borrow a car, but his visit to Coco Grimes in Miami proves disconcerting when the former athlete talks with excitement and certainty about his days on the playing field one minute and is confused and yelling at Thomas the next. The fourth book featuring this African-American grandfather and grandson whose relationship continues to grow was preceded by other equally successful books to read aloud or for newly independent readers: *Storm in the Night* (1988), *Go Fish* (1991), and *Stealing Home* (1992), all published by HarperCollins. (Ages 7–11)

Stolz, Mary. *Stealing Home.* HarperCollins, 1992. 153 pages. (0–06–021154–7) (lib. bdg. 0–06–021157–1) (pbk. 0–06–440528–1, 1994)

Thomas is happy with his life with Grandfather. Fishing, listening to baseball games, and putting together jigsaw puzzles in their small Florida home is, as Thomas puts it, "cozy." But when Grandfather's sister-in-law Linzy arrives from Chicago for an extended, perhaps permanent, visit, Thomas's sense of coziness disappears. Aunt Linzy is a vegetarian who objects to fishing, she doesn't understand baseball, and she seems obsessed with cleaning. Worst of all, Thomas's cat Ringo seems to be abandoning him in favor of the new arrival. Mary Stolz has created an appealing novel about the same African-American family in her earlier picture story *Storm in the Night* (Harper, 1988) and the beginning reader *Go Fish* (HarperCollins, 1991). (Ages 8–11)

Tate, Eleanora E. *Front Porch Stories at the One-Room School.* Illustrated by Eric Velasquez. Bantam Skylark, 1992. 98 pages. (pbk. 0–440–40901–2; Dell, 1994)

With nothing to do on a hot summer evening, Margie wishes she had gone to a Tupperware party with her mother until her Daddy takes her and her cousin Ethel to the school's front steps and starts telling stories. His stories are always good, and these are no exception as he tells scary, funny, and sad stories about what it was like when he was growing up in Missouri. The tales flow easily from the present into the past and back again, and from one story to the next, as they feature an African-American family and community. (Ages 8–11)

Taylor, Mildred D. *The Well.* Dial, 1995. 92 pages. (0–8037–1803–9, out of print)

In her latest work of short fiction in the Logan family saga, Mildred Taylor moves back a generation into the childhood of Cassie Logan's father in the early 1900s. Brothers David and Hammer Logan are seen on the brink of adolescence, trying to make sense out of a senseless social order based on race and class. During an extreme dry spell in Mississippi, nearly every family's well has run dry, except for that of the Logan family, which draws from an underground lake. The Logans willingly share their water with rich and poor, Black and white. They even share with the Simms family, a difficult pill for the Logan boys to swallow since 13-year-old Hammer and 14-year-old Charlie Simms are bitter rivals. When an argument between the two young teens comes to blows and Hammer knocks Charlie to the ground, the situation escalates into a social crisis in which Charlie's racist attitude threatens to poison the entire community. With her spare account of a single event, Mildred Taylor's extremely accomplished storytelling shows the horrific impact of segregation and racism. Like the well itself, the story is deceptively simple and one can dip below its surface to find that each character's actions are drawn from an underground reservoir of social history. (Ages 9–14)

Temple, Frances. *Grab Hands and Run.* Orchard, 1993. 165 pages. (0–531–05480–2) (lib. bdg. 0–531–08630–5) (pbk. 0–06–440548–6, 1995)

Twelve-year-old Felipe and his younger sister, Romy, literally are running for their lives. Along with their mother they are trying to escape El Salvador, haunted by fears of what has happened to their father, Jacinto, whose disappearance has propelled them into flight. Jacinto's political activities against the government had made him a target. Now that he has apparently been caught, their mother is following the advice he once gave her: "If they come for me, you and the children—grab hands and run." Felipe, Romy, and their mother, Paloma, must rely on their strength, their wits, and most of all one another to survive as they journey by any means they can find through Central America and Mexico and on into the United States, where they are fugitives still. Insight into human nature, understanding, and the political barriers to justice in many countries, including our own, are blended into this swiftly-moving first-person narrative. (Ages 11–14)

Temple, Frances. *Tonight, by Sea.* A Richard Jackson Book/Orchard, 1995. 152 pages. (0–531–06899–4) (lib. bdg. 0–531–08749–2) (pbk. 0–06–440670–9, HarperTrophy, 1996)

Darkness approaches as Paulie runs to borrow a live coal from a neighbor in Belle Fleuve on a Haitian beach. After the girl fans a flame from the ember placed on seaweed, her Grann Adeline will cook a small fish for supper. Paulie's uncle, the village coffin-maker, has begun to build a boat. Uncle will craft the vessel by cunning, construct it with used boards and nails, caulk it using pig hair with burlap, and grace it with a worship pole. Until now, Uncle, Grann, and their community have struggled to survive under the slavery of constant hunger, the shadow of a teacher's disappearance, the gradual erosion of their freedoms, and governance through terror. Paulie's parents are already "across the water" in Miami. An American journalist wants their story to reach the outside world, but his video camera holds as much danger for them as a gun. By the time Paulie and those surviving the voyage reach another shore, readers will be familiar with a folktale about hope. Like Paulie, they will find out about the Amistad, another boat dedicated to life. They will realize that one can be killed or changed by "habits of truth." Temple's fine prose, deft dialogue, and compassionate heart fill a terrific story that takes readers behind the faces in the evening news, straight to the people whose lives hang in the balance. (Ages 10–14)

Whelan, Gloria. *Goodbye, Vietnam.*
Alfred A. Knopf, 1992. 135 pages.
(0–679–82263–1) (lib. bdg. 0–679–92263–6)
(pbk. 0–679–82376–X; Random House, 1993)

Forced to flee Vietnam to avoid police persecution, Mai and her parents, siblings, and grandmother travel with many other refugees by boat to Hong Kong. The journey is arduous, as the boat experiences mechanical problems and its overcrowded occupants suffer from hunger, thirst, and illness. Upon arrival in Hong Kong, the refugees are immediately sent to a holding center where they await permission to travel to another country, or word that they will be sent back to Vietnam. This contemporary short novel contrasts the desperate situation of many economic and political refugees with their determination to lead safe and fulfilling lives. (Ages 9–12)

Woodson, Jacqueline. *I Hadn't Meant to Tell You This.* Delacorte, 1994. 115 pages.
(0–385–32031–0) (pbk. 0–440–21960–4)

"Sometimes Lena walked like somebody broken. When I found myself behind her in the crowded hallway, I wanted to punch her back straight, to yank her head up, to focus her eyes away from the floor. Other times she moved through the hallway like a steel wall, impenetrable and upright. Then I was a little bit afraid that she would turn around, see me behind her, and explode." In Chauncey, where issues of race and class mean everything, 12-year-olds Marie and Lena seem an unlikely match in friendship. Marie, who is middle class and Black, is at first irritated but eventually intrigued by the efforts of Lena, a new girl at her school who is poor and white, to be friends with her. The friendship that develops between them helps Marie deal with the hurt and confusion she feels over her mother's desertion, and gives Lena respite from life with an abusive father. Together, the two girls create a haven; for Lena, it is a place of safety and comfort, for Marie a place to build strength and find courage. For them both, it is also, quite simply, a place to be children a few moments longer. (Ages 10–13)

Woodson, Jacqueline. *Maizon at Blue Hill.*
Delacorte, 1992. 131 pages.
(0–385–30796–9) (pbk. 0–440–40899–7;
Dell, 1994)

When Maizon accepts a scholarship to a private boarding school, she leaves behind her Grandmother, her best friend Margaret, and the familiarity of the community in which she's grown up. Blue Hill School offers many things, including stimulating classes with excellent teachers in a beautiful rural setting. It also forces Maizon to consider issues of race, prejudice, elitism, and stereotypes in new ways, as she enters school as one of five African-American students. Maizon learns much about herself and the teachers and students around her, both white and Black, as she struggles to decide whether to continue at Blue Hill or return to her home in the city. First met in *Last Summer with Maizon* (Delacorte, 1990), Maizon continues to ring true as an academically gifted, multi-faceted young woman. (Ages 9–12)

Yep, Laurence. *Later, Gator.* Hyperion, 1995.
122 pages. (0–7868–0059–3)

Teddy describes his younger brother as "a walking Hallmark card." Bobby's sweet disposition and naiveté in the face of insults drive Teddy crazy. When Teddy gives Bobby a live, eight-inch alligator for his birthday, he does so as a joke that is meant to frighten him. Instead, much to Teddy's chagrin, Bobby loves the reptile. The care and feeding of Oscar, whose residence is established in the family bathtub, becomes a fascinating draw for friends and family in their San Francisco Chinatown neighborhood. Teddy grows to appreciate his younger brother's knowledge, patience, and good humor as they care for his unusual pet in a wry, funny narrative about sibling relationships set in a warm, extended Chinese-American family. (Ages 9–11)

Yep, Laurence. *The Star Fisher.* Morrow,
1991. 150 pages. (0–688–09365–5)
(pbk. 0–14–036003–4; Puffin, 1992)

In 1927, 15-year-old Joan Lee moves with her family from Ohio to a small town in West Virginia. As the only Chinese-Americans in town, the Lees face social ostracism and overt racism from townspeople who boycott the Lee family business. Joan herself feels tensions between the pressure at home to follow strict Chinese traditions and the pressure at school to assimilate into a white American mainstream. The Chinese folktale of the star fisher, a bird/woman caught between two worlds, provides the central metaphor for this rich, witty, engrossing novel. (Ages 10–13)

Yumoto, Kazumi. *The Friends.* Translated from the Japanese by Cathy Hirano. U.S. edition: Farrar Straus Giroux, 1996. 170 pages.
(0–374–32460–3)

In search of answers to questions about death, three Japanese boys learn about life and living in a beautifully unfolding novel from Japanese author Kazumi Yumoto. Kiyama, Kawabe, and Yamashita are sixth-grade friends who want to know what happens when someone dies, in the very moment of life's passing. They begin spying on a reclusive old man near their school: the most likely candidate for death that they know. But the old man, whose life is spare and lonely, who is, indeed, physically alive but barely engaged in the act of living, catches them. As if to defy the very thing the boys hope for, the old man begins to embrace life in a new and vigorous way, challenging the boys to come out from behind the wall where they spy and close the distance between them as he does so. What began as a death watch slowly transforms into a deeply felt friendship between the boys and the old man, a friendship that encourages them all—children and adult alike—to live life more deliberately. A novel set in contemporary Japan and providing a realistic portrayal of the busy, active schedules which many Japanese children maintain to meet the expectations of family and society acknowledges the ways lives are enriched when people risk coming out from behind their walls to meet the hearts and minds of others. (Ages 10–13)

FICTION FOR TEENAGERS

Baillie, Allan. *Little Brother.* U.S. edition: Viking, 1992. 144 pages. (0–670–84381–4) (pbk. 0–14–036862–0; Puffin, 1994)

When Vithy is separated from his brother Mang while trying to cross the Cambodian border into Thailand, he doesn't know how to continue. Mang had always been there to take care of Vithy, even to orchestrating their escape from the Big Paddy where they had been held captive for months. Now, faced with a treacherous journey and danger at every turn, Vithy longs for Mang's guidance. As he makes his way towards the border, Vithy gradually discovers that he, too, is capable of making wise decisions. Set in post-Vietnam War Cambodia, the story of Vithy's plight and growing self-reliance is both suspenseful and credible. (Ages 11–14)

Berry, James. *Ajeemah and His Son.* U.S. edition: A Willa Perlman Book/HarperCollins, 1992. 83 pages. (0–06–021043–5) (lib. bdg. 0–06–021044–3) (pbk. 0–06–440523–0, 1994)

Eighteen-year-old Atu and his father are abducted as they are taking a dowry to Atu's soon-to-be wife's parents. They are sent by boat from Africa to Jamaica and sold to plantation owners. Separated by just a few miles on neighboring plantations, both men spend horrendous years in captivity, never knowing that the other is so near, and never able to get word to their family in Africa of their enslavement. The author's rich prose gives depth to this unforgettable short account of loss of freedom and family. (Ages 14–16)

Buss, Fran Leeper. *Journey of the Sparrows.* With the assistance of Daisy Cubias. Lodestar, 1991. 155 pages. (0–525–67362–8) (pbk. 0–440–40785–0; Dell, 1993)

After a harrowing, dangerous journey from war-torn El Salvador to the United States, teenage Maria and her sister and brother settle in Chicago, waiting for their mother and youngest sister to join them. Welcomed into a community of Salvadoran refugees struggling to survive, Maria works hard to support her family, all the while trying to be "invisible" to lessen the risk of deportation. A gripping, provocative first novel about some of the challenges faced by the people known as "illegal aliens." (Ages 12–16)

Carlson, Lori M. editor. *American Eyes: New Asian-American Short Stories for Young Adults.* Introduction by Cynthia Kadohata. An Edge Book/Henry Holt, 1994. 144 pages. (0–8050–3544–3) (pbk. 0–449–70448–3; Fawcett, 1996)

Ten authors use "their own voices and visions—their American eyes—to Americanize all of us in new ways," according to the editor. Some of the stories involve experiences of assimilation or prejudice. Others examine the theme of Home and/or Homeland. Two are excerpted from longer works. The authors are Peter Bacho, Lan Samantha Chang, Mary Chen, Cynthia Kadohata, Marie G. Lee, Katherine Min, Nguyen Duc Minh, Faye Myenne Ng, Ryan Oba, and Lois-Ann Yamanaka. Short biographies of the authors are included; their backgrounds and experiences vary, in that their heritages are Chinese, Filipino, Korean, Japanese, and Vietnamese. (Ages 14–16)

Castañeda, Omar S. *Among the Volcanoes.* Lodestar, 1991. 183 pages. (0–525–67332–6) (pbk. 0–440–40746–X)

In his first novel for young adults, Omar S. Castañeda draws on his own heritage as a Guatemalan American for a story set in contemporary Guatemala. Teenager Isabel Pacay is a Tzutujil Indian living in Chuuí Chopaló, a small town entirely populated by the Tzutujil. As the eldest daughter, Isabel is expected to take on a lot of responsibility, particularly now that her mother is ill, and Isabel resents that she has had to leave school in order to care for the household. On the inside, Isabel is filled with conflict; on the outside, she is trying to make a smooth transition from childhood to adulthood in a town undergoing political and social changes which parallel Isabel's own growth. (Ages 13–16)

Castañeda, Omar S. *Imagining Isabel.* Lodestar, 1994. 200 pages. (0–525–67431–4)

Sixteen-year-old Isabel Pacay Choy is torn between tradition and her own longing. Newly married, Isabel makes the difficult decision to attend a government-sponsored teacher training school in the city, despite the fact that Tzutujil women traditionally care for their husbands and families. Isabel's widowed father also needs her to help care for her youngest sister. Political turmoil in Guatemala further complicates the issue. Trusting the government can be dangerous in Guatemala, especially for the Indian peoples. Isabel loves to learn, and she loves the prospect of teaching. But she doesn't know if she is strong enough to endure the challenges—and dangers—that she must face. This sequel to *Among the Volcanoes* (Lodestar, 1991) explores tense political and cultural issues in the context of a young woman's struggle to find the strength, the knowledge, and the inner peace to endure whatever choice she makes. (Ages 13–16)

Choi, Sook Nyul. *Year of Impossible Goodbyes.* Houghton Mifflin, 1991. 169 pages. (0–395–57419–6) (pbk. 0–440–40759–1; Dell, 1993)

A stupendous autobiographical novel set in Korea involves ten-year-old Sookan and her family's survival during and after World War II. They experience a devastating sequence of losses due to the physical and psychological cruelties of occupying authorities, first the Japanese military and then the Communist Russian troops. Before people were turned against each other, hunger was their common enemy; afterwards, the enemy became lack of mutual trust. But hope, even trust prevails. The stark, spare story is suspensefully paced with a single celebratory event offering relief at a critical point. Many memorable images will stand out for readers long after they finish this book, such as episodes involving the "sock girls"; the children's witnessing of an elder's abandonment of his shoes; and the bravery of an aunt who rebelled against the unwritten rules of a battle to win young minds. Sookan's story continues in *Echoes of the White Giraffe* (Houghton Mifflin, 1993) and *Gathering of Pearls* (Houghton Mifflin, 1994). (Ages 12–16)

Cofer, Judith Ortiz. *An Island Like You.* A Melanie Kroupa Book/Orchard, 1995. 165 pages. (0–531–06897–8) (lib. bdg. 0–531–08747–6) (pbk. 0–14–038068–X; Penguin, 1996)

The sounds and the sights of El Barrio and the relationships and the emotions of Puerto Rican-American family and neighborhood life form the backdrop for each of the 12 stories that comprise *An Island Like You.* For the teenagers whose hearts and minds are unmasked in this powerful collection of short stories from Latina author Judith Ortiz Cofer, El Barrio is their home and their culture, steeped in the Puerto Rican traditions of their parents and grandparents, flavored with the promise and bitterness of urban American life. El Barrio is also the world they share. Yet each of the protagonists in *An Island Like You* moves through this world in his or her own way. The range of experience which Cofer brilliantly illuminates through the singular lives of her adolescent characters reveals truths that are sometimes comforting, sometimes startling, but always dancing on the edge of enlightenment. (Ages 12–16)

Draper, Sharon M. *Tears of a Tiger.* Atheneum, 1994. 161 pages. (0–689–31878–2) (pbk. 0–689–80698–1; Simon & Schuster, 1996)

A taut novel unfolds the stories of several teenagers deeply affected by the violent car crash that caused the death of a high school basketball star who went out drinking with friends after a game. The novel opens with a news account of the accident and ends with a letter written months later by a grieving boy to the driver, his older brother, who later killed himself. Draper clearly understands and cares about teens and their worlds. This high school teacher/author successfully employs dialogue, diary entries, transcripts of loudspeaker announcements, and other epistolary devices to relate a sad tale about African-American teens real enough to walk off the page—alive. (Ages 11–16)

Hodge, Merle. *For the Life of Laetitia.* Farrar Straus Giroux, 1993. 214 pages. (0–374–32447–6) (pbk. 0–374–42444–6, 1994)

Twelve-year-old Laetitia is a promising student who's been selected to attend a government-run secondary school in the town of La Puerta on her Caribbean island home. Her family is proud and pleased, and yet will barely have enough money for books and uniforms, let alone for the long bus and taxi rides between their rural village and La Puerta each day. Enter Laetitia's long-absent father who now lives in town with a new wife and child and who has agreed to take his eldest daughter in as a boarder during the week. Although he is not on the best of terms with his former family and he and Laetitia barely know each other, he, too, is proud of his daughter's academic promise and seems happy to have her join his family. As Laetitia adjusts to a new school and a new family, she must learn to cope with the strong prejudices against rural working-class people that continually find expression in both places. Memorable characters, a strong sense of place and a thought-provoking storyline distinguish an excellent and absorbing first novel by a West Indian writer. (Ages 12–16)

Jenkins, Lyll Becerra de. *Celebrating the Hero.* Lodestar, 1993. 179 pages. (0–525–67399–7) (pbk. 0–14–037605–4; Puffin, 1995)

Seventeen-year-old Camila is the only daughter of an Anglo father and a Colombian mother. Camila has grown up in the United States and most of what she knows of Colombian heritage comes from her mother's stories of growing up in San Javier, a small town in Colombia where her mother's father was something of a local hero. Camila's maternal grandmother was rarely mentioned in her mother's stories. After her mother's death, Camila agrees to represent her at a local celebration in honor of her famous grandfather. But there is a mix-up in the flight arrangements and Camila arrives in San Javier a full 24 hours before anyone else in her family knows she's there. And that gives her just enough time to try to find out who her grandmother was and why she is never mentioned. The details she manages to uncover reveal much about her heritage that her mother probably could never have divulged, details that Camila's status as an outsider likely sharpen and amplify. Lyll Becerra de Jenkins's brilliant novel explores the depths of human identity connected to gender, culture, and age, even as she spins out all the intrigue of a great mystery story and keeps the reader riveted to the page. (Ages 12–16)

Jenkins, Lyll Becerra de. *So Loud a Silence.* Lodestar, 1996. 154 pages. (0–525–67538–8)

Layers of a family story are revealed in the midst of tense and tenuous times in Lyll Becerra de Jenkins's eye-opening, radical novel set in Colombia today. Seventeen-year-old Juan Guillermo lives in Bogotá, the oldest child of a poverty-stricken family. When he visits a woman professed to be his aunt, Doña Petrona, a landowner in a rural village in the mountains, he finds, for the first time in his life, a sense of peace and affinity for a place. But life in the mountains is not uncomplicated; indeed, beneath the pastoral beauty is the real danger: the people are caught in the war between guerrillas and the army. Even without gunfire in the streets, their lives are threatened if they speak the wrong words or express the wrong sympathies. While the elders of the village, Doña Petrona included, preach measured restraint, Juan finds himself drawn to the passionate beliefs of the young people who call for action. At the same time he finds himself in conflict with this strong yet compassionate woman, he is longing for her respect and for the insights she can give him into his family and his life in a novel that provides an uncommon political perspective for young readers in the United States. (Ages 12–16)

Johnson, Angela. *Toning the Sweep.* Orchard, 1993. 103 pages. (0–531–05476–4) (lib. bdg. 0–531–08626–7) (pbk. 0–590–48142–8; Scholastic, 1994)

In a family composed of three strong, independent African-American women (daughter, mother, grandmother), it's often what's left unsaid among them that resonates the loudest for the youngest family member, 14-year-old Emmie. Now that Grandmother Ola is dying from cancer, Emmie feels compelled to hear the truth behind their silences. She knows that something awful happened long ago that no one ever mentions. What was it? In a spare, eloquent first novel, Angela Johnson shows that silence can dull the pain of tragedy but can never really cure it. Emmie discovers that one must ring the dead into heaven with great noise, by elegizing, keening, or even by striking a plow with a hammer, a folk ritual known as "toning the sweep." (Ages 12–16)

Kim, Helen. *The Long Season of Rain.* Henry Holt, 1996. 275 pages. (0–8050–4758–1)

The start of the rainy season in June means a break in the stifling heat and humidity, but it brings a new, deeper awareness to 11-year-old Junehee of the tension that binds her family in this riveting narrative set in Korea in the 1960s. Junehee's father is a military officer who has become more and more disconnected and emotionally distant from his wife and children over the years. Her paternal grandmother, who lives with the family, has asserted more and more control over Junehee's mother and the children as a result. Junehee's mother has endured both conditions with the silence that tradition seems to dictate. But tradition clashes with desire when Junehee's mother longs to keep a boy whom the family takes in temporarily after he is orphaned as the result of a mud slide brought on by the heavy rains. Junehee, a middle child, becomes a keen-eyed observer of her mother's unrelenting sadness, a sadness that Junehee realizes has gone on far longer than the rains. Helen Kim's emotionally acute novel about a child's growing awareness of her mother's powerlessness and pain is beautifully written, and not without hope. (Age 12–adult)

Lee, Marie G. *Saying Goodbye.* Houghton Mifflin, 1994. 219 pages. (0–395–67066–7)

Cambridge, Massachusetts, is a long way from Arkin, Minnesota. Starting her freshman year at Harvard College, Ellen Sung quickly realizes that the distance from college to her home town is measured in more than miles. In Arkin, where her family was more concerned with fitting into their Midwest surroundings than emphasizing their cultural identity, she was labeled "Oriental" by members of the community. But at Harvard, she is looked upon as "Korean-American," and with this comes wonderful discoveries about her cultural heritage, but also pressures and expectations she could never have imagined. When tensions build between members of an African-American and Korean-American student group on campus, Ellen feels torn between loyalty to her closest friend—her African-American roommate, Leecia—and loyalty to her fellow Korean-American students. She must struggle with difficult decisions to come to her own point of truth. A courageous novel exploring racism, identity, and friendship continues Ellen's story, which began in *Finding My Voice* (1992) and continued in *If It Hadn't Been for Yoon Jun* (1993), both published by Houghton. (Ages 14–16)

Martinez, Victor. *Parrot in the Oven: mi vida.* Joanna Cotler/HarperCollins, 1996. 216 pages. (0–06–026704–6) (lib. bdg. 0–06–026706–2)

Manny is smart; sometimes he thinks he might be smart enough to make it out of his struggling neighborhood to a life beyond poverty, beyond the threat of apathy and violence. In his emotionally torn family, the tension of racism and economic oppression plays itself out: his father drinks to combat frustration, his brother can't keep a job, his sisters are experiencing too much too soon, and his mother strives to hold them all together even as she sometimes seems close to unraveling herself. But despite the strain in his family, Manny finds home is a place of refuge compared to the uncertainty of the outside world. The Mexican-American teenager's observations of a life filled with tension and fragile possibility are not without humor or hope, but it is his honesty in describing the experiences that unfold that gives powerful shape to his narrative voice. (Age 16–adult)

Moore, Yvette. *Freedom Songs.* Orchard, 1991. 168 pages. (pbk. 0–14–036017–4; Puffin, 1992)

In the spring of 1963, 14-year-old Shirl's thoughts are on the end of junior high school and the beginning of her freshman year of high school the following autumn. When her family travels south to stay with relatives over Easter break, Shirl experiences firsthand the pain of Jim Crow laws and witnesses the courageous resistance of her 19-year-old Uncle Pete, a freedom rider. Newspaper headlines about the civil rights struggles in the South take on new meaning for Shirl once she returns to Brooklyn, where she organizes her friends to put on a gospel concert to raise funds for Uncle Pete's cause. In this fine first novel by an African-American author, the power of fiction brings history to life and offers a fictional glimpse of northern Black church involvement in the U.S. Civil Rights Movement. (Ages 12–16)

Mori, Kyoko. *One Bird.* Henry Holt, 1995. 242 pages. (0–8050–2983–4) (pbk. 0–449–70453-X; Fawcett, 1996)

Fifteen-year-old Megumi is alone with her emotionally distant father and stern, silent grandmother after her father's unfaithfulness drives her mother away. Megumi is internally outraged at the circumstances that force her to endure an aching separation, but it is out of her pain that she begins to question who she is and what she believes in, and it is out of her loneliness that she seeks out new friendships which challenge her to define the future in her own terms. With the help of an independent woman who shows her that life is never without choices, Megumi asserts her right to defy tradition and embrace her mother in her life. A rich, multi-layered novel set in contemporary Japan. (Ages 12–16)

Mori, Kyoki. *Shizuko's Daughter.* Henry Holt, 1993. 227 pages. (0–8050–2557-X) (pbk. 0–449–70433–5; Fawcett, 1994)

"People will tell you that I've done this because I did not love you. Don't listen to them. When you grow up to be a strong woman, you will know that this is for the best." These words, left in her mother's suicide note, and memories are all that 12-year-old Yuki has to comfort her after her mother's death. Her cold, distant father provides no strength, nor does the new wife he takes one year later. Yuki becomes steeped in bitterness and anger as she grows. She feels she must fight her stepmother for the right to keep every memory of her mother that is rooted in physical things, while she becomes more and more aware of the pain her mother endured in a marriage that not only had no love, but also drained her of her strength to endure. Only art, running, and visits to her grandparents where the memory of her mother is enshrined provide respite for Yuki from the constant battles she is waging at home, and it is only in leaving home for good that she is finally able to free herself from her bitterness and grief. This emotionally intricate novel set in contemporary Japan takes place over seven years and follows Yuki from adolescence through age 19, when she has grown into the strong woman her mother knew she would someday become. (Ages 12–16)

Myers, Walter Dean. *The Glory Field.* Scholastic, 1994. 375 pages. (0–590–45897–3)

An ambitious novel tracing the history of an African-American family from its first member to come to this country in 1753—in the bonds of slavery—up to the present time. The fictitious Lewis family's story begins with a short chapter telling of the capture of 11-year-old Muhammad Bilal in Sierra Leone, Africa. Each subsequent section of the book moves the story forward in time and follows the family's journey from place to place—from the Civil War and then the turn of the 20th century on Curry Island off the coast of South Carolina, to Chicago in 1930, to Johnson City, South Carolina in 1964, and finally to Harlem in 1994. As the story moves forward in time, it is enriched with greater and greater detail about the daily life of that generation of family members and the social and political climate in which they lived. At the same time that he creates a compelling history of an extended African-American family, Myers paints an unflinching portrait of life for African Americans in the United States at various times and places throughout this nation's history. (Ages 12–16)

Myers, Walter Dean. *Slam!* Scholastic, 1996. 266 pages. (0–590–48667–5)

Slam has dreams of playing in the NBA, and the 17-year-old thinks he might have a shot. But events at high school seem to be conspiring against him: the coach doesn't like him and his grades are going down despite the video project that has captured his interest in one of his classes. Between his dad's unemployment and his mom's worries about Grandma Ellie's illness, things at home don't seem any brighter. Add to all this Mtisha, the serious young woman who may or may not be his girlfriend depending on how Slam behaves, and Ice, Slam's best friend since forever who may be getting mixed up with dangerous business in the neighborhood, and Slam feels as if he's being asked too much by too many people and getting too little respect in return. Strong characterizations and lots of play-by-play basketball action distinguish Walter Dean Myers's sensitive, well-rounded novel in which a young African-American must look both inside himself and at the people around him in order to start regaining a sense of control in his life. (Ages 14–16)

Myers, Walter Dean. *Somewhere in the Darkness.* Scholastic, 1992. 168 pages (0–590–42411–4) (pbk. 0–590–42412–2, 1993)

Jimmy has little choice when his long-absent father Crab re-enters his life and takes him off on a trip to Chicago. Crab has experienced many failures and losses in his life, but he is determined to make a last effort to connect with Jimmy. Unsure and untrusting of each other at first, often with good reason, this African-American son and father slowly develop a relationship, although neither can be completely open about his feelings with the other. Walter Dean Myers excels at creating strong characterizations and showing emotions from the outside, as readers watch Jimmy grow and develop during his time with Crab. (Ages 12–16)

Soto, Gary. *Jesse.* Harcourt, Brace, 1994. 166 pages. (0–15–240239–X) (pbk. 0–590–52837–8, 1996)

"By the time I was seventeen, in junior college, and living on fruit snatched from neighborhood trees and Top Ramen, I no longer thought God was the creaks rising from the wood floor. I knew God was found in prayer, not in the sudden closing of the hallway door just as you stepped from the bathroom." A provocative opening to a provocative novel about a young Mexican-American man coming face to face with adulthood, and the havoc it plays on his dreams. Jesse has left high school early, eager to start junior college and get an education. An aspiring artist, he lives with his older brother, Abel, and the two attend classes each weekday and then work as field laborers on the weekend to earn money for food. But Jesse sometimes wonders if he hasn't entered the adult world too quickly. His life at home with his mother and stepfather wasn't easy, but being out on his own means a struggling survival and decisions that can bring their own kind of difficulty and pain. The political struggles of César Chávez and migrant laborers figure prominently in this novel set in the early 1970s, while the Vietnam war rages quietly in the background. (Age 16–adult)

Tate, Eleanora E. *A Blessing in Disguise.* Delacorte, 1995. 184 pages. (0–385–32103–1) (pbk. 0–440–41209–9; Dell, 1996)

Living a quiet life with her aunt and uncle in a small town in South Carolina, 12-year-old Zambia is sure she would be happier with her father Snake LaRange, who has just opened up a new nightclub on the beach, much to the community's dismay. Zambia's fantasies about her father's life, however, are no match for reality. Her strong personality comes through her distinctive narrative voice as she grows in self-awareness. Eleanora Tate skillfully moves the plot along through realistic dialogue of young teenagers who are struggling with peer relationships of their own, not to mention trying to figure out the complexities of the adult world in a novel that also explores relationships and community in an extended African-American family. (Ages 11–14)

Temple, Frances. *Taste of Salt: A Story of Modern Haiti.* A Richard Jackson Book/ Orchard, 1992. 179 pages. (0–531–05459–4) (lib. bdg. 0–531–08609–7) (pbk. 0–06–447136–5, 1994)

The powerful stories of two Haitian teenagers, Djo and Jeremie, speak to the loyalty they both feel for their country. Djo was one of Father Jean-Bertrand Aristide's "boys" engaged in an ongoing street fight against military dictatorship in Haiti, until he was taken against his will to work in the sugarcane fields of the Dominican Republic. It is three long years before he is able to escape back to Haiti. Soon after his return he is badly injured in a firebombing attack on Titid's boys. As he lies in a hospital bed, Djo tells his story to Jeremie, who has a tale of her own. Jeremie and Djo's contemporary voices are a riveting testament to a country in political turmoil and to the liberating power of literacy. (Ages 12–16)

Watkins, Yoko Kawashima. *My Brother, My Sister, and I.* Bradbury, 1994. 275 pages. (lib. bdg. 0–02–792526–9) (pbk. 0–689–80656–6; Aladdin, 1996)

Continuing the story begun in *So Far From the Bamboo Grove* (Lothrop, Lee & Shepard, 1986), Yoko, now thirteen, her sister Ko, seventeen, and brother Hideyo are living in poverty in Kyoto, Japan, in the years immediately following World War II. For them, a cup of rice is precious, and a handful of vegetable greens and fruit peelings are a treat on the day Hideyo turns 21. They are also still hoping to find their father, who has been missing since the war. Their struggles are complicated after a fire destroys the warehouse in which they'd been living and seriously injures Ko. Drawing strength from one another, they never lose hope or grow bitter, and hard work and acts of kindness which they bestow upon others come full circle in their lives. (Ages 12–16)

Williams-Garcia, Rita. *Fast Talk on a Slow Track.* Lodestar, 1991. 183 pages. (0–525–67334–2) (pbk. 0–553–29594–2; Bantam, 1992)

As the eldest son in a middle-class African-American family living in Brooklyn, New York, 18-year-old Denzel finds that he has a hard act to follow—his own. Since first grade, he's been a star in his family, school, church, and community and, after graduating as valedictorian of his high school class, Denzel is on his way to Princeton. Success has always come easily to Denzel until he attends a summer orientation program for minority students and discovers that the competition in college is stiff. His fear of failure consumes his thoughts throughout the remainder of the summer as he tries to figure out a way to break the news to his dad that he's decided not to go to college. (Ages 12–16)

Williams-Garcia, Rita. *Like Sisters on the Homefront.* Lodestar, 1995. 165 pages. (0–525–67465–9)

Sent down south with her seven-month-old son to live with her aunt and uncle, 14-year-old Gayle is angry and resentful. It's bad enough being away from the girls in the neighborhood and her boyfriend, Troy, but her cousin Cookie is too prissy and perfect for words, her uncle is a stern minister, and her aunt won't even watch the baby for her. Exasperated and sometimes at odds with these members of her family, Gayle finds the only bright spot is Great, her great grandmother, and even she takes some getting used to. Great is daunting, but also sharp and sassy, something Gayle understands. Great is also the keeper of the family story, and Gayle finds herself drawn to the old woman whose words offer her a sense of the past that is larger than herself even as it embraces her. A sometimes funny, always powerful story of an African-American family finding healing in unity: one with another, present with past. In Gayle, with her eager bravado on the subject of sex and immature understanding of love, Rita Williams-Garcia creates a painfully realistic, stunningly accurate account of teenage sexuality and the need for belonging and love. (Ages 13–16)

Woodson, Jacqueline. *From the Notebooks of Melanin Sun.* Blue Sky/Scholastic, 1995. 141 pages. (0–590–45880–9)

Melanin Sun's mother named him for the pigment that makes his skin so beautiful and black, and for the sun she sees shining from his eyes. For as long as Melanin can remember, he and mama have been a family—loving close. At 13, Melanin, who keeps notebooks to record his thoughts about family, friends, and life in his urban neighborhood, has a mature appreciation for his mother's strength and character. Then she tells him something that makes him feel as if his entire world has shattered: she is a lesbian, and she is in love with a white woman, Kristin. Melanin wants to deny the truth, but to do so would deny his mama. "I couldn't stand having her touch me but if she wasn't holding me then who would I be? Where would I be?" Angry and scared ("If she was a dyke, then what did that make me?"), Melanin lashes out, no longer easy with his mother and unwilling to find room in his life—or his heart—for Kristin. There is no easy solution in this courageous novel which addresses the fear that fuels homophobia, but there is honest emotion and real love, and these are what begin to open Melanin's mind. (Ages 11–15)

Woodson, Jacqueline, editor. *A Way Out of No Way: Writings About Growing Up Black in America.* An Edge Book/Henry Holt, 1996. 172 pages. (0–8050–4570–8)

A provocative anthology offers high quality writing and reading, including excerpts from *A Lesson before Dying* by Ernest J. Gaines, *If Beale Street Could Talk* by James Baldwin, *The Friends* by Rosa Guy, *Annie John* by Jamaica Kincaid, *Betsey Brown* by Ntozake Shange, *Sula* by Toni Morrison, *A Visitation of Spirits* by Randall Kenan, and *Maud Martha* by Gwendolyn Brooks. Other authors represented by a poem, short fiction or other work are Toni Cade Bambara, Tim Seibles, Paul Beatty, Langston Hughes, Anna Deavere Smith, Claude McKay, Nikki Giovanni, and Bernice Johnson Reagon. The book title is from June Jordan's poem "Ought to Be a Woman," reprinted here. This splendid collection of literature for pleasure or study or both contains short biographical notes about the contributors. (Age 16–adult)

Wright, Richard. *Rite of Passage.* Afterword by Arnold Rampersad. HarperCollins, 1994. 151 pages. (0–06–023419–9) (lib. bdg. 0–06–023420–2) (pbk. 0–06–447111-X, 1996)

The story of 15-year-old African American Johnny Gibbs was written in the 1940s but published for the first time in 1994. A good student with a loving family, Johnny comes home from school one day to find his world is torn apart. Unknown to Johnny, his parents were really his foster parents, and welfare authorities have determined that Johnny must be moved to another family placement. Frightened and dazed, Johnny bolts into the streets of New York, entering a nighttime world of loneliness and fear wholly foreign to him. Over one night, Johnny careens on a whirlwind course of events that are survival-driven, forced to make split-second decisions that will forever change his life. Set in the 1940s, the themes of this tale of racism and urban violence are chillingly timely still. (Age 16–adult)

Yep, Laurence, editor. *American Dragons: Twenty-Five Asian American Voices.* HarperCollins, 1993. 237 pages. (lib. bdg. 0–06–021495–3) (pbk. 0–06–440603–2, 1995)

Yep organized this important anthology of short fiction and poetry into six themes or "trails" into what Virginia Hamilton has called The Great American Hopescape: Identity, In the Shadow of Ghosts, The Wise Child, World War Two, Love, and Guides. The works here demonstrate that Asian-American history and literature are not monolithic, a premise Yep states in the preface. The writers represented are Richard Haratani, Visalaya Hirunpidok, Rebecca Honma, Jeanne Wakatsuki Houston, Nicol Juratovac, Maxine Hong Kingston, Alan Chong Lau, Cherylene Lee, Amy Ling, Darrell Lum, Wing Tek Lum, Janice Mirikitani, Toshio Mori, Lensey Namioka, Judith Nihei, Lane Nishikawa, Longhang Nguyen, Ann Tashi Slater, William F. Wu, Wakako Yamauchi, Julie Yabu, and Steve Chan-No Yoon. (Age 14–adult)

SEASONS AND CELEBRATIONS

Ancona, George. *Fiesta U.S.A.* Lodestar, 1995. 48 pages. (0–525–67498–5) (pbk. 0–525–67522–1)

George Ancona profiles four Hispanic community celebrations in different parts of the United States in a lively, inviting photodocumentary. Mexican Americans in the barrio in San Francisco celebrate All Souls Day with family observances and a community parade. In Albuquerque, the processions of *Las Posadas* during the nine days before Christmas are a highlight for both Hispanic and non-Hispanic members of the community. The dance of *Los Matachines* marks the New Year for Mexican Americans in the village of El Rancho in northern New Mexico. Caribbean traditions fill the streets of East Harlem during *La Fiesta de los Reyes Magos* (Three Kings Day) on January 6. The colorful photographs and engaging narrative festively highlight these diverse cultural celebrations. (Ages 7–10)

Ancona, George. *Pablo Remembers: The Fiesta of the Day of the Dead.* Lothrop, Lee & Shepard, 1993. 48 pages. (0–688–11249–8) (lib. bdg. 0–688–11250–1)

A color photodocumentary explanation of *el Día de Los Muertos* features a Mexican family's observances of The Day of the Dead beginning October 31 or All Hallow's Eve. Bakers make special bread, candy makers create sugar skulls, marigolds are harvested, women prepare special foods, and children cut out cardboard skeletons in anticipation of the *fiesta*. Family altars are readied in advance of bell-ringing that signals the spirits' return and heralds the activities and visits that are part of the three-day family and community event. Ancona's camera and text feature Pablo, his three sisters, and parents as they honor the memory of their ancestors, especially their grandmother who died two years ago. Spanish words used in context or defined as necessary amplify Ancona's interpretation in a book measuring $8^{1}/_{4}$ x 10" in size and larger in importance. (Ages 5–9)

Ancona, George. *Powwow.* Harcourt Brace Jovanovich, 1993. 48 pages. (0–15–263268–9) (pbk. 0–15–263269–7)

Dynamic color photographs underscore Ancona's explanation about the Crow Fair in Montana, the biggest powwow in North America. Readers see how the people gather on the prairie to renew acquaintances and celebrate the shared heritage of Lakota, Ojibwa, Cheyenne, Crow, Cree, Blackfeet, Fox, and other Native peoples. The opening parade, role of the drum, and main types of dancing are explained and pictured. Whether a dancer wears Traditional, Fancy, Grass, or Jingle-dress clothing, each one has practiced long before donning the specific celebratory garments at this event. Occasionally Ancona details the enjoyment and excitement of Anthony Standing Rock, a young Traditional dancer, and other children at this annual reaffirmation of shared American Indian heritage and tradition. This striking 8 x $11^{1}/_{4}$" account pictures a community created in one place annually for a carefully prepared tribute to its common history. (Ages 5–11)

Berry, James. *Celebration Song.* Illustrated by Louise Brierley. U.S. edition: Simon & Schuster, 1994. 24 pages. (0–671–89446–3)

In a voice resonant with the love and hope and dreams held by every parent for a child, Mary tells the one-year old Jesus the story of his own birth on the occasion of his first birthday. "You were born so very quietly / and so very simply / laid in a cattle-feeding trough . . . .Your born-day is a happening day. / All day I feel a celebration, / everywhere alive in jubilation." Both Jesus's birth and his first year are a cause for joy in his mother's eyes, and in the eyes of those around him in this stirring poem that concludes with the question "When your childhood has gone— / my mothering long done / will your day still be one / *long long* celebration day?" James Berry's West Indian rhythms are perhaps the inspiration for Louise Brierley's exquisite watercolor illustrations in which the Black Jesus and Mary are welcome members of an island community. (All ages)

Bruchac, Joseph and Jonathan London. *Thirteen Moons on Turtle's Back: A Native American Year of Moons.* Illustrated by Thomas Locker. Philomel, 1992. 32 pages. (lib. bdg. 0–399–22141–7)

In many Native cultures, seasonal changes in the natural world are noted by naming a month with a descriptive phrase. The Micmac, for example, call the ninth month "the moose-calling moon" while the Cherokee call the tenth "the moon of falling leaves." Each of 13 months included in this book is illustrated with an oil painting accompanied by a three-verse poem about the distinctive features which led to its name. Potawatomi, Anishinabe (Ojibway), Menominee, and Winnebago are four of the thirteen tribes represented. (Ages 4–9)

Bunting, Eve. *Going Home.* Illustrated by David Diaz. HarperCollins, 1996. 32 pages. (0–06–026296–6) (lib. bdg. 0–06–026297–4)

After sleeping under the stars for three nights, Carlos and his family finally arrive by car in time to celebrate Christmas in La Perla, Mexico. Even though there is no work for Mama and Papa in their home village, La Perla is still home for them. Mama even blew kisses "at the sun-filled winter sky" as soon as the family car crossed the border from the USA into Mexico. Warm welcomes and celebrations of Christmas await the family in La Perla, along with expressions of pride in the English language Carlos and his sisters acquired since their last visit. The walls of Grandfather's La Perla house "bulge with talk and rememberings." Distant La Perla has never felt like home to five-year-old Nora, ten-year-old Delores and young Carlos. Home for them is the house where they live all year while working in the fields with their parents. During this visit Carlos begins to understand about the "opportunities" his parents and grandparents hold in such high regard. Exuberant paintings superimposed over full-color photographs of folk art assemblages detail the specific people and locales of a joyous reunion. The composition of several paintings suggests the traditional Christmas story. A font designed especially for the dialogue-filled text is set on sun-colored pages. This rich story for all seasons has multi-dimensional characters and a plot that does not minimize hard labor at the expense of hope. (Ages 5–9)

Burden-Patmon, Denise. *Imani's Gift at Kwanzaa.* Illustrated by Floyd Cooper. Simon & Schuster, 1992. 23 pages (pbk. 0–671–79841–3)

While Imani's grandmother M'dear braids small red, black, and green beads into her hair, they talk about the seven-day African-American December celebration they'll soon observe with family and friends. Imani looks forward to everything except being with Enna, a mean tease. How can Imani give formal Kwanzaa appreciation to Enna, one of the *watoto* (children) coming to their home tonight? M'dear tells Imani that Enna hasn't known much love; "she has had no one to believe in her . . . to tell her who she is and where she came from." Cooper's full-color illustrations show Kwanzaa details and complement this warm story created under the auspices of the Children's Museum in Boston. A glossary defines the 15 Swahili words integrated into the English text. The Seven Principles are listed at the end of this durable paperback edition. (Ages 3–8)

Chinn, Karen. *Sam and the Lucky Money.* Illustrated by Cornelius Van Wright & Ying-Hwa Hu. Lee & Low (95 Madison Ave., New York, NY 10016), 1995. 32 pages. (1–880000–13-X)

When Sam goes to Chinatown with his mother to shop for New Year's Day, he carries the four dollar bills his grandparents gave him in bright red *leisees*, just in case he should find something to buy with his newly acquired wealth. Four dollars seems like a lot of money to him until he sees the prices on things he wants in the toy shop. But the money turns out to be lucky for Sam after all when he finds just the right way to spend it. Karen Chinn's charming story of a young boy's first understanding of value is accompanied by expressive watercolors which capture the bustling excitement of Chinatown on New Year's Day, as well as Sam's many moods. (Ages 4–7)

Chocolate, Deborah M. Newton. *My First Kwanzaa Book.* Illustrated by Cal Massey. Cartwheel/Scholastic, 1992. 24 pages. (0–590–45762–4)

Easy-to-read short sentences relay basic information about Kwanzaa and are paired with brightly colored illustrations picturing a little boy, his father, and his mother each preparing for the celebration with their extended family. The full-color pictures are filled with cultural information. A brief history of Kwanzaa, its Seven Principles, definitions of symbols and words used during Kwanzaa, and a citation for an adult resource are listed at the back of this high-spirited, helpful $8^1/_4$ x $10^1/_4$" picture book. (Ages 2–7)

Clifton, Lucille. *Everett Anderson's Christmas Coming.* Illustrated by Jan Spivey Gilchrist. Revised edition: Henry Holt, 1991. 24 pages. (0–8050–1549–3) (pbk. 0–8050–2949–4)

". . . Whatever you think, / whatever you say, / a tree can grow / in 14A . . ." for Everett Anderson, his mother, and their friends. Something about the boy's thoughts during each day of the five-day countdown to Christmas is expressed in Clifton's brief, rhyming text first published 20 years ago but still very appealing. Gilchrist's new full-color artwork bordered with red shows both the robust excitement and quiet joy of an enduring, endearing urban African-American preschooler whose stories appear in several books written by the poet "about a little boy who was like the boys my children might know." (Ages 2–5)

Crews, Nina. *One Hot Summer Day.* Greenwillow, 1995. 24 pages. (0–688–13393–2) (lib. bdg. 0–688–13394–0)

Instead of playing games indoors near the fan (it's on high), a bead-braided, dark-skinned child spends the day outside. Crews's impressionistic photo-collages offer sensory interpretations of the heat and relieving rain. Rather than telling a story, the images reflect one child's hot-day play in an urban neighborhood, encouraging children to remember times when the temperature takes charge. (Ages 3–6)

Delacre, Lulu. *Vejigante Masquerader.*
Scholastic, 1993. 40 pages. (0–590–45776–4)

Since 1858, boys and men in Ponce, Puerto Rico, have celebrated Carnival for the entire month of February. These masqueraders or *vejigantes* wear clown-like costumes and *papier mâché* masks resembling animals. Delacre's English = Spanish story based upon this local custom features young Ramón, who has found ways to create his first *vejigante* costume and work in exchange for a mask so that he can participate in the merriment with the older boys. During the opening festivities, Ramón's foolhardy actions gain the boys' respect but also ruin his costume. Bilingual information about three masqueraders from Mexico, Spain and Venezuela; directions for making a *vejigante* mask; several *vejigante* chants; a glossary; and a bibliography support the story. All portions of this unique $9^1/_2$ x $10^1/_4$" picture book are illustrated in full color with art created in watercolor with colored pencils and pastels. (Ages 5–9)

Dorros, Arthur. *Tonight Is Carnaval.*
Illustrated with *arpilleras* sewn by the Club de Madres Virgen del Carmen of Lima, Peru. Dutton, 1991. 24 pages. (0–525–44641–9) (pbk. 0–14–055467-X; Puffin, 1995)

A Peruvian child describes family and community preparations during a three-day period prior to the first night of Carnaval. His story is illustrated with brightly colored folk-art wall hangings (*arpilleras*), which were sewn by women in Lima, Peru. A final double-page spread entitled "How *Arpilleras* Are Made" includes captioned color photographs of the artists at work, adding another dimension of cultural detail to the book. A Spanish language edition of this book, *Por Fin Es Carnaval*, was also published in 1991 by Dutton (0–525–44690–7). (Ages 4–8)

Flournoy, Valerie and Vanessa Flournoy.
Celie and the Harvest Fiddler. Illustrated by James E. Ransome. Tambourine, 1995. 32 pages. (0–688–11457–1) (lib. bdg. 0–688–11458-X)

It's All Hallows' Eve, "the time, it was said, when ghosts and spirits roamed the earth, and witches chanted into the night. But Celie wasn't afraid . . . ." This high-spirited girl wants to have the scariest costume for the annual costume parade. She almost succeeds, no thanks to her mischievous brother Joshua and his friend Zeke, who dress up as wolves. The rich autumn colors of Ransome's oil paintings establish a long-ago African-American community, a time of buggy wheels and storytelling contests, and a night of tension due to the mysterious Fiddler's presence. A complicated picture story with a unique perspective. (Ages 7–9)

Ghazi, Suhaib Hamid. *Ramadan.* Illustrated by Omar Rayyan. Holiday House, 1996. 32 pages. (0–8234–1254–7) (pbk. 0–8234–1275-X)

Hakeem is a Muslim living in Cairo who will fast all day long with his family during the month of Ramadan, the holiest month of the Islamic calendar. Like Muslims all over the world and throughout the U.S.A., Hakeem and his family do not eat or drink anything during the day until the sun has set. Hakeem's mother makes a variety of foods for them to eat until the break of dawn "when there is enough light to see the difference between black thread and a white thread." They then perform the first of five daily prayers, do good deeds, and repair broken relationships. Children who are not Muslim will learn much from this account illustrated in full color. Children who are Muslim will see some of their values and practices reflected in a book with information rarely published for the general public in the U.S.A. Rayyan's illustrations succeed in differentiating between contemporary and historic times. (Ages 6–9)

Goss, Lynda and Clay Goss. *It's Kwanzaa Time!* Illustrations by award-winning artists. Putnam, 1995. 71 pages. (0–399–22505–6)

This introduction to Kwanzaa includes suggestions for home decorations and a ceremony, a variety of stories and tales to read aloud, a play to dramatize, a poem, directions for making Kwanzaa cards and celebrative clothing, a game to play, three songs to sing, and eight recipes to cook. Seven full-color illustrations feature some of the leading African-American artists of children's books: Ashley Bryan, Carole Byard, Floyd Cooper, Leo and Diane Dillon, Jan Spivey Gilchrist, Jonathan Green, and Jerry Pinkney. Many of the readings can be used all year, such as Eloise Greenfield's previously published biographical prose about Rosa Parks. A resource list completes an engaging, attractive, do-it-yourself family book. A many-faceted exploration of the holiday celebrating the richness of traditional African heritage offers something for everyone. (Ages 5–12)

Greenfield, Monica. *Waiting for Christmas.*
Illustrated by Jan Spivey Gilchrist. Scholastic, 1996. 32 pages. (0–590–52700–2)

On Christmas Eve an African-American brother and sister anxiously await the end of the day and the beginning of Christmas morning. Jan Spivey Gilchrist's wintry acrylic paintings aptly capture the children's anticipatory mood, heightened by the short, lyrical lines of the rhyming text. (Ages 3–6)

Guback, Georgia. *The Carolers.* Greenwillow, 1992. 32 pages. (0–688–09772–3) (lib. bdg. 0–688–09773–1)

A group of young carolers bearing a star enters a picturesque village decorated with Christmas lights. When the carolers are outside a home singing "O Little Town of Bethlehem" the landscape of Christmas Bethlehem can be seen near them and music for the carol runs along the bottom of both pages. The next double-page picture shows a white family inside the same home decorating cookies midst other holiday preparations. The family joins the carolers to sing "The First Noel" at the next house where, once again, readers see both outside (the scene of an angel appearing to shepherds) and inside (a Black family involved in holiday activity). At each stop the carolers make, another part of the Christmas Story unfolds in a new carol, outdoor scene, and indoor family life. One family seems to be grandparents, another is a woman and two children, and yet another family has Latino decorations in its home. The six families have visibly distinctive ways of observing Christmas: some customs are religious, some are ethnic, and some are secular. Each family joins in the spontaneous outdoor community celebration. Reading the pictures as this cumulative, wordless story evolves invites singing along. The artist developed a fresh concept by creating full-color art done in cut-paper collage. (Ages 2–8)

Heath, Amy. *Sofie's Role.* Illustrated by Sheila Hamanaka. Four Winds, 1992. 32 pages. (lib. bdg. 0–02–743505–9)

The family bakery will be extremely busy on December 24th. Before dawn Sofie goes with her parents to help out. She fills pastry cases, bags orders, answers the phone, and even waits on a few customers "out front" once the shop opens. This spunky brown-skinned girl enjoys a one-time stint in the busy bakery, especially when a girl from school is one of her customers. An appetite-whetting array of baked goods is pictured in Hamanaka's oil-on-canvas paintings reproduced in full color. The illustrations display bakery workers and customers from diverse backgrounds and enliven Heath's story about a child's foray into an adult world of work. Recipes for marzipan and cinnamon star cookies are included. (Ages 4–8)

Hoyt-Goldsmith, Diane. *Celebrating Kwanzaa.* Photographs by Lawrence Migdale. Holiday House, 1993. 32 pages. (0–8234–1130–3) (lib. bdg. 0–8234–1048-X)

Eighth-grader Andiey Barnes tells how her five-generation Chicago-area family celebrates the seven-day African festival that begins on December 26th. The origin of this celebration and its founder, Dr. Maulana Karenga, are introduced, as are the Seven Principles. Expressions of cultural pride from present and past African-American leaders are quoted to underscore the Kwanzaa values expressed throughout a book appealing to older children as well as families. Sections showing Chicago's Ujamaa Market and the family's Kwanzaa Karamu, or feast, are two of several distinctive features of this striking $9^{1}/_{4}$ x $10^{1}/_{4}$" color photodocumentary account. (Ages 5–12)

Hudson, Cheryl Willis, compiler. *Hold Christmas in Your Heart: African-American Songs, Poems, and Stories for the Holidays.* Cartwheel/Scholastic, 1995. 32 pages. (0–590–48024–3)

"Carol of the Brown King" by Langston Hughes, "Christmas Is A-Comin'" by Huddie Ledbetter, "Brer Rabbit's Christmas Gift" adapted by Mia Watson, "Christmas Valentine" by Nikki Grimes, and "Tradition" by Gwendolyn Brooks are among the 13 pieces ready for recitation, reading aloud or both in this picture book anthology. The illustrators are Eric Battle, Higgins Bond, Ron Barnett, Cal Massey, James Ransome, Anna Rich, and Sylvia Walker. The music and words for two spirituals and a song are included. This user-friendly medley of selections (mostly by African-American writers) illustrated by African-American artists will be especially welcome in families with young children and in daycare and primary grade classrooms. (Ages 4–9)

Hunter, Sally M. *Four Seasons of Corn: A Winnebago Tradition.* Photographs by Joe Allen. (We Are Still Here) Lerner, 1996. 40 pages. (0–8225–2658–1) (pbk. 0–8225–9741–1)

Planting in the spring; tending in the summer; harvesting, storing, and giving thanks in the fall; food throughout the winter. These are the four seasons of corn for the Winnebago, or Hochunk, people. Twelve-year-old Russell, a member of the Hochunk Nation who lives in St. Paul, is learning about the importance of corn from his grandfather, who takes Russell, his brothers, sisters, and cousins to the country each year to plant and care for a field. But the corn is more than food for the Hochunk, it is also considered a gift from the spirits. As Russell and his family give attention to the corn every season in the midst of their busy city lives, they reaffirm ties to their heritage and knowledge of the ways of their people. Text and color photographs comprise another welcome portrayal of contemporary American Indian lives. (Ages 7–11)

Johnson, Dolores. *The Children's Book of Kwanzaa: A Guide to Celebrating the Holiday.* Atheneum, 1996. 159 pages. (0–689–80864-X)

Linoleum block prints add to the elegance of this attractive volume which includes a wealth of information on the history of Kwanzaa, the Seven Principles, crafts to make before Kwanzaa, gifts you can make yourself, recipes, suggested programs, and a suggested time-line for scheduling Kwanzaa preparations. An especially valuable feature of this book is its extensive historical background for each of the Seven Principles so that children can relate them directly to their African heritage. (Ages 8–14)

Kleven, Elisa. *Hooray, A Piñata!* Dutton, 1996. 32 pages. (0–525–45605–8)

Clara and her friend Samson go shopping for a special piñata for Clara's birthday party and they find just the one Clara wants. Trouble is, she likes it so well she can't bear the thought of breaking it! Filled with lots of intriguing visual details, Kleven's bright picture story about a young Latina girl and her African-American friend is a true celebratory delight from beginning to end. (Ages 4–7)

Lankford, Mary D. *Quinceañera: A Latina's Journey to Womanhood.* Illustrated by Jesse Herrera. Millbrook, 1994. 47 pages. (lib bdg. 1–56294–363–4)

Mexican-American teenager Martha Jimenez is joined by family and friends to celebrate her Quinceañera, a rite of passage in a Latina girl's fifteenth year that symbolizes her transition from girlhood to womanhood. Martha's Quinceañera is an elaborate event complete with attendants, a church service, and large reception, but it is rooted in traditions that go back to the indigenous cultures of Mexico and Central and Latin America. This photodocumentary provides background on the tradition of the Quinceañera and follows Martha and her family through her celebration, which includes a religious ceremony signifying an affirmation of her faith, and a party with members of her family and community. (Ages 9–12)

Levy, Janice. *The Spirit of Tío Fernando: A Day of the Dead Story = El Espíritu de Tío Fernando: Una Historia del Día de los Muertos.* Illustrated by Morella Fuenmayor. Translated from the Spanish by Teresa Mlawer. Albert Whitman, 1995. 32 pages. (0–8075–7585–2) (pbk. 0–8050–7586–0)

When he goes to the market, a little Mexican boy is reminded of the ways he can honor his uncle's spirit during All Souls' Day or *El Día de los Muertos*. Venezuelan artist Morella Fuenmayor's watercolors illustrating this sweet bilingual picture story suggest important multiple cultural details rarely seen in U.S. books. In real life a child Nando's age would not require as many explanations about the special activities in which he and his mother engage while they remember the people they love who have died. Outsiders to these observances will enjoy learning about them in this way. (Ages 6–9)

McCutcheon, John. *Happy Adoption Day!* Illustrated by Julie Paschkis. Little, Brown, 1996. 24 pages. (0–316–55455–3)

The lyrics to a children's song from John McCutcheon's album *Family Garden* provide the upbeat text for this picture book. The expressive paintings suggest a folk art style and show the family as a white mother and father who adopt an Asian child. Other family structures that appear in the book include an African-American single father and a white lesbian couple. (Ages 3–6)

Marzollo, Jean. *Happy Birthday, Martin Luther King.* Illustrated by J. Brian Pinkney. Scholastic, 1993. 32 pages. (0–590–44065–9) (0–590–72828–8)

This 11$\frac{1}{2}$ x 8$\frac{1}{2}$" picture-book biography offers fresh and vibrant images of Dr. King's life and accomplishments. An excellent selection of biographical details to interest young children makes very brief information about Dr. King's life and contributions accessible and appealing. Pinkney's lively illustrations created on scratchboard with oil pastels showcase young Martin as well as the mature leader. An author's note at the beginning explains the reason for devoting a page in a book for such young children to the assassination of the mid-twentieth century Nobel Peace Prize-winning African-American leader. (Ages 3–8)

Miles, Calvin. *Calvin's Christmas Wish.* Illustrated by Dolores Johnson. Viking, 1993. 32 pages. (0–670–84295–8) (pbk. 0–14–055866–7; Viking/Penguin, 1996)

While cutting a fresh tree, collecting holly, and gathering pine cones for decorations, Calvin and his sister imagine what Santa will bring, even though he not only suspects there is no Santa, but also that his family cannot afford a bike. A first-person story about a memorable Christmas during the 1950s in rural North Carolina suggests that a strong sense of family can be more important than having Things, no matter how much one wants a specific bicycle with all the extras. The author is inspirational in telling his own story of how he studied with Literacy Volunteers at age 39 to learn to read and write. Full-color paintings provide period and regional detail as well as bringing the autobiographical African-American characters to life in this 8$\frac{1}{2}$ x 10$\frac{1}{4}$" picture book. (Ages 5–8)

Mora, Pat. *Pablo's Tree.* Illustrated by Cecily Lang. Macmillan, 1994. 32 pages. (0–02–767401–0)

Five-year-old Pablo tries to guess how his grandfather Lito will decorate the tree he planted to celebrate Pablo's adoption as an infant. One year the little tree was covered with balloons and another with paper lanterns. As part of Pablo's birthday celebration, Lito recounts the story of the tree, which is actually the loving tale of how he and Pablo's Mamá planned and waited for Pablo. Spanish words and phrases are incorporated into the text's flow, adding substance to the Mexican-American people and setting depicted. This warm, joyous book is illustrated with images created with cut paper and dyes. (Ages 2–5)

Morninghouse, Sundaira. *Habari Gani? = What's the News? A Kwanzaa Story.* Illustrated by Jody Kim. Open Hand (P.O. Box 22048, Seattle, WA 98122), 1992. 32 pages. (0–940880–39–3)

A seven-chapter illustrated story about a contemporary family interprets information about the "only nationally celebrated, indigenous, non-heroic African-American holiday in the U.S." One full-color painting accompanies each chapter, along with a symbol representing the candles for each day. The Seven Principles and a 28-item glossary for Swahili words and Kwanzaa terms are appended at the end of this well-designed book. (Ages 4–9)

Pinkney, Andrea Davis. *Seven Candles for Kwanzaa.* Illustrated by Brian Pinkney. Dial, 1993. 32 pages. (0–8037–1292–8) (lib bdg. 0–8037–1293–6)

An easy-to-read and understand explanation of Kwanzaa features images of a contemporary U.S. family observing each of the seven days in activities recognizable to today's children. Emphasis is placed on Kwanzaa as "an American holiday inspired by African traditions . . . not intended as a religious, political, or heroic holiday, nor is it a substitute for Christmas." The striking full-color artwork for this 9$\frac{1}{4}$ x 11$\frac{1}{4}$" picture book was prepared using scratchboard and oil pastels. (Ages 3–9)

Porter, A. P. *Kwanzaa.* Illustrated by Janice Lee Porter. Carolrhoda, 1991. 56 pages. (0–87614–688–X) (pbk. 0–87614–545–4)

An easy reader briefly traces the origin of the African-American holiday created by Maulana Karenga in 1966 and then describes how it is observed by families today. Special attention is given to the historical significance of each of Kwanzaa's seven principles and to the meanings and uses of Kwanzaa symbols. Full-color illustrations appear on each double-page spread, adding appeal and accessibility to the text. A glossary of the Kiswahili words used throughout the book provides English definitions and a pronunciation guide. (Ages 5–9)

Rendon, Marcie R. *Powwow Summer: A Family Celebrates the Circle of Life.* Photographs by Cheryl Walsh Bellville. Carolrhoda, 1996. 48 pages. (lib. bdg. 0–87614–986–7) (pbk. 1–57505–011–0)

"According to Native tradition, the circle of life is endless. It has no beginning. There is no end." Marcie Rendon's text and Cheryl Walsh Bellville's many color photographs look at some of the ways in which one Anishinabe family celebrates the circle of life: by opening their arms and their hearts to welcome foster children into their family, by keeping close ties among the generations, by grieving together in the aftermath of a death. The Downwind family—parents, children, foster children—is profiled over the course of a summer, during which time they go on the powwow trail, attending two gatherings where they become part of a larger community, thus entering the circle of life in yet another way. At powwows, ceremonies and dances also mark the continuous cycle of connections and changes important in Anishinabe culture. The open, engaging narrative explains the importance of the rituals and traditions at the powwows by using comparisons that will resonate for many non-Native readers. The book also discusses how, by emphasizing the importance of family and community, the Downwinds are maintaining ties to traditional Anishinabe ways, ties that keep them strong in the wake of many challenges that Native peoples face in contemporary times. (Ages 7–11)

Rosen, Michael J. *Elijah's Angel: A Story for Chanukah and Christmas.* Illustrated by Aminah Brenda Lynn Robinson. Harcourt Brace Jovanovich, 1992. 32 pages. (0–15–225394–7)

A first-person narrator tells of the year he, a nine-year-old Jewish boy, regularly visited the shop of an 84-year-old African-American barber and woodcarver. His parents told their son that some of Elijah Pierce's carvings from the *Bible* represented what might be considered "graven images." The boy never spoke of this while he and Elijah shared "time together the way Chanukah and Christmas shared the same day that year." One December after Elijah gave him a polka-dotted guardian angel, the boy hid it. His parents helped him to cherish the gift as an angel of friendship; in that spirit, the boy gave Elijah a menorah he had made at Hebrew school. Rosen based the moving personal story on the "character and vision" of Elijah Pierce (1892–1984), a woodcarver, lay minister, barber, and personal friend to many of his visitors. Robinson grew up in the same Columbus, Ohio, neighborhood and spent long hours in Elijah's barbershop modeling clay and quilting while Elijah carved and varnished. Her full-color paintings were done in house paint on scrap rag. (Ages 7–11)

Say, Allen. *Tree of Cranes.* Houghton Mifflin, 1991. 32 pages. (0–395–52024–X)

A Japanese boy "not yet old enough to wear long pants" catches a cold playing at a neighbor's carp pond and is put to bed by his mother after a hot bath. The mother seems unusually preoccupied and even severe as she folds origami figures; she then, inexplicably, digs up and brings inside the little pine tree belonging to her son. As she hangs tiny origami birds on the tree, the mother reminisces about Christmas during her own childhood in warm California, long before she came to Japan and met the boy's father. Two stories about promising and giving overlap in an unusual full-color 11^1/$_4$ x 10^1/$_4$" book evoking two past generations, two cultures, and traditional early–20th century Japanese domestic life. (Ages 5–7)

Schur, Maxine Rose. *Day of Delight: A Jewish Sabbath in Ethiopia.* Illustrated by Brian Pinkney. Dial, 1994. 32 pages. (0–8037–1413–0) (lib. bdg. 0–8037–1414–9)

For more than 1,000 years, Jews have inhabited the high mountains of Ethiopia. Using the narrative voice of a young boy, Menelik, Schur describes the hardworking inhabitants of one of these Jewish communities. The villagers make pottery, prepare raw cotton or weave, work the soil they sharecrop, grind grain into flour, and forge the iron for which they are known. Children help by collecting cow-dung for fuel or harvesting honey. The work and worries of the week are set aside for the Sabbath. Menelik tells how his mother bakes *dabo* (white Sabbath bread) and makes *wat* (peppery chicken stew). Families bathe and don clean *shammas* before the Sabbath eating, singing, rest, and worship begin. Pinkney's full-color artwork contains important cultural details and was prepared using scratchboard, black ink, oil pastels, oil paints, and gouache. (Ages 5–9)

Seymour, Tryntje Van Ness. *The Gift of Changing Woman.* Illustrated by Apache artists. Henry Holt, 1993. 38 pages. (0–8050–2577–4, out of print)

A coming-of-age ritual that transforms Apache girls into women is the focus of an unusual book respectfully written by a non-Native woman with the permission, cooperation, and approval of Apache elders. Although the first two days of the ceremony are private and sacred (and are not described in the book for this reason), the last two days consist of a public celebration. First-person accounts by Apache women recalling details of their own ceremonies and explanations of ritual meaning by Apache medicine man Philip Cassadore are woven together with a straightfoward narrative by the author, who has been an invited guest at many of the ceremonies. Visual interpretations of the proceedings by ten Apache artists add another layer of authenticity to the book as a whole. (Ages 9–14)

Spohn, David. *Starry Night.* Lothrop, Lee & Shepard, 1992. 32 pages. (0–688–11171–8, out of print)

When Nate, Matt, and Dad went camping near their house in August, everyone helped with preparations. Nate assembled snacks, Matt packed his stuffed animal, and Dad took a harmonica. They established their campsite, built a fire, and settled in for singing, stories and locating the Big Dipper, the Great Bear, and Cassiopeia. Observant readers will notice practical details about camping unobtrusively woven within the brief, quiet 8 x 6 ¼" book about two boys and their father. The same biracial (African-American/white) family pictured in the full-color illustrations appears in *Home Field* (Lothrop, 1993), *Nate's Treasure* (Lothrop, 1991), and *Winter Wood* (Lothrop, 1991). (Ages 3–7)

Spohn, David. *Winter Wood.* Lothrop, Lee & Shepard, 1991. 32 pages. (0–688–10093–7, out of print)

It's a cold Saturday morning, but Matt and Dad bundle up and venture outside to cut wood. Boots, jackets, scarves, and mittens go on to protect them from the cold. Out at the woodpile they begin to chop and stack wood, and soon scarves and jackets come off as the hard work warms them. Later, as Matt is loading the stove at home, Dad reminds him of what Grandpa used to say: "Winter wood warms you twice—once when you cut it . . . and again when you burn it." The time shared by the father and son in this biracial (African American/white) family is as much about being together as it is about getting work done. (Ages 3–7)

Swamp, Chief Jake. *Giving Thanks: A Native American Good Morning Message.* Illustrated by Erwin Printup, Jr. Lee & Low (95 Madison Ave., New York, NY 10016), 1995. 24 pages. (1–880000–15–6)

Based on what is known as the Iroquois Nation's Thanksgiving Address, the text of this picture book carries the "ancient message of peace and appreciation of Mother Earth and all her inhabitants" to her family. The words are still used at contemporary governmental and ceremonial gatherings of the Six Nations: Mohawk, Oneida, Cayuga, Onondaga, Seneca, and Tuscarora. Children of these Native peoples are taught the concept of greeting the world each morning by saying thank you to all living things, which is what this picture book expresses. Chief Jake Swamp has delivered the Thanksgiving Address at the United Nations and throughout the world. The illustrations rendered in acrylic on canvas show images of Native people with Earth's creatures. Mr. Printup is a Cayuga/Tuscarora painter. (Ages 5–10)

Thomas, Joyce Carol. *Gingerbread Days.* Illustrated by Floyd Cooper. Joanna Cotler Books/HarperCollins 1995. 32 pages. (0–06–023469–5) (lib. bdg. 0–06–023472–5)

From a "gingered" January to a firelit December, a boy experiences who he is: a beloved son and grandson, a unique individual, a proud young man of African-American heritage. In January, Grandma tells the lad that the gingerbread man looks just like him. During August, ". . . Grandpa spreads a pallet / stitched with Buffalo Soldiers / for a bed / 'Oklahoma cowboys,' he says, / 'With a dark man at the head.'" And in December, Daddy's ". . . chapped hands are brave / With work / Rough with knowing / How to keep a family from freezing / How to keep a young mind growing . . ." Cooper's paintings and Thomas's poems form a picture-book companion to their earlier collection, *Brown Honey in Broomwheat Tea* (HarperCollins, 1993), which features an African-American girl. (Ages 3–7)

Van Laan, Nancy. *La Boda: A Mexican Wedding Celebration.* Illustrated by Andrea Arroyo. Little, Brown, 1996. 32 pages. (0–316–89626–8)

The traditional Zapotec wedding ceremony borrows elements from both Native and Catholic traditions. Here a young girl learns about them by asking her patient *abuela* countless questions as the two participate in the wedding ceremony of Alfonso and Luisa. The curved lines of Arroyo's stylized illustrations suggest sweeping movement as the entire town participates in this joyous community event. Even the typography helps to tell the story. (Ages 4–7)

Walter, Mildred Pitts. *Kwanzaa: A Family Affair.* Lothrop, Lee & Shepard, 1995. 95 pages. (0–688–11553–5) (pbk. 0–380–72735–8; Avon, 1995)

The author of *Have a Happy . . .* (Lothrop, 1989), a novel about a boy and his family celebrating Kwanzaa, has been celebrating Kwanzaa for 30 years. In this user-friendly handbook she interprets the background, seven principles, and the symbols of Kwanzaa, a special African-American time between December 26 and January 1. Daily activities are described, and a helpful crafts section contains directions for making games, gifts, and other items needed during Kwanzaa. Four recipes are included along with a glossary, pronunciation key, and a list of related books. Most of these activities can be undertaken by a reliable older child or teenager, although Ms. Walter encourages readers to secure a parent's permission. Walter is the author of many children's books, including *Justin and the Best Biscuits in the World* (Lothrop, 1986), *Mariah Loves Rock* (Bradbury, 1988), *Mariah Keeps Cool* (Bradbury, 1990), and *Trouble's Child* (Lothrop, 1985), a novel for young teenagers. (Age 9–adult)

Weiss, Nicki. *On a Hot, Hot Day.* Putnam, 1992. 28 pages. (0–399–22119–0, out of print)

"On a rainy day / On a rainy fall day / Mama says, 'Sip slow. Sip slow.' / So they blow on their cocoa in the luncheonette. / As the passersby outside get wet. / In the fall / The rainy fall / Mama twirls her Angel." Throughout four seasons, Mama and her little son Angel come and go in their city neighborhood. They read books inside when it's cold, and they cool off outside when it's hot. The rhythmic text moves Mama and Angel outside and inside and outside again, offering a lilting cadence when read aloud. This perfectly paced patterned story shows what it's like to be a parent and child doing ordinary things together. Mama and Angel are a Latino family, according to visual clues in illustrations that also celebrate the seasons and—most of all—their joy in being together. Parallels in the construction of the text are paired with images of family and neighborhood, demonstrating Weiss's deep understanding of and genuine affection for preschoolers. (Ages 1–4)

Woodtor, Dee Parmer. *Big Meeting.*
Illustrated by Dolores Johnson. Atheneum, 1996. 32 pages. (0–689–31933–9)

"It happens the third week of August, in some places the second, when people get together Down Home." Extended families from most heritages hold regular family gatherings, but reunions have particular significance for many African-American families. Readers are reminded of or introduced to this special experience through one family's visit Down Home, "a place to run free" according to the young narrator. Grandma Bessie's place and the Little Bethel A.M.E. Church serve as the geographic locales for Down Home family events rich in emotion and memory. Johnson's characters have distinctive faces and great body language. Her etchings and aquatints with watercolor and colored pencil illustrations are wonderfully effective in this warm story celebrating and elevating small, happy moments in a conscious echo of the mid–20th century. (Ages 3–8)

Yerxa, Leo. *Last Leaf First Snowflake to Fall.*
U.S. edition: Orchard, 1994. 32 pages. (0–531–06824–2) (lib. bdg. 0–531–08674–7)

A Woodland Indian child travels by canoe and on foot with a parent to an island campsite. During a day and a night, autumn becomes winter. Details of the familiar transition seem new within a wondrous, sophisticated account distinctive in design and voice. The text opens with a lengthy poetic commentary on creation: "before seeing, before being / before valentines and wild flowers . . . snow was born." A unique naturalistic first person narrative follows: "The blanket of leaves that yesterday / covered the earth / was now covered with a blanket / of snow / to keep her warm during her long winter sleep / My blanket was also covered in snow / I brushed the snow away / Gone were the colors of yesterday / I arose from the earth / and walked into the light / of a new season." Neither uses conventional punctuation. Stunning full-color collage assemblages sometimes fill double-page spreads and at other times decorate one corner of a full page of text. Illuminated letters and images of falling leaves assist in expressing the delicate instant when the season changes. (Age 10–adult)

FOLKLORE, MYTHOLOGY AND TRADITIONAL LITERATURE

Aardema, Verna. *Borreguita and the Coyote.*
Illustrated by Petra Mathers. Alfred A. Knopf, 1991. 32 pages. (0–679–80921–X) (lib. bdg. 0–679–90921–4)

Hungry Coyote thinks that Borreguita, the little lamb, would make a tasty meal but every time he meets her she manages to outsmart him, leaving him not only hungry but humiliated as well. Petra Mathers's glowing, boldly colored illustrations are ideally suited to this well-paced retelling of an amusing Mexican folktale about brain winning out over brawn. (Ages 4–8)

Aardema, Verna, reteller. *The Lonely Lioness and the Ostrich Chicks: A Masai Tale.* Illustrated by Yumi Heo. Alfred A. Knopf, 1996. 32 pages. (0–679–86934–4) (lib. bdg. 0–679–96934–9)

Mother Ostrich leads four miniatures of herself—single file—to feed under a tree where a lioness happens to be sleeping. The chicks become confused and run, *pamdal*, in every direction. The lioness lures them to follow her—single file—to her den. Mother Ostrich implores Gazelle, Hyena, Jackal, and Mongoose to come to her aid. Interlaced with ono-matopoeia, this highly entertaining tale is only a tad scary because its creatures simply cannot be taken seriously. Heo's extraordinarily effective paintings cleverly extend the Masai story. Visual humor stems from the way each creature looks and moves and from the hapless chicks, in particular. The unusual combination of colors and shapes com-bines with an overall page layout exactly suiting the action. (Ages 4–9)

Aldana, Patricia, editor. *Jade and Iron: Latin American Tales from Two Cultures.* Translated by Hugh Hazelton. Illustrated by Luis Garay. U.S. edition: Groundwood/ Douglas & McIntyre, 1996. 64 pages. (0–88899–256–4)

This unique anthology contains 14 tales from Native and Latin sources. The title refers to "worlds that co-exist in Latin America and are still struggling to find a way to live together." The tales are told or retold here by various Latin American authors and folk-lorists, including Carmen Diana Dearden. Each tale is four pages or less in length. Their origins vary: an Indian legend from southern Brazil and a Chimane Indian tale from the Brazilian Amazon; a Pemon legend and two folktales from Venezuela; three legends from individually distinct peoples of Chile; a legend of the Cora Indians of western Mexico and a tale from colonial Mexico; a folktale from Zapatera in Lake Nicaragua; and a Gua-temalan folktale. Seventeen full-page illustrations created in pen and ink and watercolor are reproduced in full color. The editor is originally from Guatemala, while the illustra-tor was born in Nicaragua. (Ages 9–12)

Begay, Shonto. *Ma'ii and Cousin Horned Toad: A Traditional Navajo Story.* Scholastic, 1992. 32 pages. (0–590–45391–2, out of print)

The distinguished Navajo artist retells a folktale from his own tribal heritage. In this coyote teaching tale, lazy Ma'ii always manages to call on one of his cousins at mealtime. Although Cousin Horned Toad is an accommodating fellow, he can't get any farm work done with Ma'ii around demanding food, so he comes up with an idea to teach the coy-ote to have some respect for a hard-working horned toad. Begay's earth-toned water-color, goauche, and colored pencil illustrations capture the humor of a traditional story in which the coyote meets his match. (Ages 4–8)

Bierhorst, John, compiler. *Lightning Inside You, and Other Native American Riddles.* Illustrated by Louise Brierley. Morrow, 1992. 104 pages. (0–688–09582–8)

Over 100 riddles from 35 North, South, and Central American Indian nations are arranged into five categories: Natural World, Human Body, Animals, Things that Grow, and Things Made to Be Used. The answer and source for each riddle is given on the bot-tom of the page on which the riddle appears and sophisticated black-and-white line drawings are included on every other page. The book concludes with two longer story riddles, one from the Pawnee and one from the Pehuenche of Chile. (Ages 7–11)

Bierhorst, John, editor. *The White Deer and Other Stories Told by the Lenape.* Morrow, 1995. 137 pages. (0–688–12900–5)

The Lenape, also called Delaware Indians by the European colonists, once lived throughout what is today known as New Jersey, southeastern New York, eastern Pennsyl-vania and northern Delaware. The traditional tales appearing in this volume include myths and stories about lost children, boy heroes, tricksters, dogs, and prophecies. One of the most distinctive features of this collection is the credit that has been given to the ten elders from whom the 25 tales were originally collected. Black-and-white photo-graphs and brief biographical sketches of each elder are interspersed throughout the book to accompany the stories which have been recorded in the tellers' conversational narrative styles. (Ages 8–14)

Bierhorst, John. *The Woman Who Fell from the Sky: The Iroquois Story of Creation.* Illustrated by Robert Andrew Parker. Morrow, 1993. 32 pages. (0–688–10680–3) (lib. bdg. 0–688–10681–1)

Sky Woman possesses the power of creation. When she falls from the sky and lands on Turtle's back in the water, the mud on Turtle's back begins to grow, and so the earth is formed. Later, Sky Woman gives birth to Sapling and Flint, who share their mother's power. Sapling's gentle nature and Flint's hard-edged ways imbue the world with both opportunity and hardship as they combine together to create life from the earth. Bier-horst retells this creation tale of the Native peoples who comprise the six Iroquois nations in simple, elegant prose that is complimented by Parker's stirring illustrations brimming with color and life. (Ages 6–10)

Bruchac, Joseph, reteller. *The Boy Who Lived with the Bears and Other Iroquois Stories.* Illustrated by Murv Jacob. HarperCollins, 1995. 63 pages. (0–06–021288–8) (lib. bdg. 0–06–021287-X)

In his introduction, Bruchac writes about the People of the Longhouse and the five Iro-quois nations: Mohawk, Seneca, Onondaga, Oneida, and Cayuga. He comments on some of what can be learned today from the People: efficient farming systems, their Great League of Peace, the balanced leadership roles of women and men, stories. The six winter stories Bruchac gained permission to share here are easy to read due to the large typeface, relatively short lines and plenty of white space. Bruchac's experience in telling them results in lively dialogue and action. Seven of Jacob's luminous full-color paintings grace the pages that unfold "Rabbit and Fox," "How the Birds Got Their Feathers," "Turtle Makes War on Man," "Chipmunk and Bear," "Rabbit's Snow Dance," and the title tale. *Ho? Hey.* (Ages 5–9)

Bruchac, Joseph, reteller. *Native American Animal Stories.* Foreword by Vine Deloria, Jr. Illustrated by John Kahionhes Fadden and David Kanietakeron Fadden. Fulcrum (350 Indiana St., Suite 350, Golden, CO 80401), 1992. 135 pages. (pbk. 1–55591–127–7)

The traditional stories from the author and Michael J. Caduto's *Keepers of the Animals* (Fulcrum, 1991) are excerpted for this handsomely designed, well-organized volume. With skill and vitality, Bruchac respectfully retells 24 animal stories from 18 North American tribes. Each story, illustrated with a culturally accurate line drawing, is carefully documented and put into a cultural context by the author's scholarly notes at the book's end. A glossary and pronunciation guide will prove helpful for storytellers. Overall, the careful attention to detail on the part of both the author and the illustrator provides an exemplary model from which other retellers of Native folktales could learn. (Ages 7–14)

Bruchac, Joseph and Michael J. Caduto. *Native American Stories.* Illustrated by John Kahionhes Fadden. Fulcrum (350 Indiana St., Golden, CO 80401), 1991. 145 pages. (pbk. 1–55591–094–7)

Twenty-four stories from the traditions of peoples indigenous to what is now called North America entertain and teach about the family relationship of native people with the Earth. The tales are reprinted in a readable typeface, illustrated with black and white artwork and presented within a visual framework signifying geographic origins and cultural symbols. The book contains a map designating American Indian cultural areas and tribal locations as they appeared around 1600, a glossary, and a substantial paragraph about each of the sixteen nations from which the tales originated. Short introductions contain facts and insights about the tales essential for all who wish to read, tell, or teach them. These stories first appeared in *Keepers of the Earth* (Fulcrum, 1988). (Ages 5–14)

Brusca, María Cristina and Tona Wilson. *When Jaguars Ate the Moon and Other Stories about Animals and Plants of the Americas.* Illustrated by María Cristina Brusca. Henry Holt, 1995. 40 pages. (0-8050-2797-1, out of print)

Thirty one-page tales arranged from A to Z are bordered with drawings that introduce more than 100 plants and animals indigenous to North and South America. In a brief introduction, the retellers refer to the disappearance of specific species and cultures and ask readers to "listen to each other's stories and find that plants and animals frighten, touch, or amuse us in many of the same ways" they have done for thousands of years. This unique cultural alphabet of flora and fauna includes a small map of the Americas, short notes on the tales and a selected bibliography. (Ages 6–11)

Bryan, Ashley. *The Story of Lightning & Thunder.* Atheneum, 1993. 32 pages. (0–689–31836–7)

Ma Sheep Thunder and Sun Ram Lightning have worked out an arrangement with The People: when the farmers need to irrigate their crops, mother and son run to the mountain top and call their friend Rain to come down out of the clouds. But during his leisure hours, Son Ram often gets restless and runs through the village, sparking trouble. The solution to which everyone eventually agrees explains why thunder and lightning now live in the sky. Ashley Bryan's appealing retelling of a Nigerian *pourquoi* tale is accompanied by his brightly jewel-colored stylized paintings. (Ages 4–7)

Compton, Patricia A. *The Terrible Eek.* Illustrated by Sheila Hamanaka. Simon & Schuster, 1991. 32 pages. (pbk. 0–671–87169–2, 1993)

A Japanese tale begins with a child asking his father if he is ever afraid. Yes, he responds, he's fearful of a thief, a wolf, and a leak in the roof. A nearby thief and wolf mistake what they partially overhear and spend the remainder of the tale trying to escape from an imaginary "eek." The action-packed story involves increasing confusion for its characters and glee for its readers and listeners. Hamanaka's cinematic, rocketing perspectives convey the rushing motions for a fast-moving tale with a truly happy ending. Perfect for classroom groups and library story hour sharing. (Ages 5–8)

Crespo, George, reteller and illustrator. *How Iwariwa the Cayman Learned to Share: A Yanomami Myth.* Clarion, 1995. 32 pages. (0–395–67162–0)

Iwariwa the Cayman has something called fire, with which he can cook sweet potatoes until they are crispy and warm. Unwilling to share it with the other animals, he keeps it hidden in a magic basket in his mouth. When the animals find out, they hatch a plot to make Iwariwa laugh so that the fire will come shooting out. An intriguing tale written and illustrated with humor incorporates many plants and animals indigenous to the Yanomami homeland in the Amazon. An extensive note provides information on the Yanomami people and the tale's origins. (Ages 7–10)

Cruz Martinez, Alejandro. *The Woman Who Outshone the Sun: The Legend of Lucia Zenteno = La Mujer Que Brillaba Aún Más que el Sol: La Leyenda de Lucía Zenteno.* From a poem by Alejandro Cruz Martinez. Story by Rosalma Zubizarreta, Harriet Rohmer and David Schecter. Illustrated by Fernando Olivera. Children's Book Press (246 First St., Suite 101, San Francisco, CA 94105), 1991. 32 pages. (0–89239–101–4) (pbk. 0–89239–126–X, 1994)

Cruz was a young Zapotec poet who collected this tale prior to being killed in 1987 while organizing his people to regain their water rights. After the Mexican painter Fernando Olivera heard the story from Cruz, he created paintings about the legendary Lucia Zenteno. Olivera's stunning full-color paintings illustrate this bilingual 8 1/4 x 9 1/4" edition of the tale featuring a woman who, when she mysteriously arrived at a village ". . . brought thousands of dancing butterflies and brightly colored flowers on her skirts. She walked softly yet with quiet dignity, her long, unbraided hair flowing behind her. A loyal iguana walked at her side . . . Everyone felt a little afraid of someone so wonderful and yet so strange . . . ." When Lucia was driven from the village by misunderstanding and cruelty, the river she loved and all its creatures left with her. The resulting drought caused the villagers to search for Lucia and ask her forgiveness. They found out that just as the river once gave water to all, so, also, were they to "treat everyone with kindness, even those who seem different . . . ." (Ages 5–11)

Dee, Ruby. *Tower to Heaven.* Illustrated by Jennifer Bent. Henry Holt, 1991. 32 pages. (0–8050–1460–8)

Talkative Yaa and the people of her village fall just short of reaching the great god of the sky with their tower of mortars. To this day it is possible to see Yaa at the top of the tower, telling Onyankopon what she thinks he needs to know and calling for one more mortar to complete the tower. This interpretation of a tale well-known in many African regions has Ghanian roots in its narrative details and also in the elements of its full-color illustrations created with concentrated inks on scratchboard. (Ages 5–9)

Delacre, Lulu, reteller and illustrator. *Golden Tales: Myths, Legends & Folktales from Latin America.* Scholastic, 1996. 73 pages. (0–590–48186-X)

After much research Delacre selected 12 classic tales for this volume, bringing 13 nations and four native cultures together. The tales are from the lands of the Taino (a Taino myth, a Puerto Rican legend, a Dominican legend, and a Cuban folktale); the land of the Zapotec (a Chatino myth, a Zapotec myth, and a Mexican legend); and the land of the Muisca (an Inca/Quechua myth, a Quechua folktale from Bolivia, and a Quechua legend from Bolivia). Delacre's 37 paintings were done in oil and are reproduced in full color. Her linocuts recreate selected motifs of ancient Latin American rock and textile artists. The source notes and index/pronunciation guide increase enjoyment and use of the collection. A Spanish language edition, *De Oro y Esmeraldas: Mitos, Leyendas y Cuentos Populares de Latinoamérica* (0–590–67683–0), was published simultaneously. (Ages 8–12)

Ehlert, Lois. *Mole's Hill.* Harcourt, Brace, 1994. 32 pages. (0–15–255116–6)

Fox, Skunk, and Raccoon have a problem. Mole's hill is in the way of the path they're planning to make to the pond before the next winter. Because Mole is attached to her home and doesn't want to move it, she thinks of a plan to help her three neighbors appreciate the beauty of her hill. A perfectly spare retelling of a traditional Seneca tale is appropriately illustrated with brilliantly colored, stylized art inspired by sewn beadwork and ribbon appliqué from Woodland Indian traditions. (Ages 3–9)

Ehlert, Lois. *Moon Rope: A Peruvian Folktale = Un Lazo a la Luna: Una Leyenda Peruana.* Translated into Spanish by Amy Prince. Harcourt Brace Jovanovich, 1992. 32 pages. (0–15–255343–6)

Ehlert's brilliant use of ancient Peruvian color and form creates a stunning picture book with an avant-garde appearance. The simple bilingual text tells the story of Fox and Mole's attempt to reach the moon by climbing up a rope made of grass. Mole is so embarrassed when he loses his grip and falls back to earth that he burrows into the ground and to this day only comes out at night. And Fox? Many say they can still see him up there sometimes when the moon is full. A bold palette of blue, red, orange, green, purple, and black constrasts sharply with the luminous silver color of the Fox and the moon, proving Ehlert to be one of the most gifted colorists working in contemporary picture books. (Ages 3–7)

Garland, Sherry. *Why Ducks Sleep on One Leg.* Illustrated by Jean and Mou-Sien Tseng. Scholastic, 1993. 32 pages. (0–590–45697–0)

When the earth was young, all creatures were newly created and all were content except for three ducks in a rice-farming village. These unhappy but clever ducks had only one leg each, so it wasn't long before they developed a petition about the matter to take to the Jade Emperor. The humorous, absorbing *pourquoi* tale explains how the ducks each received a special second leg and also why, once they figured out how to hide it, this manner of sleeping became so comfortable that the custom spread elsewhere. The water-color illustrations employ an unconventional palette fitting both the tale and its ancient feudal Vietnamese locale. This 11¹/₂ x 8⁵/₈" book can be seen well by a group as well as enjoyed by individuals. (Ages 5–8)

Gershator, Phillis. *Tukama Tootles the Flute: A Tale from the Antilles.* Illustrated by Synthia Saint James. A Richard Jackson Book/Orchard, 1994. 32 pages. (0–531–06811–0) (lib. bdg. 0–531–08661–5)

Tukama ignores his grandmother's warning to stay away from the rocks near the sea. He would much rather play there all day than stay home and help her with the chores, despite her fear that he'll meet the same fate as other children who've played there: capture by the two-headed giant. Tempting fate once too often, Tukama falls into the giant's clutches, but he is able to use his wits—and his flute-playing—to trick the giant's wife into helping him escape. Synthia Saint James's oil paintings, with their bold use of color and form, highlight the telling of this cautionary tale. (Ages 4–7)

Goble, Paul. *Crow Chief: A Plains Indian Story.* Orchard, 1992. 32 pages. (0–531–05947–2) (lib. bdg. 0–531–08547–3) (pbk. 0–531–07064–6, 1995)

Long ago, in the days before horses, crows were jealous of people and sought revenge on them by warning buffaloes whenever human hunters were nearby. The people would have died out completely had it not been for their savior, Falling Star, who figured out a way to outsmart the chief of the crows. The bossy character of the crow chief adds touches of humor to this Lakota legend, illustrated in Goble's trademark style which seems to be inspired by the traditional 19th century ledger art of Native artists. (Ages 4–8)

Goble, Paul. *Iktomi and the Buzzard.* A Richard Jackson Book/Orchard, 1994. 32 pages. (0–531–06812–9) (lib. bdg. 0–531–08662–3)

It seems that with each retelling of an Iktomi tale, Goble refines his style a little further, so that art and text are blended into a seamless aesthetic whole. Here he employs three different typography styles to tell this humorous Lakota trickster tale in three different voices: that of the narrator, that of the narrator's critical alter-ego, and that of the vain Iktomi himself. In this particular tale, Iktomi manages to hitch a ride across a river on a buzzard's back. In spite of the buzzard's generosity, Iktomi cannot resist making rude signs behind the bird's back, unaware that the buzzard is seeing it all by watching their shadows on the ground. Iktomi gets his comeuppance but, as usual, bounces back to find another unsuspecting sucker. But that's another story . . . (Ages 4–9)

Goble, Paul, reteller and illustrator. *The Return of the Buffaloes: A Plains Indian Story about Famine and Renewal of the Earth.* National Geographic Society, 1996. 32 pages. (0–7922–2714-X)

The winter food supplies of the Lakota people are depleted. The children are too weak from hunger to play. Even though spring has already arrived, the buffalo have not returned to the Great Plains. Two young men are dispatched to go far into the hills and find the buffaloes for their starving people. They meet a mysterious and wonderful woman who leads them into a cave, addresses each as Grandson and causes the famine to end. Extensive author's notes and details about both *parfleches* and buffalo hunting make this volume especially valuable to anyone wanting information about the Lakota people. Goble's illustrations were created in India ink and watercolor. His earlier book *Buffalo Woman* (Bradbury, 1984) featured a tale about a different visitation of this holy Mother Earth figure. (Ages 8–12)

González, Lucía M. *The Bossy Gallito = El Gallo de Bodas.* Illustrated by Lulu Delacre. Scholastic, 1994. 32 pages. (0–590–46843-X)

On his way to his uncle's lavish wedding, a showy rooster cannot resist two kernels of corn he sees in the street, even though eating them dirties his beak. He commands the grass to clean his beak and when it refuses, he tells the goat to eat the grass but the goat refuses as well. Each refusal leads to another demand from the bossy little rooster in this cumulative folk story from Cuba. Side-by-side bilingual text (with the Spanish set in a darker typeface to distinguish it from the English) is accompanied by full-color mixed media paintings that aptly capture the character of the arrogant *gallito*, as well as the exasperated neighbors he attempted to rule. Endnotes include a pronunciation guide and extensive notes about the story's background, cast, and setting in Little Havana, Miami. (Ages 3–6)

Hall, Nancy Abraham and Jill Syverson-Stork. *Los Pollitos Dicen: Juegos, Rimas y Canciones Infantiles de Países de Habla Hispana = The Baby Chicks Sing: Traditional Games, Nursery Rhymes, and Songs from Spanish-Speaking Countries.* Illustrated by Kay Chorao. Little, Brown, 1994. 32 pages. (0–316–34010–3)

Seventeen songs and rhymes from a variety of Spanish-speaking countries are presented in Spanish with English translation in this appealing collection. Kay Chorao's lovely, lively color illustrations span each double-page spread, which feature one or two songs or rhymes with musical notation and directions for any accompanying hand-clapping, jump-roping, pantomiming, or other activity involved. (Ages 9 months–4 years)

Hamanaka, Sheila. *Screen of Frogs: An Old Tale.* Orchard, 1993. 32 pages. (0–531–05464–0) (lib. bdg. 0–531–08614–3)

A wealthy but lazy boy named Koji lived long ago in Japan, and when he became a man he was a lazy man—so lazy that rather than manage his property, he sold whatever possessions might provide the money he needed. Finally a frog as large as a man appeared to Koji, telling him what would become of the wildlife on the mountain if the woodcutters were to chop down the trees. Excellent use of white space and distinctive perspectives earmark the dramatic story. The full-color illustrations for the fast-moving $8^1/4$ x $10^1/2$" tale of transformation and gratitude are acrylic and collage on handmade *kozo* paper. (Ages 5–9)

Hamilton, Virginia, reteller and author. *Her Stories: African American Folktales, Fairy Tales, and True Tales.* Illustrated by Leo and Diane Dillon. Blue Sky/Scholastic, 1995. 109 pages. (0–590–47370–0)

In a companion volume to *The People Could Fly: American Black Folktales* (Knopf, 1985), Hamilton retells 19 tales with female protagonists that have been passed down from generation to generation by African-American women. The tales are divided into five sections: animal stories; fairy tales; the supernatural; folkways and legends; and true tales. Each section is introduced by an author's note and includes three or four stories. Each tale is told in a distinctive voice and followed by commentary that places the story in a historical and cultural context. Leo and Diane Dillon's distinguished color paintings add to the overall elegance of this beautifully designed volume. (Ages 7–14)

Hamilton, Virginia, reteller. *When Birds Could Talk & Bats Could Sing: The Adventures of Bruh Sparrow, Sis Wren, and Their Friends.* Illustrated by Barry Moser. Blue Sky/Scholastic, 1996. 63 pages. (0–590–47372–7)

Unforgettable winged creatures practically fly off the pages of this elegant volume. Virginia Hamilton has selected and retold eight African-American folktales first written down in heavy black dialect by folklorist Martha Young, who collected the stories from former slaves on her father's plantation in Alabama. In each of the brief stories, the creatures behave like humans with human weaknesses: pride, selfishness, and just plain nosiness. The stories are written in a prose style known as *cante fable*, meaning that songs and verses are woven into the story and each one ends with a moral. The characters themselves are brilliantly characterized by a combination of Hamilton's perfectly crafted dialogue and Barry Moser's stunning watercolor paintings. In spite of the human attributes Moser gives Miss Bat and the birds through the facial expressions and the hats they wear, we never forget that they are creatures of the sky, thanks largely to a page design which causes viewers' eyes to sweep upward as they follow the characters' antics, making an inevitable fall from grace all the more dramatic. (Ages 7–12)

Han, Suzanne Crowder, reteller. *The Rabbit's Escape.* Illustrated by Yumi Heo. Henry Holt, 1995. 32 pages. (0–8050–2675–4)

Fresh, distinctive artwork characterized by innovative perspectives and a unique and wonderful attention to detail enhance the telling of this delightful bilingual (Korean-English) tale. Rabbit is eager to travel to the underwater world of the East Sea. Luckily Rabbit is wily as well as curious, for he must use his wits to escape when the ailing underwater Dragon King demands Rabbit's liver, which, the King has been told, will cure him. An author's note provides information on the tale's origin, and the Korean language translation appears above the English on each page of text in a tale that follows Rabbit's debut in *The Rabbit's Judgment* (Henry Holt, 1994). (Ages 5–8)

Haskins, James. *The Headless Haunt and Other African-American Ghost Stories.* Illustrated by Ben Otero. HarperCollins, 1994. 116 pages. (0–06–022994–2) (lib. bdg. 0–06–022997–7) (pbk. 0–06–440602–4, 1995)

An outstanding collection of ghost stories from African-American traditions is superbly organized by type, including sections on Who Can See Ghosts; Plat-Eyes; Precautions to Take When Someone Dies; Ghosts and Buried Treasure; Jack-O'-Lantern Tales; and Civil War Ghosts. Each section includes an intriguing excerpt from interviews conducted in the 1930s by the Georgia Writers Project, in which African-American elders were asked to speak about their folk beliefs concerning ghosts. In addition, Haskins' notes provide further analytical information about European and African influences on African-American ghost stories and point out qualities that are unique to the African-American tradition. (Ages 8–14)

Heo, Yumi, reteller and illustrator. *The Green Frogs: A Korean Folktale.* Houghton Mifflin, 1996. 32 pages. (0–395–68378–5)

"Long ago when tigers still smoked pipes . . ." a pair of naughty frogs always did the opposite of what their mother told them to do. This *pourquoi* tale explains why frogs always cry "Gaegul! Gaegul! Gaegul!" whenever it rains and why—in Korea—"children who don't listen to their mother are called *chung-gaeguri* or green frogs." Heo remembers hearing the story of the green frogs when she was a little girl in Korea. Her humorous illustrations suggest swampy, underwater, and microscopic images. They were created with oil paint and pencil and are reproduced in full color— mostly shades of green. (Ages 3–8)

Hong, Lily Toy. *How the Ox Star Fell from Heaven.* Albert Whitman, 1991. 32 pages. (lib. bdg. 0–8075–3428–5) (pbk. 0–8075–3429–3, 1995)

Long ago, the Ox Star was sent to Earth to deliver a message from the Emperor of the Heavens. He was instructed to tell the people that the Emperor promised they'd eat once every three days, but he garbled the message and instead told them that the Emperor promised they'd eat three times a day. Of course, the people would need help in order to produce enough food to feed themselves so often. Bold, stylized paintings illustrate the Chinese folktale which explains how oxen came to be beasts of burden. (Ages 4–7)

Jaramillo, Nelly Palacio. *Grandmother's Nursery Rhymes: Lullabies, Tongue Twisters, and Riddles from South America = Las Nanas de Abuelita: Canciones de Cuna, Trabalenguas y Adivinanzas de Suramérica.* Illustrated by Elivia. Henry Holt, 1994. 32 pages. (0–8050–2555–3) (pbk. 8050–4644–5, 1996)

Familiar Hispanic nursery rhymes and riddles are presented in their original Spanish versions, along with outstanding translations into English which truly capture the spirit and usually the meanings of the originals. Watercolor illustrations enhance the playful exuberance of the rhymes. (Ages 18 months–6 years)

Joseph, Lynn. *The Mermaid's Twin Sister: More Stories from Trinidad.* Illustrated by Donna Perrone. Clarion, 1994. 63 pages. (0–395–64365–1)

Amber's grandaunt, Tantie, has marvelous stories based on her life in Trinidad, the Caribbean island where Tantie was born. Tantie tells five tales within the context of contemporary family experiences that read like chapters in a short novel. Before the book ends, Amber accepts the new role of storyteller for her generation by telling a story herself. A two-page note at the end provides a cultural context for the tales. (Ages 9–12)

Joseph, Lynn. *A Wave in Her Pocket: Stories from Trinidad.* Illustrated by Brian Pinkney. Clarion, 1991. 51 pages. (0–395–54432–7) (pbk. 0–395–81309–3, 1996)

A collection of tales written from the perspective of a young girl in Trinidad shows her and her cousins delighting in listening to her great aunt's stories from traditional folklore. Each tale is framed by family events and activities which inspire Tantie to remember a fitting story: some of them teach, some of them amuse, and some of them scare, but all of them entertain and delight listeners and readers. (Ages 6–11)

Kurtz, Jane. *Fire on the Mountain.* Illustrated by E.B. Lewis. Simon & Schuster, 1994. 28 pages. (0–671–88268–6)

The wealthy landowner whom Alemayu and his sister work for is a bragging, boastful man. When he tells of surviving an entire night on the cold mountain with nothing to keep him warm, he expects his servants to be impressed, but Alemayu is not. As a sheep-herder, the boy has done the same many times, and he accepts the landowner's challenge to spend an entire night on the mountain with only his thin *shemma* to keep him warm. If he wins the challenge, Alemayu will get four cows and a bag of money. Alemayu does succeed, but the wealthy man claims the boy has cheated by looking at a far-off fire to stay warm. "Looking at a fire on the mountain is the same as building a fire," he claims. Alemayu's sister and the rest of the servant's use the landowner's own logic against him to set things right in Jane Kurtz's satisfying retelling of an Ethiopian folktale illustrated with E.B. Lewis's watercolor paintings washed in tones of the earth. The author, who grew up in Ethiopia, added the character of Alemayu's sister to her retelling based on a tradition of strong women in Ethiopian stories. (Ages 7–10)

Kurtz, Jane, reteller. *Pulling the Lion's Tail.* Illustrated by Floyd Cooper. Simon & Schuster, 1995. 32 pages. (0–689–80324–9) (pbk. 0–671–88183–3)

According to Kurtz, who grew up in a southwest Ethiopian village, "respect for elders is almost the most important thing every child needs to learn." Interpreting a traditional Ethiopian tale often called "The Lion's Whiskers," Kurtz writes about Almaz, a young girl grieving over her mother's death. Her attempts to welcome her father's new wife seem futile until grandfather advises Almaz to get hair from a lion's tale. To do this, she must be patient. Almaz learns to approach her shy, young, homesick stepmother slowly and is rewarded by the possibility of a new relationship. Kurtz's story involves important cultural and geographic references, such as the beeswax candles and woven baskets in Almaz's home, *wat* (peppery stew), and *injera* (thin bread eaten with *wat*). Cooper's illustrations are painted in oils, revealing the expressive faces of a family in transition. (Ages 6–9)

Lester, Julius. *John Henry.* Illustrated by Jerry Pinkney. Dial, 1994. 40 pages. (0–8037–1606–0) (lib. bdg. 0–8037–1607–9)

The mythic railroad worker from the African-American oral tradition comes to life in this outstanding retelling that recounts his extraordinary accomplishments. Julius Lester's use of anthropomorphism and anachronism marks the story with his own distinctive flair as a skillful storyteller for contemporary children. Jerry Pinkney's vibrant colored pencil and watercolor paintings depict John Henry as an ordinary mortal, just a little taller than everybody else. This is in keeping with Lester's historical note concerning the academic research into whether or not the legendary John Henry was based on a real man. The story retold for this picture-book account was based on three specific versions of the African-American folk ballad about the famous contest between John Henry and a steam drill in the building of Big Bend Tunnel in the Allegheny Mountains. Visual images of rainbows and meteors add cosmic scope throughout. The final page combines John Henry with another icon of power: the White House. (Ages 4–12)

Lester, Julius. *The Last Tales of Uncle Remus.* Illustrated by Jerry Pinkney. Dial, 1994. 156 pages. (0–8037–1303–7) (lib. bdg. 0–8037–1304–5)

Lester's incomparable storytelling shines once again in a collection of 39 tales that wholly honors and embraces the African-American oral tradition from which the stories emerged. Vibrant and witty, Lester's language resonates with voices of the past while firmly establishing the stories as tales for today. In his introduction, Lester writes that "storytelling is a human event, an act of creating relationship," and in his storytelling he creates a bond between storyteller and reader that is direct and friendly. Lester also notes in the introduction that while the character of Uncle Remus is sometimes criticized as a stereotype, "it is the same Uncle Remus who preserved the culture through the tales. Without Uncle Remus, how much of black folk culture would have survived?" Lester continues to preserve that culture in this volume of lively tales that are illustrated with Jerry Pinkney's black-and-white drawings, as well as full-color paintings that span across the two-page spread of some stories. Readers familiar with Lester's earlier Uncle Remus collections, *The Tales of Uncle Remus* (Dial, 1987), *More Tales of Uncle Remus* (Dial, 1988) and *Further Tales of Uncle Remus* (Dial, 1990) will welcome this collection chronicling additional adventures of Brer Rabbit, Brer Bear, Brer Fox and many others, while new readers to the tales will eagerly seek out the predecessors. (Ages 8–12)

McKissack, Patricia C. *The Dark-Thirty: Southern Tales of the Supernatural.* Illustrated by Brian Pinkney. Alfred A. Knopf, 1992. 122 pages. (0–689–81863–4) (lib. bdg. 0–679–91863–9) (pbk. 0–679–88335–5; Random House, 1997)

Ten original stories based in African-American history combine supernatural elements with an oral style that reads like traditional storytelling. Whether it's the mysterious disappearance of a slave being sold away from his family, or the ghostly revenge of a man lynched by the Ku Klux Klan, all of these well-written stories are satisfyingly eerie, exactly right to be told and re-told during the "dark-thirty"—the half hour just before nightfall. (Ages 7–12)

McLellan, Joe. *Nanabosho, Soaring Eagle, and the Great Sturgeon.* Illustrated by Rhian Brynjolson. Pemmican Publications (1635 Burrows Avenue, #2, Winnepeg, Manitoba R2X 0T1 Canada), 1993. 48 pages. (pbk. 0–921827–23–7, out of print)

When two Ojibway girls go fishing with their grandfather, they brag about the number of fish they'll catch as they ride in their grandfather's truck to the lake. After listening to the two girls, grandfather shares a Nanabosho story about a time the trickster hero and his friend Soaring Eagle were greedy when they stocked up on fish for the winter. Engaging watercolor illustrations capture the humor and the wisdom of this story within a story. They even take the story one step further by including border illustrations which depict the challenges faced by an older brother who was left home to do the laundry. (Ages 4–8)

Medearis, Angela Shelf. *The Singing Man: Adapted from a West African Folktale.* Illustrated by Terea Shaffer. Holiday House, 1994. (0–8234–1103–6) (pbk. 0–8234–1208–3)

A folktale from the Yoruba people in Nigeria tells the story of a third son who is cast out from his village for wanting to be a musician instead of a farmer or blacksmith or something else his village elders value. Traveling with only his flute and a few coins, Banzar meets Sholo, a musician who teaches him the history and traditions of praise singers, who compose songs to honor village chiefs and their ancestors. An author's note informs readers that praise singing is the means by which the stories and the history of the African peoples were preserved. "Long before African history was written in books, it was sung." Richly colored oil paintings depict the Nigerian people and landscapes of the story, while borders inspired by the textile patterns of West Africa frame each page. (Ages 5–8)

Merrill, Jean. *The Girl Who Loved Caterpillars.* Illustrated by Floyd Cooper. Philomel, 1992. 32 pages. (lib. bdg. 0–399–21871–8)

An adaptation of a 12th-century Japanese story left unfinished by its anonymous author has a startlingly modern ring. As the daughter of a nobleman in the Emperor's court, Izumi is expected to conform to standards of behavior and beauty which will assure her a place as a lady-in-waiting or as the wife of a nobleman. But Izumi has no interest in fashion or femininity; instead she is fascinated with worms, toads, insects and, most especially, caterpillars. While other nobles find Izumi disgusting and ridiculous, "scruffy-looking boys from families of low standing" find her admirable. The boys (to whom Izumi assigns nicknames such as Worm Boy and Mantis Man) line up to present her with gifts—unusual insects or caterpillars they have found. And one day a nobleman overhears Izumi talking to a caterpillar as he is passing by . . . but what, if anything, developed from their chance meeting has been lost to history. Floyd Cooper's lush oil paintings capture the strength of character and individuality of a girl living 800 years ago who might have been much more comfortable growing up in the late 20th century. (Ages 6–11)

Mollel, Tololwa M. *Orphan Boy.* Illustrated by Paul Morin. Clarion, 1991. 32 pages. (0–89919–985–2) (0–685–53587–8) (0–395–72080–X), 1996. (pbk. 0–395–72079–6, 1995)

One night as an old man gazes at the sky, he notices that one of the stars is missing. His attention is soon diverted, however, when he is startled by Kileken, a young boy who seems to appear out of nowhere. After he offers Kileken a place to stay, the old man is amazed by the work the boy manages to accomplish, and he begins to question where the boy came from. His curiosity turns out to be a fatal flaw. This hauntingly beautiful traditional Maasai story, retold by an Arusha Maasai writer who grew up in Tanzania, is accompanied by breathtaking textured oil paintings. (Ages 4–7)

Namioka, Lensey, reteller. *The Loyal Cat.* Illustrated by Aki Sogabe. Browndeer/Harcourt Brace, 1995. 40 pages. (0–15–200092–5)

A Japanese fairy tale involves a holy man named Tetsuzan and Huku, his amazing cat. Soft-spoken Tetsuzan cares little about importance and has few material needs. In fact, the modest priest has hardly noticed that few gifts are brought to his temple. Enter Huku, a cat with magical powers and a normal appetite. Seeing that even the mice have left because there were few morsels to steal, Huku attempts to upgrade his master's life. Huku proves to be loyal as well as smart in a beautifully designed, humorous story about greed and humility. Sogabe created each picture in this elegant $11^3/8$ x $8^3/4$" book from one sheet of black paper, cut freehand and placed over rice papers that were colored using airbrush or watercolor. An endnote indicates that today one can visit the Cat Temple in northern Japan. (Ages 5–9)

Rosen, Michael. *South and North, East and West: The Oxfam Book of Children's Stories.* Introduction by Whoopi Goldberg. U.S. edition: Candlewick, 1992. 95 pages. (1–56402–117–3)

The global scope of these tales distinguishes this anthology, as does the generally eerie and delightfully scary tone of many of the tales introduced. The collection was developed from suggestions by Oxfam staff members who heard the stories from people with whom they work in nations such as Bolivia, Botswana, Indonesia, Korea, Mali, Nepal, and Vietnam. A creation story, "The Beginning of History," came from a Brazilian Indian story source. The volume was published to coincide with the 50th birthday of this international aid and development organization to benefit self-help projects in Africa, Asia, Latin America, and the Caribbean. Brief identifications are provided for the 22 mostly British artists who contributed full-color illustrations. Two pages of information about Oxfam complete the book. (Ages 9–12)

Ross, Gayle and Joseph Bruchac, retellers.
The Girl Who Married the Moon: Tales from Native North America. BridgeWater, 1994.
127 pages. (0–8167–3480–1)
(pbk. 0–8167–3481-X, 1996)

American Indian storytellers Gayle Ross and Joseph Bruchac set out to dismantle stereotypes of American Indian women too often perpetuated in the movies and other media in this singular collection of folklore. The sixteen stories in *The Girl Who Married the Moon* come from American Indian Nations across Native North America and honor and celebrate the valued and varied roles of women in these cultures. Arranged by geographic region, each section begins with a brief introduction to the American Indian nations of that area from which the stories come. Source information for the tales is provided in an Afterword and Acknowledgments section at the end of the book. (Ages 11–14)

Ross, Gayle, reteller. *How Turtle's Back Was Cracked: A Traditional Cherokee Tale.*
Illustrated by Murv Jacob. Dial, 1995.
32 pages. (lib. bdg.0–8037–1729–6)
(0–8037–1728–8)

A Cherokee legend from "the days when the people and the animals still spoke the same language" begins when Possum and Turtle search for persimmons. When a wolf spoils their feast, Possum retaliates, but it's vain Turtle who claims the credit. Turtle not only makes a pair of wolf-ear spoons, but then he shows off this "tribute," prevailing upon friends and even on strangers to respond with hospitality. After Turtle gorges himself on corn soup, the insulted wolves serve him a comeuppance for such bad behavior. This *pourquois* tale is beautifully illustrated with Jacobs's detailed, intricately patterned artwork done in acrylics that suggest a dark forest full of an active community of talking creatures. Ross is an accomplished storyteller and a descendent of the principal chief of the Cherokee Nation during the time of the Trail of Tears. Her endnotes briefly summarize the history of that Indian Removal (1838–39) and also point out accomplishments of the Cherokee Nation. (Ages 7–10)

Ross, Gayle, reteller. *The Legend of the Windigo: A Tale from Native North America.*
Illustrated by Murv Jacob. Dial, 1996.
(0–8037–1897–7) (lib. bdg. 0–8037–1898–5)

Trouble comes to the ancient inhabitants of a North American woodland village when a Windigo arrives. This "giant creature made of stone with eyes like deep caves that hypnotize human beings" also feeds on them, too. Although the people outwitted it then, their method causes the Windigo to exist now in the form of mosquitoes. It continues to eat humans—one bite at a time. Jacob's detailed, intricately patterned artwork suggest a dark forest full of activity. His illustrations were rendered in acrylics on watercolor paper. In an endnote Ross tells about the time when she first began to think about this trickster tale. She was with Utah Phillips and other storytellers gathered about a Northern Wisconsin campfire. (Ages 7–10)

Taylor, C. J. *The Ghost and Lone Warrior: An Arapaho Legend.* Tundra, 1991. 24 pages.
(0–88776–263–8) (0–516–08167–5; Children's Press, 1991)

In the days before horses, the people had to walk everywhere, even when they were hunting buffalo. When Lone Warrior injures his ankle on such a hunt, he is left behind by the rest of the hunting party, who promise to return in a few days. Months pass and they never return, nor does Lone Warrior's ankle heal. But his struggle to survive is eventually rewarded one night when he is visited by the spirit of an ancestor who has an explanation for everything that has happened. This fine retelling of an Arapaho legend is accompanied by full-color paintings by a Mohawk artist. (Ages 5–9)

Taylor, C.J. *Little Water and the Gift of the Animals: A Seneca Legend.* Tundra, 1992.
24 pages. (lib. bdg. 0–88776–285–9)

A Mohawk artist retells and illustrates a legend from another Iroquois tribe, the Seneca. Little Water was respected by his people as a good hunter; however, he especially loved to spend time alone in the woods, observing the animals rather than hunting them. When tragedy befalls his village in the form of a mysterious disease, Little Water calls on the spirits of his animal friends to help him bring medicine to his people. Full-color oil paintings accompany an eloquent traditional tale about the interconnectedness of all life forms. (Ages 4–8)

Temple, Frances. *Tiger Soup: An Anansi Story from Jamaica.* A Richard Jackson Book/ Orchard, 1994. 32 pages. (0–531–06859–5) (lib. bdg. 0–531–08709–3)

An engaging folktale from Jamaica features the trickster Anansi from African traditions. Here, Anansi plays two tricks: first he tricks Tiger into a swimming lesson so he can eat the good soup Tiger's spent the day cooking; next, he tricks a group of playful monkeys into taking the blame by teaching them a song with the chorus: "Just a little while ago / We ate the Tiger soup / Yum, yum, yum . . ." Illustrated with brightly colored collages, it is as satisfying as Tiger soup itself, and perfect for sharing in a preschool story hour. (Ages 3–6)

Vidal, Beatriz and Nancy Van Laan. *The Legend of El Dorado: A Latin American Tale.*
Illustrated by Beatriz Vidal. Alfred A. Knopf, 1991. 32 pages. (0–679–80136–7, out of print)

The mythical kingdom of gold, a widespread legend among the Native peoples of South America, was accepted as reality by Europeans from the time of first contact 500 years ago. In their lust for gold, generations of outsiders and explorers have searched in vain for El Dorado, seeking out and recording many versions of the legend to guide them in their quest. Argentinian Beatriz Vidal's haunting retelling of a Chibcha version, first recorded by Benalcázar in 1541, attributes the building of El Dorado to a long-ago Chibcha king. Despondent after the drowning of his wife and daughter, the king initiates an annual ritual in which he throws gold and jewels into Lake Guatavita to remind the water spirit of his promise to reunite the family upon the king's death. The lush colors of Vidal's exquisite paintings provide a perfect contrast to gold highlights scattered throughout the illustrations, making the glittering objects seem both precious and mundane. (Ages 4–8)

Vuong, Lynette Dyer and Manabu Saito. *The Golden Carp and Other Tales from Vietnam.* Illustrated by Manabu Saito. Lothrop, Lee & Shepard, 1993. 128 pages. (0–688–12514-X)

The Golden Carp contains six stories of ancient Vietnamese and Chinese origin: "A Friend's Affection," "The Ogre's Victim," "Tears of Pearl," "Third Daughter," "Second in Command," and the title story. The author's introduction explains the ways she learned about Vietnamese folklore; her extensive notes and pronunciation guide add to the value of this unusual compilation. The small typeface indicates a certain reading challenge. One full-page illustration reproduced in full color decorates each story. (Ages 9–13)

Vuong, Lynette Dyer and Manabu Saito. *Sky Legends of Vietnam.* Illustrated by Vo-Dinh Mai. HarperCollins, 1993. 103 pages. (0–06–023000–2) (lib. bdg. 0–06–023001–0)

Six stories, each one about the sun, the moon or the stars, are featured in this collection of Vietnamese tales. The typeface is large, the illustrations are black-and-white and the overall book production modest. However, Vuong's meticulous attention to cultural detail and notes make this a worthy collection. (Ages 7–11)

Yen, Clara. *Why Rat Comes First: A Story of the Chinese Zodiac.* Illustrated by Hideo C. Yoshida. Children's Book Press (246 First St., Suite 101, San Francisco, CA 94105), 1991. 32 pages. (lib. bdg. 0–89239–072–7)

As a second-generation Chinese-American, the author heard many folktales about the Chinese zodiac when she was growing up, but her favorite was a story that her father made up. To satisfy his curiosity about Earth's animals, the Jade King sends his messenger down from heaven, carrying invitations to a great feast for each and every animal. But the messenger trips and the invitations scatter; as a result only 12 animals arrive as guests at the feast. After their host decides to honor them by naming a year after each of the 12, the animals hold a contest to see which of them will come first. The amusing antics of the clever, ambitious Rat win the hearts of the contest judges—Earth's children. Yen's perfectly paced text combines with brightly colored cartoon-like illustrations to create an appealing story for reading aloud. (Ages 3–7)

Yep, Laurence. *The Ghost Fox.* Illustrated by Jean and Mou-Sien Tseng. Scholastic, 1994. 70 pages. (0–590–47204–6)

Little Lee becomes determined to outsmart a ghostly fox, even if he must defy the adults in his family and neighborhood. According to information provided by the publisher, an ancient Chinese literary tradition involved ghost storytelling. Yep adapted this tale from one collected by a seventeenth century scholar. The small volume looks like an easy "chapter book." Yes, it is easy, and it is also scary! (Ages 8–11)

Yep, Laurence. *Tongues of Jade.* Illustrated by David Wiesner. HarperCollins, 1991. 194 pages. (0–06–022470–3, out of print)

These 17 stories, once gathered in San Francisco's Chinatown, have been retold by a writer well attuned to today's young readers as well as to his own heritage. The intriguing tales are organized into sections titled Roots, Family Ties, The Wild Heart, Face, and Beyond the Grave. This collection is a welcome companion to Yep's *The Rainbow People* (Harper, 1989). (Age 9–adult)

HISTORICAL PEOPLE, PLACES AND EVENTS

Balgassi, Haemi. *Peacebound Trains.*
Illustrated by Chris K. Soentpiet. Clarion,
1996. 46 pages. (0–395–72093–1)

During these years while her mother, or *umma*, is away in the U.S. Army, young Sumi lives with her grandmother, or *harmuny*. Sumi feels particularly lonesome for Umma one day, so Harmuny tells the girl what happened when Umma was a baby in Seoul, Korea, in 1951. Fleeing from Seoul and increasing dangers, Harmuny and Sumi's grandfather, or *harabujy,* took their children and the belongings they could carry and started walking toward far away Pusan. Finally Harabujy decided that the best chance his wife and their children might have for survival would be to ride with hundreds of other desperate refugees on top of the last train going South. The family made it safely, but they never saw Harabujy again. The story is based on actual experiences in the lives of Balgassi's mother and grandmother. Both she and Soentpiet were born in Seoul. Soentpiet's marvelous watercolors grace each page, expanding the contemporary and historical scenes and specifying cultural details. This compelling fictional account is divided into eight short sections. (Ages 8–12)

Chang, Ina. *A Separate Battle: Women and the Civil War.* Lodestar, 1991. 103 pages. (0–525–67365–2) (pbk. 0–14–038106–6; Puffin, 1996)

Women played an important part in the U.S. Civil War, serving such varied roles as volunteers and nurses, soldiers and spies in both the North and the South. Drawing on 19th century women's letters, diaries, speeches, and essays, Ina Chang eloquently tells their stories, placing them within the historical context of the abolitionist movement and the struggle for women's rights. The handsome volume, generously illustrated with photographs and prints from the era, is exemplary nonfiction for young readers. (Age 9–adult)

Coerr, Eleanor. *Sadako.* Illustrated by Ed Young. Putnam, 1993. 48 pages. (0–399–21771–1)

Sadako Sasaki is the child honored by the monument of a girl holding a large origami crane in the Hiroshima Peace Park. The monument is a strong expression for peace, representing the many who perished in Japan as a result of the atomic bombs dropped on Hiroshima and Nagasaki in 1945. As she suffered from radiation sickness, Sadako and her friends are reported to have folded origami cranes, in accordance with the Japanese legend holding that if a sick person folds 1,000 cranes, the gods will restore her health. The same author who wrote the moving short fiction book *Sadako and the Thousand Paper Cranes* (Putnam, 1977) presents this adaptation of the script for a film of the same name. The striking 9 1/4 x 11 1/4" book includes a selection of the almost three hundred images artist Ed Young created for the film using pastels, many of which reflect images of origami cranes or cranes from nature. (Ages 8–11)

Cooper, Michael. *Playing America's Game: The Story of the Negro Baseball League.* Lodestar, 1993. 96 pages. (0–525–67407–1)

John Henry Lloyd . . . Cool Papa Bell . . . Smokey Joe Williams . . . Josh Gibson. These are baseball players of whom many people have never heard, and yet they were among the best in their day, some of them contemporaries of more well-known players such as Babe Ruth and Ty Cobb. In a country in which sports heroes are elevated to the rank of superstar, these men, too, held their places of honor among their fans. The fact that their names are unfamiliar to so many today has nothing to do with their talent and ability, only with the color of their skin—they were Black and played in the Negro League. Unlike the major league teams and players, theirs has not been a history held in high national esteem, even though they were revered by many in their time. This history traces Negro League baseball, which was played for almost the entire first half of the 20th century, from its early days when it grew out of the segregation of baseball teams in the late 19th century (during the 1880s, Blacks and whites did play together on professional baseball teams), to its collapse in the late 1940s when players like Jackie Robinson, Larry Doby, and Satchel Paige integrated professional baseball once again. Black-and-white photographs marking "the beginning of an important public record" are used throughout the text of this important and fascinating history. (Ages 11–14)

Cox, Clinton. *Undying Glory: The Story of the Massachusetts 54th Regiment.* Scholastic, 1991. 167 pages. (pbk. 0–590–44171-X, 1993)

As the first African-American soldiers to serve in the U.S. Civil War, the members of the 54th had much at stake other than the usual life and death struggle of the soldier: not only were they fighting to free their brothers and sisters from captivity, but also to prove themselves as equals in the eyes of all Americans. A fast-paced, action-packed history focuses on the human side of this seldom-told story. (Age 9–adult)

Feelings, Tom. *The Middle Passage: White Ships / Black Cargo.* Dial, 1995. 80 pages. (0–8037–1804–7)

Tom Feelings worked ten years to complete the agonizing art that would become *The Middle Passage*, an achingly powerful 10¹/₂ x 13¹/₂" wordless book for older readers and adults that chronicles the forced journey of Africans into slavery. Feelings created 64 images that detail the experience of Africans captured at gunpoint and shackled and herded onto ships of death, disease and cruelty, where they endured, and often didn't survive, the crossing to North America, South America or the Caribbean. Seeringly painful images of inhuman conditions in which living people were stacked like so much cargo, cruelly worked, brutally raped and tortured, haunt the pages. A hard journey for the reader, *The Middle Passage* was a difficult journey for Tom Feelings to make as an artist as well, and he writes in the preface about his experience researching and creating the images. An introduction by John Henrik Clarke discusses the slave trade and places the artist's images in their deeply disturbing historical context. (Age 14–adult)

Feelings, Tom. *Tommy Traveler in the World of Black History.* Black Butterfly/Writers & Readers (Box 461, Village Station, New York, NY 10014), 1991. 42 pages. (0–86316–202–9) (pbk. 0–86316–211–8, 1993)

Significant historical events in the lives of Phoebe Fraunces, Emmet Till, Aesop, Frederick Douglass, Crispus Attucks, and Joe Louis are dramatized in a comic-strip format. Each event is introduced by Tommy Traveler, an African-American child fascinated with the private library collection of his neighbor, Dr. Gray, who has had a life-long interest in collecting books, magazines and newspaper clippings related to Black history. As Tommy reads, he is transported back in time and becomes a first-hand observer and participant in the events he describes. Originally published as a weekly comic strip in 1958–59, this presentation of Black history is as fresh and original today as it was 20 years ago and will appeal to a new generation of children. (Ages 7–11)

Hamilton, Virginia. *Many Thousand Gone: African Americans from Slavery to Freedom.* Illustrated by Leo and Diane Dillon. Alfred A. Knopf, 1993. 151 pages. (0–394–82873–9) (lib. bdg. 0–394–92873–3) (pbk. 0–679–87936–6, 1995)

Here are Sojourner Truth, Harriet Tubman, and Frederick Douglas. Here, too, are Chloe Cooley, Addison White, and Jackson of Alabama. Hamilton has gathered together stories of individuals living in the time of slavery and laid them out in a powerful presentation that chronicles this chilling era in American history and the endurance of a people. Some of the names may be familiar to children, many others will not, but each vignette—each life—is compelling and lends itself to a greater understanding of the whole, such as how laws to protect free African Americans were often ignored, while others were passed to strengthen the grip of slave owners in the south. In some cases, the vignettes are only fragments, pieces of a life, as if this is all that is known, and these serve as striking, painful reminders of how much has been lost, the "many thousand gone." Modifying her usual descriptive prose style, Hamilton pares language to a minimum here, writing in short, explosive sentences that propell people and events to the forefront, while the Dillons's moody black-and-white illustrations give shape to sorrow, grief, anger, bravery, and pride, and visual expression to the overwhelming desire to be free. (Age 8–adult)

Hansen, Joyce. *The Captive.* Scholastic, 1994. 195 pages. (0–590–41625–1) (pbk. 0–590–41624–3, 1995)

Kofi was 12 seasons old in 1788 when his father, a royal man within the Ashanti Kingdom, was betrayed by a trusted slave. The boy's subsequent bondage followed several captures and escapes, each expertly unfolded through a first-person narrative, carefully developed action, and colorful historical details. Moving from West Africa to New England and back in 1811, Kofi's story addresses the involvement of Africans in the slave trade, indentured servants, cultural differences, and the incongruity of Christian doctrine. Hansen based her fast-paced novel on "The Life of Olaudah Equiano or Gustavus Vassa, the African," and of what is known about the real Captain Paul Cuffe. Showing valuable glimpses of the rich cultural past brought by African captives to North America, *The Captive* offers unique depictions of late 18th century life in West Africa and in Massachusetts. (Ages 11–16)

Haskins, Jim. *Against All Opposition: Black Explorers in America.* Walker, 1992. 86 pages. (0–8027–8137–3) (lib. bdg. 0–8027–8138–1)

Nine chapters chronicle Black sailors and travelers known to have accompanied white adventurers and explorers and also some of the historic explorations initiated or implemented by Africans and African Americans throughout the centuries. Men cited include James P. Beckwourth, Guion Stewart Bluford, Jr., George W. Bush, Estevanico, Matthew Henson, Ronald McNair, Jean Baptiste Point du Sable, and York. The indexed book contains a brief bibliography. (Ages 9–14)

Levine, Ellen. *A Fence Away from Freedom: Japanese Americans and World War II.* Putnam, 1995. 260 pages. (0–399–22638–9)

In an important and powerful documentary, Japanese Americans who were children and young adults just prior to and during World War II tell what happened in their lives after the bombing of Pearl Harbor, when they were labelled "enemy" and made domestic prisoners of war. Comprised primarily of interview's Levine conducted with dozens of Japanese Americans, the text is arranged chronologically, with specific chapters that address the experiences of those in the camps, homeless children, Japanese-American soldiers and draft resisters, and Japanese Peruvians who were deported to the United States for internment. Each chapter opens with an informative discussion that provides a historical framework for the stirring comments that follow. (Ages 12–15)

Levine, Ellen. *Freedom's Children: Young Civil Rights Activists Tell Their Own Stories.* Putnam, 1993. 167 pages. (0–399–21893–9) (pbk. 0–380–72114–7; Avon, 1994)

Thirty African-American men and women who were children during the mid–20th century Civil Rights Movement recall its impact on them: what it was like to have your home bombed; to be jailed for civil disobedience; to be the first African-American youth integrated into an all-white classroom or school; to witness or take part in non-violent acts; to be inspired by the actions of the community. Recounted with invaluable first-hand insight and commentary and well organized in a meaningful sequence, the remembered experiences range from Segregation, the Montgomery Bus Boycott, Integration, Sit-ins and Freedom Rides to the Children's Crusade, Mississippi Freedom Summer, and the Selma Movement. Readers the same ages as these former "children of crisis" can glimpse moral courage and principled action through the compelling accounts. (Age 10–adult)

Lyons, Mary E. *Letters From a Slave Girl: The Story of Harriet Jacobs.* Scribner's, 1992. 146 pages. (0–684–19446–5) (pbk. 0–689–80015–0; Aladdin, 1996)

In 1842, 22-year-old Harriet Jacobs hid between the roof and ceiling of Gran's home in Edenton, North Carolina; her confinement lasted seven years. Drawing upon Jacobs's autobiography and writings by historians, Lyons created a sequence of matter-of-fact letters the remarkable woman might have written about her life. The fictionalized letters tell Harriet's dramatic story: they reflect anguish over her physical suffering, grief over the inability to live with her children, and anger at all whose deceptions and cruelties led to the injustices and dangers filling her long life. Harriet's courage and the moral bravery of several women who were part of her experience can inspire readers, some of whom will find a contemporary parallel in the sexual harassment experienced by young Harriet Jacobs. Lyons displays discretion concerning the young audience she respects and subject matter she does not sensationalize. The book includes Lyons's note about her writing process, maps, drawings of the house in which Harriet lived, archival photographs, two family trees (the white and Black Horniblow families), a glossary of 19th century words, and a bibliography of scholarly resources. (Ages 12–16)

McKissack, Patricia C. and Fredrick McKissack, Jr. *Black Diamond: The Story of the Negro Baseball Leagues.* Scholastic, 1994. 184 pages. (0–590–45809–4) (pbk. 0–590–45810–8, 1996)

After being shut out of major league baseball for nearly a century, African Americans formed their own leagues. Any reliable recounting of this history must include examples of the heroes on and off the diamond, the scoundrels who sabotaged efforts to provide talented Black athletes with a way to compete for audiences across the nation, and the conditions of pay and daily life endured by all involved in the Negro leagues. The authors meet that challenge by using primary source documents, oral histories, archival visual materials, and unflinching details about acts of racism. (Ages 9–16)

McKissack, Patricia C. and Fredrick L. McKissack. *Christmas in the Big House, Christmas in the Quarters.* Illustrated by John Thompson. Scholastic, 1994. 68 pages. (0–590–43027–0)

To depict daily life for the two communities living in parallel realities on a Virginia plantation during December, 1859, the authors gained access to primary source materials from Tidewater plantation records and held interviews there to find out more family histories. Wisely setting their text immediately before the outbreak of the Civil War, the McKissacks offer an amazing balance of perspectives while they report the distinctive culture of the Quarters. Showing the misery as well as the dignity of families in captivity, they allow readers to draw their own conclusions. Thompson's detailed paintings rendered in acrylic and reproduced in full color recreate the season and the buildings as well as some of the individually distinct Afrocentric head-wraps of enslaved women and holiday decorations in the Big House. Both the text and the illustrations move far beyond conventional media-induced images of plantation life. Incomparable in scope, content, and emotional impact, this well designed, easy-to-read account furnishes provocative information and offers dynamic year-round reading. (Ages 8–13)

McKissack, Patricia C. and Fredrick L. McKissack. *Rebels Against Slavery: American Slave Revolts.* Scholastic, 1996. 181 pages. (0–590–45735–7)

Contrary to typical early Hollywood portrayals of chattel slavery as it was practiced in the Americas, people of African heritage were not contented in enslavement. The McKissacks' award-winning *Christmas in the Big House, Christmas in the Quarters* (Scholastic, 1994) demonstrates that historic reality. *Rebels Against Slavery* introduces young readers to some of the brave "men and women, slaves and free blacks, Northerners and Southerners, whites and Native Americans" who knowingly risked their lives in active revolt against slavery. The defiance of individuals such as Toussaint Louverture, Gabriel Prosser, Harriet Tubman, Nat Turner, Denmark Vesey, and the rebels on the *Amistad* are described. Black-and-white archival photos document this carefully researched, compelling account. A chronology and extensive bibliography are included. (Ages 11–16)

McKissack, Patricia C. and Fredrick L. McKissack. *Red-Tail Angels: The Story of the Tuskegee Airmen of World War II.* Walker, 1995. 136 pages. (0–8027–8292–2) (lib. bdg. 0–8027–8293–0)

The McKissack's write a testament to dreams and ability in a history of the Tuskegee Airmen, the only African-American pilots to fly in World War II. Opening chapters on the history of human flight and of African Americans in the U.S. military set the stage for the hopes and struggles embraced and endured by the Red-Tail Angels and their supporters as they fought racist attitudes for the right to learn to fly in the U.S. military and, later, for the chance to use their skills in the war that was raging overseas. The Tuskegee Airmen eventually earned an outstanding reputation for their abilities. The text is illustrated with black-and-white photographs from archives and personal collections: the faces of pioneers. (Ages 11–14)

McKissack, Patricia and Fredrick McKissack. *The Royal Kingdoms of Ghana, Mali, and Songhay: Life in Medieval Africa.* Henry Holt, 1994. 142 pages. (0–8050–1670–8) (pbk. 0–8050–4259–8, 1995)

The ancient civilizations of the Western Sudan flourished between 500 and 1700 C.E. Drawing upon recent scholarship in archeology, anthropology, linguistics, and history, the McKissacks present a compelling Afro-centric interpretation of what is now known about these important kingdoms and trading centers. Extensive notes and a long bibliography document the authors' sources for this important book. (Age 10–adult)

Medearis, Angela Shelf. *Our People.* Illustrated by Michael Bryant. Atheneum, 1994. 32 pages. (0–689–31826-X)

An African-American girl proudly compares the realities of her everyday life to the accomplishments of people of African descent throughout history. The stories her daddy has told her of builders, explorers, inventors, adventurers, and heroes influence her present-day play and inspire her dreams for the future. The connections between past and present are imaginatively drawn with watercolor and colored pencil illustrations for this cheerful picture book. (Ages 4–8)

Mitchell, Margaree King. *Uncle Jed's Barbershop.* Illustrated by James Ransome. Simon & Schuster, 1993. 32 pages. (0–671–76969–3)

Mitchell's first-person narrative relates how her granddaddy's brother Jedediah Johnson, the only Black barber in the county, was her favorite relative. She tells about his Wednesday night visits to her family, how he paid for the operation she needed to save her life, and how the Depression caused him to lose money he saved for a barbershop. This heartwarming story is the portrait of a generous, indomitable man whose personal dream was finally fulfilled when he was 79 years old. The $11^3/4$ x $9^1/4$" picture story is also a straightforward account of segregation and its impact on one family during a crisis; and of one man plying his trade to make a living. Ransome's dramatic illustrations created with oil paint on paper are reproduced in full color. (Ages 5–9)

Mochizuki, Ken. *Baseball Saved Us.* Illustrated by Dom Lee. Lee & Low (95 Madison Ave., New York, NY 10016), 1993. 32 pages. (1–880000–01–6) (pbk. 1–880000–19–9)

The treatment of Japanese Americans during World War II is the subject of this remarkable first picture book. Shorty, a young Japanese-American boy, has a hard time understanding why he and his family had to move out of their house and into a camp in the desert. "We weren't in a camp that was fun, like summer camp. Ours was in the middle of nowhere, and we were behind a barbed-wire fence. Soldiers with guns made sure we stayed there . . ." Everything at camp is different—and more difficult—than life back home: there are dust storms, the buildings have no privacy (even for going to the bathroom), and there is nothing for anyone to do. The day Shorty's dad decides they need a baseball diamond marks a turning point in camp life as, first building the field and later competing in the games themselves, adults and children finally have something to hope and work for. Shorty, who has never been good at baseball, practices hard and eventually makes a game-winning hit in the camp championship. "But it wasn't as if everything was all fixed." Returning home after the war, he finds that he still must persevere against prejudice and his own fears to succeed. The straightforward narrative movingly captures a young boy's bewilderment over events which make no logical sense to adults, let alone to children. Sepia-toned color illustrations by Lee evoke a sense of a past that is washed in sadness. (Ages 7–11)

Myers, Walter Dean. *Now Is Your Time! The African-American Struggle for Freedom.* HarperCollins, 1991. (lib. bdg. 0–06–024371–6) (pbk. 0–06–446120–3), 1992.

Walter Dean Myers writes "Before you go forward, you must know where you have been." Myers's dynamic rendering of African-American history provides three distinct dimensions for such self-knowledge and progress: a general chronological summary, specific biographical accounts, and a striking patchwork of personal ancestry. Throughout his overview of events and conditions of the captivity of the African peoples, Myers interweaves compelling human stories. "What we understand of our history is what we understand of ourselves," he says, and so he interprets the necessary creation of the African-American extended family and the prevalence of certain means of expression within African-American life. His ringing conclusion challenges readers to think of African Americans past and present as a people fully deserving of rights and equally blessed with the gifts necessary for success. "I bring as much truth as I know," writes the author. Myers's account of the Plantation Society, his biography of the chief's son Abd al-Rahman Ibrathima, and his interpretation of the contributions of individuals such as Ida B. Wells exemplify the three-fold way this powerful 23-chapter book contributes new information, fresh insight and—ultimately—hope to all readers. (Age 9–adult)

Myers, Walter Dean. *One More River to Cross: An African American Photograph Album.* Harcourt Brace, 1995. 166 pages. (0–15–100191-X)

Walter Dean Myers's assemblage of black-and-white archival photographs demonstrate dignity, the key word in his visual documentary account of the history of people of African descent in the U.S.A. Myers's spare, lyrical text employs only a few words to accompany the striking visual images he located in personal and research collections. According to Myers's introduction, the $12^1/4$ x $9^1/2$" album offers a perspective rarely seen, one showing "our struggles but also our joy and the sense of communion we experience in family gatherings, in religious services, in music, in holiday celebrations." The hard work within this hard history is shown along with images of life enjoyment and—most especially—of dignity. A powerful, empowering history. (Age 12–adult)

Osofsky, Audrey. *Dreamcatcher.* Illustrated by Ed Young. Orchard, 1992. 32 pages. (0–531–05988–X) (lib. bdg. 0–531–08588–0)

". . . A dream net for baby / like a small spiderweb / spun of nettle-stalk twine / stained dark red with the bark of wild plum . . ." hung by the Ojibway people of centuries ago on babies' cradleboards. Such a net might serve as a charm to catch "dark dreams . . . like flies in a spider's web" before a bad dream could reach a slumbering infant. Good dreams "drift through the hole in the center of the web: dreams of . . . white shells tinkling in the breeze / pheasant feathers ruffling / sucking maple sugar in a birchbark cone . . ." Young's decorative page borders pay tribute to the floral patterns of Ojibway artists and his images of clothing and other objects allude to this cultural history. Ojibway language references and names are accurate. The full-color illustrations were created in pastel for this 9 ³/₄ x 10 ¹/₂" picture book. (Ages 4–9)

Roop, Peter and Connie Roop. *Ahyoka and the Talking Leaves.* Illustrated by Yoshi Miyake. Lothrop, Lee & Shepard, 1992. 60 pages. (0–688–10697–8) (0–688–13082–8; Beech Tree, 1994)

By developing a writing system for use by the Cherokee people, the Cherokee leader Sequoyah did "what no one person had ever done before—he had created a written language from a spoken language." Sequoyah's accomplishments come to life throughout an original story featuring Sequoyah's young daughter Ahyoka. The easy-to-read six-chapter book is illustrated with 18 black-and-white drawings. The 86-symbol Cherokee syllabary appears at the beginning of the story. A short bibliography follows the authors' epilogue that provides facts about the famous American Indian leader, in whose honor the "towering majestic redwoods" were named, Sequoia National Park was created, and the annual Sequoyah Children's Book Award is given by Oklahoma children. (Ages 7–10)

Say, Allen. *Grandfather's Journey.* Houghton Mifflin, 1993. 32 pages. (0–395–57035–2)

Wearing European clothes for the first time, a young Japanese man traveled alone across the Pacific and then throughout the U.S. during the early 20th century. He marveled at the expanses of ocean and land. "The endless farm fields reminded him of the ocean he had crossed." Finally returning to Japan years later with his wife and daughter, he established a life in his birth nation and culture but never quite settles there emotionally. This young man was the grandfather of the narrator/artist who, like his elder, now understands longing for the home left behind and yet living where one has also experienced wonder. The juxtaposition of deep feeling with emotional distance underscores the theme. Say's full-page watercolor paintings present an 11³/₄ x 9³/₄" album-like sequence of landscapes and people with effective uses of light in this unique perspective on immigration. (Ages 8–12)

Shemie, Bonnie. *Houses of Adobe: The Southwest.* (Native Dwellings) Tundra, 1995. 24 pages. (pbk. 0–88776–330–8)

The "great houses" of Chaco Canyon, the cliff dwellings of Mesa Verde, and Hopi pueblos are examples of the enduring architectural structures built over hundreds of years by the indigenous peoples of what is now the southwest United States. These buildings, and what is known about the peoples who constructed them, are the subject of an appreciative text emphasizing the unique function and form of the ingenious designs. Like those in her other excellent books in this valuable series, Shemie's black-and-white drawings illustrate art and architectural elements, and two-page color spreads show how people lived in the buildings. Other books in the Native Dwelling series include *Houses of Snow, Skin and Bones: The Far North* (1989), *Houses of Bark: Tipi, Wigwam and Longhouses—The Eastern Woodlands* (1990), *Houses of Hide and Earth: Tipi and Earthlodges—The Plains* (1991), *Houses of Wood: The Northwest Coast* (1994), and *Mounds of Earth and Shell: Native Sites—The Southeast* (1993). (Ages 9–11)

Sisulu, Elinor Batezat. *The Day Gogo Went to Vote: South Africa, April 1994.* Illustrated by Sharon Wilson. U.S. edition: Little, Brown, 1996. 32 pages. (0–316–70267–6)

A six-year-old black child tells how her 100-year-old *gogo* (grandmother) is determined to vote in the first general election in South Africa. Gogo has not left home for years, not even to attend church. The family is incredulous. "Do you want me to die not having voted?" Gogo asks her astonished relatives, and so she goes to the polls. The child's-eye view of the historic election is an effective device for including information in context about the voting procedures in the unprecedented 1994 election. Sisulu was born in Zimbabwe and now lives in Capetown, South Africa. Wilson visited South Africa before creating the artwork for this inspiring picture story with pastels on sanded board. (Ages 7–10)

Tunnell, Michael O. and George W. Chilcoat. *The Children of Topaz: The Story of a Japanese Internment Camp, Based on a Classroom Diary.* Holiday House, 1996. 74 pages. (0–8234–1239–3)

Journal entries kept by Miss Hori's third grade class from March 8 to August 12, 1943 provide the springboard for an account of day-to-day life in the Topaz Relocation Center as it was experienced by Japanese-American children. Their brief, upbeat entries describing camp life stand in stark contrast to the grim realities described in the text and shown in the accompanying documentary black-and-white photographs. (Ages 8–14)

Turner, Glennette Tilley. *Running for Our Lives.* Illustrated by Samuel Byrd. Holiday House, 1994. 198 pages. (0–8234–1121–4)

Escaping from slavery in Missouri, Luther and his younger sister, Carrie, are separated from their parents during their journey north on the Underground Railroad. Hoping to be reunited with them, the two continue on, guided by "conductors" and others whose commitment to the cause of abolition is as strong as the children's own desire for freedom. Among those they meet on their way are Frederick Douglass and Alan Pinkerton. An uplifting novel that follows one family as they build a new life that is rooted in freedom. (Ages 8–11)

Uchida, Yochiko. *The Bracelet.* Illustrated by Joanna Yardley. Philomel, 1993. 32 pages. (0–399–22503–X) (pbk. 0–698–11390–X)

Emi and her family are Japanese American and because America is at war with Japan, they are being sent to a prison camp. Emi's best friend Laurie gives her a gold bracelet just before Emi and her family leave for the camp, and the gift gives Emi something to touch and hold on to as she leaves the comfort of home and familiarity behind. Soon after arriving at the holding camp—a former racetrack where she and her family are assigned to a stall in one of the stables—Emi discovers she has lost the bracelet and fears she has lost her connection to her best friend as well. But as memories come flooding back of times she has spent with Laurie, she realizes she can never lose the feelings in her heart. A simply written picture story illustrated in full-page watercolor art introduces this aspect of United States history to young readers on an accesssible emotional level while an Afterword provides brief information about the internment of Japanese Americans during World War II and the United States's eventual admission of the injustice of what was done. (Ages 5–8)

Walter, Mildred Pitts. *Mississippi Challenge.* Bradbury, 1992. 205 pages. (lib. bdg. 0–02–792301–0) (pbk. 0–02–045641–7; Macmillan, 1996) (pbk. 0–689–80307–9; Aladdin, 1996)

A powerful account of the century of struggle by African Americans for the right to vote in Mississippi uses well-selected quotations from the generations of people who suffered under the "planned social and economic conditions that white Mississippians forced upon black Mississippians" and from those who perpetuated those conditions. Chapters relate the economic, political, and social circumstances facing the descendants of African captives following the Civil War. Each chapter is preceded by excerpts from spirituals, blues, freedom songs, and spoken words and illustrated with carefully chosen reprints of archival material. Complex events such as the Freedom Summer and the creation of the Mississippi Freedom Democratic Party are explained with directness and clarity, revealing the organizational genius of the men and women involved. Walter shows the "disastrous consequences of closing one's eyes to oppression and refusing to actively insist that laws guaranteeing freedom, justice and peace are upheld." (Age 11–adult)

Walter, Mildred Pitts. *Second Daughter: The Story of a Slave Girl.* Scholastic, 1996. 214 pages. (0–590–48282–3)

The author's meticulous research undergirds a fictional account of the actual case in 1781 of Mum Bett, the woman who won a lawsuit against her owner after suing for her freedom under the Massachusetts Constitution. The narrator Aissa is Mum Bett's sister, a strong-willed teenager nameless in the history books but fully alive within the pages of a novel contributing an essential complexity to the particulars of enslavement. "And I have now learned that no one can set you free. Freedom is living with realities in a way that they don't overcome you . . . Hold on steady! Until we know ourselves, we will never be free!" (Ages 13–16)

Williams, Sherley Anne. *Working Cotton.* Illustrated by Carole Byard. Harcourt Brace Jovanovich, 1992. 32 page. (0–15–299624–9) (pbk. 0–15–201482–9, 1997)

Sherlan, the next-to-the-youngest daughter in an African-American family, describes a typical day working in the fields with her parents and three sisters. Although the author has fond memories of her family (most particularly her father), there is not the smallest hint of nostalgia in this reminiscence of her childhood spent as a migrant worker. Byard's expressive full-color paintings brilliantly evoke the summer heat, the immensity of the cotton fields, and the strain of hard work on child and adult. In the midst of adversity, the strength of Sherlan's family comes through in both the lyrical language and the illustrations depicting tenderness in the facial expressions of Byard's characters. (Ages 6–9)

BIOGRAPHY AND AUTOBIOGRAPHY

Ada, Alma Flor. *Where the Flame Trees Bloom.* Illustrated by Antonio Martorell. Translated from the Spanish by Rosalma Zubizarreta. Atheneum, 1994. 75 pages. (0–689–31900–2) (0–689–80631–0, 1996)

In 11 wonderfully entertaining chapters Ada recreates scenes and characterizes people from her childhood in Cuba. Readers meet members of Ada's extended family and become acquainted with some of the stories she heard. Today's children can gain a sense of the lovely land and loving people she recalls. All but three of the chapters were translated by the author's daughter. The occasional illustrations are reproduced in brown and white. (Ages 9–12)

Adler, David A. *A Picture Book of Jesse Owens.* Illustrated by Robert Casilla. Holiday House, 1992. 32 pages. (lib. bdg. 0–8234–0966–X) (pbk. 0–8234–1066–8)

An easy biography of the Olympic medal-winning sprinter and champion of the long jump recounts some of the childhood barriers overcome by the amazing African-American athlete with "lucky legs." Jesse Owens's accomplishments at the 1936 Olympics in Berlin led to him being called the "World's Fastest Human" for many years. Adler's brief biography and page of notes point out racist and anti-Semitic occurrences during the 1936 Olympics, as well as the fact that prejudice was faced by this honored son of a former sharecropper afterward at home. Profusely illustrated with Casilla's watercolor paintings, there is also a brief chronology. (Ages 5–9)

Allen, Paula Gunn and Patricia Clark Smith. *As Long as the Rivers Flow: The Stories of Nine Native Americans.* Scholastic, 1996. 328 pages. (0–590–47869–9)

Native American leaders and achievers in politics, entertainment, athletics, and the arts are the subject of this collective biography featuring nine individuals who affirm American Indian accomplishments, traditions, and values through their success in a wide variety of arenas. The women and men profiled come from American Indian nations across what is now the United States. They include the woman warrior Weetamoo (Pocasset), tribal leader Geronimo (Apache), humorist Will Rogers (Cherokee), athlete Jim Thorpe (Sac and Fox), ballet dancer Maria Tallchief (Osage), United States Senator Ben Nighthorse Campbell (Northern Cheyenne), tribal leader Wilma Mankiller (Cherokee), artist Michael Naranjo (Santa Clara Pueblo), and writer Louise Erdrich (Turtle Mountain Chippewa). (Ages 11–14)

Cooper, Floyd. *Coming Home: From the Life of Langston Hughes.* Philomel, 1994. 32 pages. (lib. bdg. 0–399–22682–6)

Cooper's lyrical prose and striking full-color paintings are combined in a brief, moving portrait about a prominent writer of the Harlem Renaissance. His grandma took care of young Langston Hughes in Kansas; she had once worked on the Underground Railroad, and so he heard those stories, along with ones she told him about John Brown, the Buffalo soldiers, and his own grandfather. Although Hughes apparently felt emotionally homeless as a youth, his life and works continue to offer both hope and home to many. A *tour de force* by Floyd Cooper. (Ages 4–12)

Fradin, Dennis Brindell. *Hiawatha: Messenger of Peace.* Margaret K. McElderry, 1992. 40 pages. (0–689–50519–1)

After briefly explaining the series of historical errors and misunderstandings that led to the fictional character of Longfellow's famous poem, the author provides a concise account of the life of the flesh-and-blood Hiawatha. Along with his Huron friend, Degandawida, Hiawatha convinced five warring tribes (Mohawk, Oneida, Onondaga, Cayuga, and Seneca) to lay down their weapons and form the Iroquois Federation, a representative system of government that is often credited with providing a model for American colonists 300 years later. In addition to reproductions of historical prints by European and American artists, the text is illustrated with paintings by four contemporary Iroquois artists: John Fadden, Arnold Jacobs, Cleveland Sandy, and Ernest Smith. (Ages 7–11)

Freedman, Russell. *The Life and Death of Crazy Horse.* Drawings by Amos Bad Heart Bull. Holiday House, 1996. 166 pages. (0–8234–1219–9)

Russell Freedman's thoughtful narrative on the life of the great Sioux leader portrays a man of dignity, conviction, and courage who spent his life resisting the United States government in its efforts to displace, restrain, and destroy his people. Crazy Horse is seen as an individual of destiny from the time he was a child, but how that destiny would play itself out was unknown. He neither gloried in nor turned his back on the warfare that was an inevitable part of the Sioux's battle for survival. He never signed a treaty with the whites. The description of Crazy Horse's elderly parents riding off with their son's body after he was murdered cannot be forgotten. Black-and-white reproductions of ledger art created by Oglala Sioux artist Amos Bad Heart Bull in the late 19th century are used to illustrate this stirring biography. (Ages 11–15)

Igus, Toyomi, editor. *Great Women in the Struggle.* Contributing writers: Toyomi Igus, Veronica Freeman Ellis, Diane Patrick and Valerie Wilson Wesley. (Book of Black Heroes, Volume 2). Just Us Books (356 Glenwood Ave., 3d Floor, East Orange, NJ 07017), 1991. 107 pages. (0–940975–27–0) (pbk. 0–940975–26–2, out of print)

The accomplishments of 84 African and African-American women from past centuries and present decades are chronicled in 84 inspiring, straightforward paragraphs, each illustrated with a black-and-white photographic or hand-rendered portrait. Chapter headings convey the import and spirit of their achievements: Freedom Fighters—Breaking Down Barriers; Educators—Building Strong Foundations; Writers & Fine Artists—The Power of Creativity; Performing Artists—Bearing Witness through Self-Expression; Athletes—The Spirit of Champions; Entrepreneurs—Taking Care of Business; Lawyers & Policy Makers—Forging Equal Justice; and Scientists & Healers—Exploring without Boundaries. An African-American historical chronology, a bibliography of related children's books, an index, and source notes for quoted material enrich a book for reading, reference, and reflection. (Ages 7–14)

Klausner, Janet. *Sequoyah's Gift: A Portrait of the Cherokee Leader.* HarperCollins, 1993. 111 pages. (lib. bdg. 0–06–021236–5)

An intriguing, lively portrayal of Sequoyah and his tireless effort to develop and perfect a written language for the Cherokee people, and then the means by which that language was put to use, is woven into a history of the Cherokee Nation that encompasses the late 18th and much of the 19th century. The Cherokee Nation once covered much of what is now the southeastern United States. Expanding migration by white settlers had a devastating effect, however, not only forcing the Cherokee from their homes and land, but also, Sequoyah noticed, leading them to abandon the Cherokee traditions. It was this that led him to consider how he might preserve the Cherokee spoken language and traditions by creating a means to record them. According to to the author, Sequoyah was convinced that if his people gave up their language for that of the white's, as he saw many doing, "they would become separated from themselves, from what it meant to be Cherokee." A well-researched, compassionate telling of Sequoyah's life includes a copy of the Cherokee Alphabet he developed and is illustrated with black-and-white photographs of artwork portraying the revered Cherokee leader whose syllabary is still in use among the Cherokee people today. (Ages 11–14)

Krull, Kathleen. *Wilma Unlimited: How Wilma Rudolph Became the Fastest Woman in the World.* Illustrated by David Diaz. Harcourt Brace, 1996. 40 pages. (0–15–201267–2)

Wilma Rudolph defied the odds to win three gold medals at the 1960 Summer Olympics in Rome, a record for American women. Rudolph's Olympic achievement resulted from incredible determination, and in this strikingly illustrated picture-book biography, she is profiled as an individual of remarkable energy and fortitude from the time she was a small girl. Disabled by polio as a child, it was thought that Wilma Rudolph would never walk again, let alone run her way into the history books. With bold full-color illustrations set against intriguing sepia-toned photographs depicting the text's background elements, artist David Diaz captures Rudolph's spirit, power, and pride, as well as the loving, supportive African-American family and community in which she was raised. The author grounds the story with details of Rudolph's family life, her wishes and dreams, and the times in which she lived, so that the athlete's extraordinary accomplishments never overwhelm the human story that is at the heart of the book. (Ages 5–10)

Lowery, Linda. *Wilma Mankiller.* Illustrated by Janice Lee Porter. Carolrhoda, 1996. 56 pages. (0–87614–880–1) (pbk. 0–87614–953–0)

The first woman Chief to lead the Cherokee Nation did not have an easy path to her distinguished office. She endured displacement and racism as a child, and continued prejudice, including sexism among her fellow Cherokee, as she reached adulthood. But Wilma learned to believe in herself and her ability to help her people. Linda Lowery uses short, simple sentences to skillfully tell Wilma Mankiller's story, resulting in an inspiring biography for new readers. Janice Lee Porter's splendid full-color artwork appears on each two-page spread. (Ages 6–8)

McKissack, Patricia C. and Fredrick McKissack. *Sojourner Truth: Ain't I a Woman?* Scholastic, 1992. 186 pages. (0–590–44690–8) (pbk. 0–590–44691–6, 1994)

When she was 46 years old, an African-American woman called Belle who had been born into slavery renamed herself. She became Sojourner Truth, a pilgrim who spoke, sang and recited long passages from the *Bible* before white and Black audiences wherever matters concerning freedom were discussed and debated. The McKissacks trace how Sojourner Truth became a staunch abolitionist and effective advocate for women's rights, and they relate the tragic personal losses suffered by this amazing leader. This outstanding biography is documented with photographs, a bibliography, and capsule biographies of 14 of the women and men who were Sojourner's contemporaries in 19th century movements for liberation. (Ages 10–14)

Miller, William. *Frederick Douglass: The Last Day of Slavery.* Illustrated by Cedric Lucas. Lee & Low (95 Madison Ave., New York, NY 10016), 1995. 32 pages. (1–880000–17–2)

An understated picture book for older readers dramatizes a critical moment in the life of the young Frederick Douglass who was born into slavery in 1817. After setting the scene by briefly telling us what Douglass's childhood was like, the author describes a confrontation between the 20-year-old Douglass and an overseer, the moment at which Douglass chose a life of active resistance against the cruel and immoral institution of slavery. Cedric Lucas's somber pastel paintings perfectly capture the serious tone of the text and show Frederick Douglass thinking and working, and ultimately fighting back. (Ages 8–12)

Mohr, Nicholasa. *Growing Up in the Sanctuary of My Imagination.* (In My Own Words) Julian Messner, 1994. 118 pages. (0–671–74171–3, out of print)

An autobiographical memoir of a major U.S. author unfolds many of the experiences and insights that later fueled her outstanding novels and short fiction for youth, including *El Bronx Remembered, Felita, In Nueva York* and *Nilda*, all initially published by Harper, as well as her varied works for adult readers. Providing the same strong sense of place and people and the emotional content one discovers in her fiction, Mohr's selection of details underscore her memories, her strong sense of family, and the spirituality of her mother's culture. Mohr's imagination offered deliverance and salvation throughout the years when she (along with many other Puerto Rican-American children whose first home was New York City and first language was English) found herself discounted by the educational system and invisible in the larger society. (Age 12–adult)

Myers, Walter Dean. *Malcolm X: By Any Means Necessary.* Scholastic, 1993. 224 pages. (0–590–46484–1) (pbk. 0–590–48109–6, 1994)

A riveting opening chapter relates the now-legendary nonviolent standoff between the Black Muslims and precinct police following a street incident in Harlem and introduces Malcolm's multi-faceted authority. Carefully selected archival photographs and other illustrative material, a chronology, a bibliography, and an index contribute to the considerable substance of this compelling volume illuminating the life of an African-American man whose mid–20th century deeds and writings continue to inspire many youth and adults today. Myers draws implicit parallels between today's challenges for some African-American youth and some of the experiences during the early years of the self-made survivor who became Malcolm X by showing how, in his youth, Malcolm expressed the universal need to belong. In showing the changes Malcolm made in his own life, Myers demonstrates that youth do not have to fail themselves even though people and institutions fail them. An absorbing biography introduces this important leader to youth not yet ready for *The Autobiography of Malcolm X.* (Ages 9–14)

Myers, Walter Dean. *Toussaint L'Ouverture: The Fight for Haiti's Freedom.* Illustrated by Jacob Lawrence. Simon & Schuster, 1996. 40 pages. (0–689–80126–2)

Toussaint L'Ouverture dreamed of freedom for the people of African descent in Haiti, and when Blacks started to revolt against their French and Spanish oppressors in the late 18th century, he proved to be a brilliant military strategist whose leadership was invaluable and inspiring to his people. Jacob Lawrence created 41 bold, harrowing paintings to tell the story of Toussaint and slavery and the struggle for freedom in Haiti. His dramatic, emotional art is balanced by Walter Dean Myers's skillful, measured narrative that serves to tell a riveting story while pacing the runaway power of the images. (Ages 9–12)

Neuberger, Anne E. *The Girl-Son.* Carolrhoda, 1995. 131 pages. (0–87614–846–1)

Induk Pak was born in Korea in 1896, at a time when education was a priority for boys only. Thankfully, Induk's remarkable mother, Onyu, had little use for aspects of tradition that would prevent her and her daughter from leading independent lives. Author Anne Neuberger brings Induk's fascinating story to life in a compelling biographical novel based largely on Induk's own writings, previously published as books for adults. Neuberger skillfully translates Induk's story into engaging fiction for children. (Ages 10–14)

Oodgeroo. *Dreamtime: Aboriginal Stories.* Illustrated by Bronwyn Bancroft. U.S. edition: Lothrop, Lee & Shepard, 1994. 96 pages. (0–688–13296–0)

An original and unusual collection that begins with a series of stories that are humorous, revealing and unflinching reminiscences of Oodgeroo's childhood with her Aboriginal family on Stradbroke Island off the coast of Queensland, Australia. In Part II, Oodgeroo retells a number of Aboriginal legends and in doing so places her own story firmly in their midst. Bancroft draws upon her own Aboriginal heritage in her full-page black-and-white and color paintings and detail artwork that beautifully capture both the natural and emotional landscape of the stories. (Ages 11–14)

Osofsky, Audrey. *Free to Dream, The Making of a Poet: Langston Hughes.* Lothrop, Lee & Shepard, 1996. 112 pages. (0–688–10605–6)

An engaging narrative chronicles the life of the celebrated African-American poet who rose to fame during the Harlem Renaissance but whose words endure today in poems that talk of high hopes and hard times for his people. Langston's childhood, early adulthood, and writing career are all addressed with avid attention to the thoughts, feelings, and experiences that he wove into his writing. Beautiful design elements such as bordered black-and-white photographs and reproductions of publications in which Langston's poems appeared add to the elegance of cream-colored pages and the overall design of this handsome volume that pays tribute to the life and voice of Langston Hughes. (Ages 10–14)

Parks, Rosa and Jim Haskins. *Rosa Parks: My Story.* Dial, 1992. 92 pages. (0–8037–0673–1)

Rosa Parks wasn't tired when she decided not to move to a different seat in the bus. She knew exactly what she was doing and what the NAACP would probably do as a result in December, 1955, in Montgomery, Alabama. According to Dr. Martin Luther King, Jr., Mrs. Parks's action was a "creative witness." According to the world today, she is the mother of the U.S. Civil Rights Movement. Mrs. Parks sets the record straight here about several matters recorded inaccurately for decades concerning the Montgomery Bus Boycott and other actions in which she participated. She also relates details about her childhood, her education, and many other aspects of her long, productive life. She is now a "symbol," not a role she chose, but one that fits this honorable woman whose courageous activism took many forms and made all the difference. (Ages 11–14)

Pinkney, Andrea D. *Bill Pickett: Rodeo-Ridin' Cowboy.* Illustrated by Brian Pinkney. Gulliver/Harcourt Brace, 1996. 32 pages. (0–15–200100–X)

The child of former slaves, Bill Pickett grew up on the wide open Texas prairie. "He was quick as a jackrabbit, more wide-eyed than a hooty owl—and curious." The eager boy developed his own unique style of cow wrestling in which he sunk his teeth into the animal's lip to keep it under control. Observer's called it bulldogging, and it was to become Bill's trademark in a distinguished career as a cowboy and rodeo rider. Almost one in four cowboys who rode the western states in the 19th century was Black, author Andrea Pinkney notes in historical information that follows the text of this lively biography. Bill Pickett was among the most famous of them all. Brian Pinkney's scratchboard illustrations capture the expansive feeling of the western landscape and the energy of humans and animals in motion on the pages of this $11^1/4$ x $9^1/2$" book. (Ages 7–10)

Pinkney, Andrea Davis. *Dear Benjamin Banneker.* Illustrated by Brian Pinkney. Gulliver/Harcourt, Brace, 1994. 32 pages. (0–15–200417–3)

Beginning to teach himself mathematics and astronomy at age 57, Benjamin Banneker later became known for his scientifically developed predictions concerning the weather. He was the first black person to create a published almanac. Banneker can also be remembered for the forthright letter he wrote in 1791 to Secretary of State Thomas Jefferson concerning slavery and the need for equal opportunity for all people. This $11^1/4$ x $8^1/4$" picture biography created by a wife-and-husband team brings to life Banneker's early years and later accomplishments. The full-color illustrations were rendered using scratchboard colored with oil paint. (Ages 5–9)

St. George, Judith. *Crazy Horse.* Putnam, 1994. 180 pages. (0–399–22667–2)

St. George recreates several decades of this famous leader's life by describing what is known about *Tashunka Witko*, his people, and the battles in which they fought. This highly readable, compelling portrait of a man who consistently refused to be photographed and whose most famous battle offers continuing controversy shows him to be a man "of and for his people" and "only secondly as the celebrated Oglala warrior of Sioux Wars fame." In addition to traveling throughout the Northern Great Plains where "Crazy Horse" and his people had camped, hunted, wintered, and fought, St. George made extensive use of primary source material at the Nebraska State Historical Society, such as transcripts of interviews with people who had known him and other documentation from people who had survived the Sioux Wars. (Ages 10–16)

Schroeder, Alan. *Minty: The Story of Young Harriet Tubman.* Illustrated by Jerry Pinkney. Dial, 1996. 40 pages. (0–8037–1888–8) (lib. bdg. 0–8037–1889–6)

"I'm gonna run away," the sad, angry Minty tells her mother after the Missus throws her rag doll into the fire. Later, after she is beaten by the overseer, the young girl who is a slave on a Maryland plantation tells her parents once again that she will flee. Realizing their daughter's determination, they subtly but deliberately begin to show her things she will need to know to survive: how to find her way north by moss on trees and one shining star; how to swim a river; how to find food in the forest. Alan Schroeder's moving story never strays from what is possible in this fictional biography of the life of young Harriet Tubman. Jerry Pinkney's full-color paintings are rendered in pencil, colored pencil, and watercolor. Light and dark dance across the pages of this $11^3/4$ x $9^3/4$" book as he skillfully and beautifully brings his vision of Minty's story to life. (Ages 7–10)

Swanson, Gloria M. and Margaret V. Ott. *I've Got an Idea: The Story of Frederick McKinley Jones.* Runestone/Lerner, 1994. 95 pages. (lib. bdg. 0–8225–3174–7) (pbk. 0–8225–9662–8)

From the time he was a small child taking apart his father's watch, Frederick McKinley Jones showed a fascination and genius for things mechanical. By the time he was 14, the young African American was admired for his expertise with car engines. By the time he was 17, he was designing and building racing cars. Jones's inventive mind was never quiet, and over the course of his life, from 1893 to 1961, he acquired over 60 patents for his ideas, which ranged from movie theater ticket machines and sound systems to mobile refrigeration units that enabled perishable food to be carried long distances. An appealing biography focusing on his personal and professional life and containing numerous black-and-white photos of Frederick Jones in his wide and varied creative pursuits. (Ages 9–11)

Towle, Wendy. *The Real McCoy: The Life of an African-American Inventor.* Illustrated by Wil Clay. Scholastic, 1993. 32 pages. (0–590–43596–5) (pbk. 0–590–48102–9, 1995)

Born in Canada in 1844, Elijah McCoy, the son of former slaves, patented over 50 inventions throughout his life. This simply told history of an African-American inventor focuses on McCoy's achievements without minimizing the barriers he faced because he was Black. Full-page illustrations by Clay show a man wholly dedicated to his work and his dreams. A role model for many African Americans while he was alive, McCoy is once again a source of pride and inspiration. (Ages 7–10)

Turner, Glennette Tilley. *Lewis Howard Latimer.* (Pioneers in Change) Silver Burdett, 1991. 128 pages. (0–382–09524–3)

An absorbing, highly readable biography tells about a great thinker, scientist and inventor who is best known for his invention of the carbon filament light bulb. Turner's many hours of painstaking primary research of unpublished materials housed in the Schomburg Collection and extensive interviews with experts (including Latimer's grandchildren) make the life and work of Lewis Howard Latimer particularly valuable. Her style makes the information easily accessible. (Ages 9–12)

Uchida, Yoshiko. *The Invisible Thread.*
Julian Messner, 1991. 136 pages.
(0–671–74164–0) (pbk. 0–688–13703–2;
Beech Tree/Morrow, 1995)

With a brisk narrative style full of lively dialogue, Uchida writes of two decades of American life thrown into sharp contrast during a 1930s family visit to Japan, where she and her sister felt totally foreign. The author's experiences as a girl growing up in Berkeley, California, were thoroughly American; she had a bicultural childhood, as well, because of the unseen thread she describes as binding her parents to the Japan they left behind long before World War I. Her account of the family's forced internment in 1942, just as she was completing her university degree, unfolds within the context of their previous lives as U.S. citizens. Uchida emphasizes her youth, the internment, and a bit about early vocational attempts, rather than her development as a writer and her successful career yielding more than two dozen published books. Two of Uchida's novels for children concern the internment: *Journey to Topaz* (Scribner's, 1971) and *Journey Home* (Atheneum, 1978). Several of her other novels fictionalize Japanese-American California life during the 1930s. (Ages 9–14)

Ward, Glenyse. *Wandering Girl.* U.S. edition:
Henry Holt, 1991. 183 pages.
(0–8050–1634–1, out of print)

A rare glimpse into the life of a mid–20th century Australian Aboriginal woman is offered in this autobiographical account which reads like a novel. After being taken from her mother in infancy and raised in a Catholic mission, Glenyse Ward is hired out as a domestic servant to an upper-class white family when she is 15. Working for an employer who refers to her as "my dark slave," Ward successfully struggles to maintain dignity and an identity in harsh, humiliating circumstances. (Age 13–adult)

Yep, Laurence. *The Lost Garden.*
Julian Messner, 1991. 117 pages.
(pbk. 0–688–13701–6;
Beech Tree/Morrow, 1996)

Yep compares his life to a jigsaw puzzle and describes the process of growth and maturation as a search for all the pieces—some sought out intentionally, others found by serendipity but recognized at the moment of discovery as pieces of the puzzle. The absorbing autobiographical narrative introduces facts about this highly-regarded author's San Francisco childhood and Chinese-American heritage to readers who already know some of his many novels, including *Child of the Owl* (Harper, 1975) and *Dragonwings* (Harper, 1977). (Ages 9–14)

CONTEMPORARY PEOPLE, PLACES AND EVENTS

Ancona, George. *The Golden Lion Tamarin Comes Home.* Macmillan, 1994. 40 pages. (0–02–700905–X)

The coastal rain forest in southeastern Brazil is the only known natural habitat of the *mico* or golden lion tamarin, a small monkey about the size of a squirrel. With 98 percent of the Brazilian rain forest depleted, wild *micos* are becoming scarce, but thanks to the tireless efforts of Andreia Martins and other Brazilian conservationists, *micos* born in captivity in zoos are slowly and successfully being introduced back into the wild. A lively text and color photographs document the painstaking work of Andreia, in addition to describing the habits of the *mico* and the reasoning behind human efforts to protect its native home. (Ages 7–11)

Ancona, George. *The Piñata Maker = El Piñatero.* Harcourt, Brace, 1994. 40 pages. (0–15–261875–9) (pbk. 0–15–200060–7)

In Ejutla de Crespo, a village in southern Mexico, 77-year-old Don Ricardo makes piñatas for all the festive occasions. Tio Rico, as the children call him, is clearly valued among children and adults alike in the community. Color photographs and text show how Tio Rico makes both traditional and unusual piñatas for parties and holiday celebrations. A brief author's note at the end of this bilingual book provides suggestions for making simple piñatas. (Ages 8–10)

Angelou, Maya. *Kofi and His Magic.* Photographs by Margaret Courtney-Clarke. Designed by Alexander Isley Design. Clarkson Potter, 1996. 36 pages. (0–517–70453–6) (lib. bdg. 0–517–70796–9)

A dazzling photoessay combines an energizing, poetic text with crisp, colorful photographs and an engaging, playful design. Seven-year-old Kofi lives in Bonwire, the West African village known for its beautiful Kente cloth. Kofi likes to weave, and he likes to travel. "I sit down, Close my eyes, Open my mind," Kofi explains, and he is transported to other places in Africa that he has always wanted to see. Kofi's magic is his vivid imagination, but his journey comes alive for readers through words and images depicting both his own life and each place he visits with a joyous sense of appreciation and discovery. (Ages 6–8)

Angelou, Maya. *My Painted House, My Friendly Chicken, and Me.* Photographs by Margaret Courtney-Clarke. Clarkson Potter, 1994. 40 pages. (0–517–59667–9) (pbk. 0–517–88815–7, 1996)

In Angelou's engaging first-person narrative young readers meet Thandi, an eight-year-old Ndebele girl in South Africa. Thandi relates details of her own life and of Ndebele culture, and these details are brought into focus through Courtney-Clark's shining, colorful photographs of Ndebele people. The Ndebele custom of painting houses with intricate, colorful patterns forms the inspiration for the design of this vibrant book that is an invitation to friendship. (Ages 5–8)

Atkin, S. Beth. *Voices from the Fields: Children of Migrant Farmworkers Tell Their Stories.* Joy Street/Little Brown, 1993. 96 pages. (0–316–05633–2)

First-person narratives and/or poems present ten voices representative of Hispanic migrant children and teenagers working in the Salinas Valley of California. This unparalleled photodocumentary book originated in migrant programs or in the fields where some of the children and teenagers agreed to tell their stories and be photographed. Atkin's brief introductory passages establish a context for each commentary. These children of Mexican heritage speak about work, family, fitting in, the gang, teen parents, and other topics. Spanish was used in most of the interviews, the English translations of which offer an urgent witness and testimony to certain realities and experiences and, sometimes, to hopes, as well. (Ages 9–14)

Banish, Roslyn and Jennifer Jordan-Wong. *A Forever Family.* HarperCollins, 1992. 44 pages. (lib. bdg. 0–06–021674–3) (pbk. 0–06–446116–5)

An eight-year-old Amerasian girl briefly describes events leading up to her adoption the previous year by an interracial (Asian/white) couple. The first-person account, accompanied by black-and-white photographs, includes details of the court proceedings, as well as of her earlier life with her African-American foster family and her current life with her new extended family. (Ages 6–11)

Bash, Barbara. *In the Heart of the Village: The World of the Indian Banyan Tree.* Sierra Club, 1996. 32 pages. (0–87156–575–7)

Beneath a banyan tree's broad, expansive covering, the people of a small village in India find a center for community life. School children gather for a class, traders exchange goods, and villagers seek shelter from the midday sun. Later in the day, children will play in and around the tree and old men will gather to talk. All the while, high up in its branches, egrets and owls nest, langur monkeys play, and rose finches, fairy bluebirds and other birdlife feast on ripe red figs. The human and wildlife activity in around this tree that is sacred to the people of India is followed from dawn to dusk to dawn in a singular, informative text with full-color illustrations that stretch across each two-page spread. (Ages 8–11)

Braine, Susan. *Drumbeat . . . Heartbeat: A Celebration of the Powwow.* (We Are Still Here) Lerner, 1995. 48 pages. (0–8225–2656–5) (pbk. 0–8225–9711–X)

Author Susan Braine shares her own anticipation of and excitement for the powwow with readers in an inviting, informative photoessay. Braine, a member of the Assiniboine Tribe in Montana, talks about the importance of the powwow to American Indian culture and its significance in uniting Native and non-Native peoples. Her enthusiasm is infectious as she takes readers through a typical day at a powwow, which might include a parade, a rodeo, and many related activities in addition to the steps and spins of the dancers and the rhythm of the drum. Engaging color photographs capture both the high energy and the reflective, quiet times of a powwow gathering. (Ages 7–11)

Brusca, María Cristina. *My Mama's Little Ranch on the Pampas.* Henry Holt, 1994. 32 pages. (0–8050–2782–3)

An autobiographical picture book continues the story Brusca started in *On the Pampas* (Holt, 1991) about her childhood in Argentina. In this volume, young Cristina's determined mother purchases her own small ranch and a herd of cattle. Cristina and her brother Guillermo continue living with their father in the city during the week so they can attend school but on weekends and throughout their long, hot winter vacations, the children enjoy helping out on their mother's ranch. Filled with realistic details of daily life on an Argentinian ranch, Brusca's book also paints a portrait of a very strong, independent-minded Latina woman in Cristina's mama, who is always shown actively conducting the business of running a ranch. (Ages 7–11)

Brusca, María Cristina. *On the Pampas.* Henry Holt, 1991. 32 pages. (0–8050–1548–5) (pbk. 0–8050–2919–2, 1993)

A young girl from Buenos Aires, Argentina, spends the summer on her grandmother's ranch on the pampas, enjoying a thrilling camaraderie with her cousin and age-mate, Susanita, who knows "everything about horses, cows, and all the other animals that live on the pampas." Together the two girls ride horses, go swimming, search for *nandu* eggs, and listen to the *gauchos* tell ghost stories. There are plenty of activities to fill the days of these tireless and adventuresome cousins, both of whom aspire to be *gauchos* some day themselves. This autobiographical reminiscence by Argentinian María Cristina Brusca is filled with visual and textual details about life on a South American ranch. (Ages 7–11)

Cooper, Martha and Ginger Gordon. *Anthony Reynoso: Born to Rope.* Clarion, 1996. 32 pages. (0–395–71690–X)

Anthony Reynoso is nine years old and lives with his parents in Guadalupe, Arizona. Like his father and grandfather before him, Anthony is practicing to become a *charro*, or Mexican cowboy. He is a skilled rider and roper, but there is always more to learn from his father, with whom he also performs in exhibitions. Anthony's first-person voice provides the narrative for this engaging photoessay in which readers get a glimpse into other aspects of Anthony's life and community as well, from his interest in basketball, to the importance of extended family gatherings, to his excitement at the pending arrival of a new baby brother or sister. (Ages 7–10)

Crum, Robert. *Eagle Drum: On the Powwow Trail with a Young Grass Dancer.* Four Winds, 1994. 48 pages. (0–02–725515–8)

"I almost can't remember a time when I wasn't a dancer," says nine-year-old Louis Pierre. Louis, a Pend Oreille Indian, lives on the Flathead Reservation in Montana. Louis's knowledge of traditional dance has been passed on to him from his grandfather, along with an understanding of the importance of dance to the history and culture of his people. This photodocumentary shows Louis as he learns a new dance—the grass dance—and dances it in a powwow for the first time. (Ages 8–11)

Hewett, Joan. *Public Defender: Lawyer for the People.* Photographs by Richard Hewett. Lodestar, 1991. 48 pages. (0–525–67340–7)

A photoessay describes typical activities in the worklife of Janice Fukai, an Asian-American lawyer in Los Angeles County. Black-and-white photographs accompany the straightforward account of an individual public defender's work with clients who have been charged with serious crimes. (Ages 8–11)

Hirshfelder, Arlene B. and Beverly R. Singer, compilers. *Rising Voices: Writings of Young Native Americans.* Scribner's, 1992. 115 pages. (lib. bdg. 0–684–19207–1) (pbk. 0–8041–1167–7; Ivy, 1993)

A collection of 62 letters, poems, essays, and other writings of contemporary youth is thematically grouped: Identity, Family, Homelands, Ritual and Ceremony, Education, and Harsh Realities. The young men and women represent many American Indian heritages and nations in expressing themselves about their bicultural experiences. A brief biographical paragraph introduces each writer. Each section is introduced by the compilers with background information helpful to non-Indian readers of this important anthology. (Age 11–adult)

Hoyt-Goldsmith, Diane. *Arctic Hunter.* Photographs by Lawrence Migdale. Holiday House, 1992. 30 pages. (0–8234–0972–4) (pbk. 0–8234–1124–9)

For most of the year, ten-year-old Reggie lives with his family in a modern three-bedroom house in Kotzebue, Alaska, but every summer, he and his family spend several weeks in a traditional Iñupiaq camp where they fish and hunt to store up food for the long winter months ahead. Through color photographs and first-person narration, Reggie introduces the basic values and traditions of his people, the Inupiat, which represent perhaps the most ingenious human adaptations to an ungiving natural environment. (Ages 9–13)

Hoyt-Goldsmith, Diane. *Cherokee Summer.* Photographs by Lawrence Migdale. Holiday House, 1993. 32 pages. (lib. bdg 0–8234–0995–3)

Bridget is a ten-year-old Cherokee girl who lives in a mobile home near Tahlequah, Oklahoma, with her parents, brother, and sister. An up-beat first-person text describes Bridget's typical summer activities: drawing pictures, hunting for crawdads, spending time with her grandparents, studying the Cherokee language on a computer at the library, and attending a summer stomp dance. Information about Cherokee history, culture, and contemporary issues is woven throughout Bridget's discussion, accompanied by color photographs of this energetic girl. (Ages 7–11)

Hoyt-Goldsmith, Diane. *Hoang Anh: A Vietnamese-American Boy.* Photographs by Lawrence Migdale. Holiday House, 1992. 32 pages. (lib. bdg. 0–8234–0948–1)

A photoessay uses color photographs and a short first-person text to describe the day-to-day life of a young Vietnamese-American boy living in San Rafael, California. Hoang Anh briefly recounts the circumstances of his family's escape from Vietnam in 1978, their life in a refugee camp, and details of his family's bicultural lifestyle in the United States. Roughly one-half of the book is devoted to Hoang Anh's observances of the New Year (TET), making this a useful source for information about the Vietnamese holiday. (Ages 8–12)

Jenness, Aylette. *Come Home with Me: A Multicultural Treasure Hunt.* Illustrated by Laura DeSantis. Photographs by Max Belcher. The New Press (450 W. 41st St., New York, NY 10036), 1993. 48 pages. (1–56584–064–X)

Abdus is African American, Annie is Irish American, Marcos is Puerto Rican and Terri is Cambodian. These four friendly, appealing tour guides take readers on an exploration of the ethnically diverse Boston neighborhoods in which they live in a different kind of adventure story that combines lively, informative text with photographs and colorful graphics. Readers must turn back and forth through the pages as they make decisions about where to go and what to see next, accompanied each step of the way by one of the four children, who share information about their cultural heritages throughout the journey. Additional facts about the African-American, Irish-American, Latino and Cambodian cultures are provided in stimulating asides that will challenge children to consider the people and world around them. Inspired readers will want to follow some of the tips at the end of the text for exploring new neighborhodds and making a video like the one on which this book is based. (Ages 7–12)

King, Sandra. *Shannon: An Ojibway Dancer.* Photographs by Catherine Whipple. (We Are Still Here) Lerner, 1993. 48 pages. (0–8225–2652–2) (pbk. 0–8225–9643–1)

Photographs and text depict the life of a 13-year-old Ojibway girl, Shannon Anderson, who lives with her grandmother, sisters, and cousins in Minneapolis. Shannon's life is firmly rooted in her cultural heritage. A fancy dancer belonging to two drum and dance groups, Shannon goes through detailed preparations to get her intricate costumes ready for performances, and she is proud of her skills in the traditional ways of her people. "It's a good thing I'm Indian," she says to her grandmother, and her grandmother replies, ". . . always remember to be glad. Remember that wherever you go, all that you are goes with you." (Ages 7–11)

Krull, Kathleen. *One Nation, Many Tribes: How Kids Live in Milwaukee's Indian Community.* Photographs by David Hautzig. (A World of My Own) Lodestar, 1995. 48 pages. (0–525–67440–3)

Eleven-year-old Thirza and 12-year-old Shawnee are students at the Milwaukee Community Indian School, which is distinctive for a number of reasons discussed in the text: its urban location, its funding through Potawatomi bingo hall profits, and its inclusion of five Wisconsin tribes in the student body. Within this context, both children are presented as unique individuals: Shawnee dreams of becoming an architect and returning to the reservation, while Thirza, an aspiring actress, is headed for Broadway or Hollywood. An upbeat text and appealing color photographs show the two children in their day-to-day activities in and out of school. (Ages 8–12)

Krull, Kathleen. *The Other Side: How Kids Live in a California Latino Neighborhood.* Photographs by David Hautzig. (A World of My Own) Lodestar, 1994. 48 pages. (0–525–67438–1) (pbk. 0–14–036521–4; Puffin, 1996)

Twelve-year old Cinthya Guzman and brothers Francisco and Pedro Tapia, ages eight and 12, all were born in Mexico and are living now in Castle Park, a Latino neighborhood in Chula Vista, California. For all three, moving to the United States meant making many adjustments, but because Chula Vista is only seven miles from Tijuana, Mexico, they have also been able to remain grounded in their cultures of birth, regularly returning to visit family. Text and photographs examine the similarities and differences of the children's lives and communities on both sides of the border. (Ages 7–11)

Kuklin, Susan. *Going to My Gymnastics Class.* Bradbury, 1991. 32 pages. (lib. bdg. 0–02–751236–3)

A photoessay shows Gaspar as he and eight other children enjoy their weekly beginner gym class. The culturally diverse boys and girls engage in a sequence of activities co-taught by Bill Hladik, a recreational gymnastics enthusiast and expert, with Jackie Pazmiño, the Ecuadoran athlete who competed at age 13 in the Pan American Games. The positive self-esteem engendered by the instructors' approach is conveyed in Kuklin's marvelous color photographs of Gaspar and the other children and also within the first-person narrative. (Ages 3–5)

Kuklin, Susan. *How My Family Lives in America.* Bradbury, 1992. 32 pages. (0–02–751239–8)

Three young children whose parents immigrated to the United States (from Senegal, Puerto Rico, and Taiwan) are featured in this appealing photoessay which allows the children to speak for themselves about what they are learning from their parents and grandparents. In an author's note at the end of the book, Kuklin explains her intent: ". . . to show how families impart a sense of identity to their young children." The book concludes with a simple recipe from each child's culture. (Ages 4–7)

Kuklin, Susan. *Kodomo: Children of Japan.* Putnam, 1995. 48 pages. (0–399–22613–3, out of print)

An engaging photoessay provides a colorful portrait of children in modern Japan. Divided into two parts, the first, entitled A Way of Life, introduces U.S. children to three of their counterparts living in Hiroshima: eight-year-old Eri and nine-year-old Nozomi both describe their day-to-day lives at school and at home, while 14-year-old Ai tells readers about the tradition of dressing in a special kimono on New Year's Day. Part Two is titled Traditional Activities and shows four children in Kyoto observing Japanese traditions, including martial arts, calligraphy, and the tea ceremony. (Ages 5–11)

Lankford, Mary D. *Hopscotch around the World.* Illustrated by Karen Milone. Morrow, 1992. 47 pages. (0–688–08419–2) (lib. bdg. 0–688–08420–6) (pbk. 0–688–14745–3, 1996)

Hopscotch has a long history worldwide and children in most parts of the world still play it today. Directions for 19 hopscotch variants played in 16 nations follow brief notes which place each of the variants in their historical and geographical contexts. Each description is illustrated with a full-page, full-color illustration of contemporary children playing the game. (Ages 6–9)

Lourie, Peter. *Everglades: Buffalo Tiger and the River of Grass.* Boyds Mills, 1994. 47 pages. (1–878093–91–6)

Writer-photographer Peter Lourie's desire to learn about the Everglades takes him on a journey into the "River of Grass." His guide is Buffalo Tiger, chief of the Miccosukee Indians, who grew up in the Everglades more than 60 years ago, when the area was not yet polluted and the tribe could still live off the land. Lourie's appreciation for this unique and fragile environment, and for Buffalo Tiger's willingness to share his personal experience and expertise, unfolds through full-color photos and a text that skillfully weaves a brief, fascinating history of the Miccosukee into a compelling portrait of nature in the "grassy water," an environment which is in danger of dying. (Ages 9–11)

Onyefulu, Ifeoma. *A Is for Africa.* Cobblehill, 1993. 28 pages. (0–525–65147–0)

A Nigerian photographer selected 26 photographs from her homeland to illustrate this introduction to Africa. While the images she chose are specific to Nigeria, she states in an author's note that she attempted to capture what the people of Africa have in common: "traditional village life, warm family ties, and above all the hospitality for which Africans are famous." The color photographs were also chosen with the interests of young children in mind, as they show objects (drums, lamps, houses) and individuals (children) that will appeal to them greatly. (Ages 3–7)

Onyefulu, Ifeoma. *Emeka's Gift: An African Counting Story.* U.S. edition: Cobblehill/ Dutton, 1995. 20 pages. (0–525–65205–1)

Photographic images of village life among the Igala people in Nigeria shine from the pages of this unique counting book that follows the short journey of ONE small boy to his grandmother's house. Along the way, Emeka passes people and objects numbered from two to ten (FOUR brooms, SIX beaded necklaces, SEVEN musical instruments, etc.). Brief sidebars provide information on the items and activities shown in the lively color photographs in this wonderful companion to the author's earlier work, *A Is for Africa* (Cobblehill/Dutton, 1993). (Ages 4–7)

Onyefulu, Ifeoma. *Ogbo: Sharing Life in an African Village.* U.S. edition: Gulliver/ Harcourt, 1996. 24 pages. (0–15–200498–X)

A singular, shining book features Obioma, a six-year old girl in eastern Nigeria who tells readers about ogbos, or age groups, in her community. From the time they are young, children of the same general age identify with their ogbos, which extend beyond family ties to embrace the community as a whole. Members of ogbos play and work together and help one another in times of need. It is a connection that lasts throughout their lives, regardless of where they later live. Through text accompanied by lively color photographs, Obioma tells about the ogbo to which each member of her immediate family belongs in a beautifully designed and realized book. (Ages 7–10)

Peters, Russell M. *Clambake: A Wampanoag Tradition.* Photographs by John Madama. Foreword by Michael Dorris. (We Are Still Here) Lerner, 1992. 48 pages. (lib. bdg. 0–8225–2651–4) (pbk. 0–8225–9621–0)

One of the first titles in this excellent series about the observance of tribal traditions by contemporary Native children features a Wampanoag boy in Plymouth, Massachusetts. Twelve-year-old Steven learns the traditions of the *appanaug* (clambake) from his grandfather who has been selected as the "bakemaster" for this special ceremony to honor an important person in the tribe. Both the text and the color photographs reinforce Steven's sense of pride in his heritage, his closeness to family and friends, and his great respect for his elders and the knowledge they share with him. (Ages 7–13)

Raimondo, Lois. *The Little Lama of Tibet.* Scholastic, 1994. 40 pages. (0–590–46167–2)

A child is recognized as the new incarnation of Ling Rinpoche, the late tutor of the Dalai Lama. He lives in exile in the mountains of Dharamsala, India, studying scriptures, reading religious stories, and otherwise preparing spiritually to pass on Buddhist teachings to his people. This young monk was six years old during the year when Raimondo was granted permission to interview and photograph him. Her photographs are reproduced in full color, providing unparalleled glimpses of his daily discipline and that of those who teach him. The Tibetan alphabet is reproduced on the endpapers. (Ages 7–10)

Regguinti, Gordon. *The Sacred Harvest: Ojibway Wild Rice Gathering.* Photographs by Dale Kakkak. Foreword by Michael Dorris. (We Are Still Here) Lerner, 1992. 48 pages. (lib. bdg. 0–8225–2650–6) (pbk. 0–8225–9620–2)

A narrative by an Ojibway writer and color photographs by a Menominee photographer recount 11-year-old Glen Jackson's first time gathering wild rice with his father near their home on the Leech Lake Reservation in Minnesota. In addition to showing the harvest from start to finish, the author continually links the tradition to Glen's Ojibway heritage and the teachings of his elders, placing the harvest in a broader cultural context. (Ages 7–13)

Roessel, Monty. *Kinaaldá: A Navajo Girl Grows Up.* (We Are Still Here) Lerner, 1993. 48 pages. (0–8225–2655–7) (pbk. 0–8225–9641–5)

Thirteen-year-old Celinda McKelvey is about to participate in her Kinaaldá, a Navajo coming-of-age ceremony for girls. Over two days, with the support of her extended family and friends, she will run a race, prepare a corncake to be baked in the earth, and stay up through the night as traditional prayers are sung, all the while learning more about the Navajo culture. Celinda's preparations for and participation in this important event are recorded through documentary photographs and text that unite the history of the ceremony and the Navajo people with a girl's transition into womanhood. (Ages 7–11)

Roessel, Monty. *Songs from the Loom: A Navajo Girl Learns to Weave.* (We Are Still Here) Lerner, 1995. 48 pages. (lib. bdg. 0–8225–2657–3) (pbk. 0–8225–9712–8)

Jaclyn Roessel is learning how to weave in the traditional Navajo way. Her grandmother, Ruth, is teaching her how to shear the sheep, dye the wool, and work the loom. At the same time, she is teaching her the stories and songs of weaving that are part of the Navajo culture. Without them, her grandmother makes clear, Jaclyn's education as a Navajo weaver will be incomplete. Monty Roessel, Jaclyn's father, documents his daughter's education in photographs taken when she was between the ages of ten and 12. In accompanying text, he describes Jaclyn's experience and shares the stories and songs that she learns. (Ages 7–11)

Sandoval, Dolores. *Be Patient, Abdul.* Margaret K. McElderry, 1996. 32 pages. (0–689–50607–4)

Abdul lives in Freetown, the capital of Sierra Leone. The seven-year-old sells oranges to earn money for his school fees, but when business is slow, he has a hard time being patient: he loves to learn and wants to be sure he'll be able to continue his education. The day that Momma marches in the big parade to celebrate the anniversary of Sierra Leone's independence, Abdul's worries come to an end, but not before he's learned to appreciate what patience can bring, and not before readers have learned a little about contemporary life for a child in this West African nation. A picture book featuring full-page, full-color acrylic illustrations and a text well-suited for emergent readers. (Ages 5–7)

Schmidt, Jeremy and Ted Wood. *Two Lands, One Heart: An American Boy's Journey to His Mother's Vietnam.* Photographs by Ted Wood. Walker, 1995. 44 pages. (0–8027–8357–0) (lib. bdg. 0–8027–8358–9)

Seven-year-old T.J. Sharp is accompanying his mother on a journey to Vietnam—the homeland she fled as a child in the midst of the war. T.J. is eager to meet his Vietnamese grandparents, aunts, uncles, and cousins and see the country about which he has been hearing for so long. Color photographs and text document T.J.'s experience as he travels to a far-away land where the language and customs differ from his own, but which holds the familiar embrace of family. (Ages 7–10)

Strom, Yale. *Quilted Landscape: Conversations with Young Immigrants.* Simon & Schuster, 1996. 80 pages. (0–689–80074–6)

Writer and photographer Yale Strom turns a keen and understanding eye on children and young adults who are recent immigrants to the United States. Twenty-six young people who range in age from 11 to 17 discuss when, how, and why they came to the United States; what their life is like here; who and what they left behind; and their plans and hopes for the future. Though the children come from countries all over the world, and from diverse social and economic backgrounds, their experiences in this country are often similar as they must meet the challenges of culture and language barriers and discrimination and prejudice, and deal with the conflicts that can arise when family and cultural expectations clash with a new way of life. Each profile includes black-and-white photographs of the child and a brief summary of facts about the country from which he or she came. The featured nations of origin include Bangladesh, China, Dominican Republic, Egypt, Ethiopia, Mexico, Peru, Philippines, Puerto Rico, El Salvador, and Thailand. An important book that encourages readers to consider what it means to be a newcomer and what sustains us as a nation. (Ages 11–14)

Swentzell, Rina. *Children of Clay: A Family of Pueblo Potters.* Photographs by Bill Steen. Foreword by Michael Dorris. (We Are Still Here) Lerner, 1992. 40 pages. (lib. bdg. 0–8225–2654–9) (pbk. 0–8225–9627–X)

Eliza, Zachary, and Devonna are Tewa children living in Santa Clara Pueblo, New Mexico, who are learning the traditions of making clay pottery from their grandmother, Gia Rose. Together the family members dig for clay, clean it, and mix it with sand to make it ready for sculpting. Later they will sand, polish, and fire the pottery they have made. Even the youngest children in this large, extended family have a job to do and everyone is delighted to see the final results of all their hard work. (Ages 7–13)

Wittstock, Laura Waterman. *Ininatig's Gift of Sugar: Traditional Native Sugarmaking.* Photographs by Dale Kakkak. (We Are Still Here) Lerner, 1993. 48 pages. (0–8225–2653–0) (pbk. 0–8225–9642–3)

A legend of the Ojibway people tells the story of Ininatig, the man-tree who saved the people from starving when he showed them how to collect the sap that flowed from his skin when it was cut. The tradition of maple sugarmaking and thanking the trees each spring is continued at a sugarbush outside of Minneapolis by a 73-year-old Ojibway man named Porky, a member of the Loon clan, who has turned the annual event into a hands-on learning experience for adults and children alike. Text and photographs follow Porky, his family and friends, and countless visitors to the camp through the step-by-step process of sugarmaking, from collecting the proper tools to tapping the trees to boiling the clear sweet liquid into golden maple syrup or sugar. (Ages 7–11)

Wood, Ted and Wanbli Numpa Afraid of Hawk. *A Boy Becomes a Man at Wounded Knee.* Walker, 1992. 42 pages. (lib. bdg. 0–8027–8175–6) (pbk. 0–8027–7446–6)

A photoessay with color photographs traces the dramatic journey made in December, 1990, by the descendants of survivors of the Wounded Knee Massacre. The account is told from the point of view of eight-year-old Wanbli Numpa, the youngest Lakota to make the trip. Throughout their treacherous six-day journey on horseback in subzero temperatures, they are continually reminded of the suffering of their ancestors along this same trail 100 years ago and of the seriousness of their mission: to mend the sacred hoop of the world that was broken at Wounded Knee in 1890. (Ages 8–13)

ISSUES IN TODAY'S WORLD

Atkins, Jeannine. *Aani and the Tree Huggers.* Illustrated by Venantius J. Pinto. Lee & Low (95 Madison Ave., New York, NY 10016), 1995. 32 pages. (1–880000–24–5)

A fictionalized picture story, told from the point of view of young Aani, recounts the origins of the Chipko Andolan (Hug the Tree) Movement in northern India in the 1970s. When men from the city came into rural areas to cut down the trees, women villagers successfully stopped them by embracing individual trees. Indian artist Venantius J. Pinto explains in a note at the end how and why his pictures for this book were influenced by five different styles of traditional miniature painting that were used in northern India in the 17th century. (Ages 4–9)

Bunting, Eve. *Smoky Night.* Illustrated by David Diaz. Harcourt, Brace, 1994. 36 pages. (0–15–269954–6) (0–15–201035–1, 1995)

A young African-American child describes a night of fear when rioting occurs in his city neighborhood. "Rioting can happen when people get angry," his mother explains to him. "They want to smash and destroy. They don't care anymore what's right and what's wrong." In the middle of the night, a fire forces the boy and his mother to flee their apartment building and take refuge in a shelter, where African-American, Korean-American, and Latino neighbors, some of who are strangers to one another, have gathered in the confusion. Tensions between African-American and Korean-American residents of the neighborhood are specifically addressed. The child's anxiety is soothed but not extinguished by his mother's deliberate calm for the sake of her child, and these are the most powerful elements of the text. David Diaz's explosive artwork is a powerful complement—he sets his intense paintings against a multi-media backdrop that is suggested by elements of the text and created with items culled from everyday life. (Ages 6–10)

Echo-Hawk, Roger C. and Walter R. Echo-Hawk. *Battlefields and Burial Grounds: The Indian Struggle to Protect Ancestral Graves in the United States.* Lerner, 1994. 80 pages. (lib. bdg. 0–8225–2663–8) (pbk. 0–8225–9722–5, 1996)

In Part I of this thought-provoking text, the authors discuss the significance of burial practices to American Indian cultures and examine the history of Indian burial ground desecration in the United States, exploring the centuries-old double standard that has seen white graves respected and protected by law while American Indian graves were being legally robbed, and even destroyed. In Part II, they chronicle the successful efforts of their own tribe, the Pawnee, to reclaim and rebury their dead. A book remarkable in both tone and content, explaining events and actions in light of the attitudes toward indigenous peoples that prevailed at various times throughout United States history, but never excusing injustice. Illustrated with historical and contemporary photographs. (Age 12–adult)

Hamanaka, Sheila, coordinator. *On the Wings of Peace: Writers and Illustrators Speak Out for Peace in Memory of Hiroshima and Nagasaki.* Clarion, 1995. 144 pages. (0–395–72619–0)

Writing and art from 60 authors and artists forms a stunning anthology concerning the 1945 bombings of Hiroshima and Nagasaki and visions of peace. Handsome full-color art created in a variety of media accompanies history, poetry, short stories, and memoirs. This important assemblage can be read a bit at a time, in any order, in any year. As a whole, the volume energizes, rather than assessing blame or creating melancholy. A reliable resource list for children and adults suggests further reading. Brief biographical information placed next to tiny black and white photos marks the credentials of contributors. They include Marjorie Agosín, Joseph Bruchac, Ashley Bryan, Omar S. Castañeda, Edwidge Danticat, Jean Durandisse, Tom Feelings, Shinya Fukatsu, Nikki Grimes, Hushang Moradi Kermani, Marie G. Lee, George Littlechild, Ana Maria Machado, Kam Mak, Kyoko Mori, Junko Morimoto, Walter Dean Myers, Keiko Narahashi, Jerry Pinkney, James E. Ransome, Enrique O. Sánchez, Virginia Driving Hawk Sneve, Rigoberta Menchu Tum, Yoko Kawashima Watkins, and Ed Young. Royalties from sales of *On the Wings of Peace* are designated for three organizations devoted to these issues. (Age 8–adult)

Hoose, Phillip. *It's Our World, Too! Stories of Young People Who Are Making a Difference.* Little, Brown, 1993. 166 pages. (pbk. 0–316–37245–5)

A collection of profiles documenting the efforts of 14 contemporary children and teenagers from diverse backgrounds who have successfully taken a stand on issues such as racism, sexism, the environment, and violence, or who have undertaken projects to help others in their communities. Each of the children or groups of children profiled saw something happening that was unfair or frightening which compelled them to take action, and this understanding of injustice and fear is something with which children reading the book will immediately identify. The means to turn understanding into action is displayed in the profiles themselves, and in the Handbook for Young Activists section which tells children how they can replicate many of the techniques used by the young people, and emphasizes the ability children have to affect change. (Ages 8–14)

Kuklin, Susan. *Irrepressible Spirit: Conversations with Human Rights Activists.* Putnam, 1996. 230 pages. (0–399–22762–8) (pbk. 0–399–23045–9)

Kuklin begins by summarizing the processes she used to conduct interviews and gather information about human rights activism, claiming no intention to single out or condemn any one nation or ideology. *Irrepressible Spirit* is organized according to types of human rights: Freedom of Expression, Freedom from Communal Violence, The Right to One's Life, Freedom from Bondage, The Rights of the Child, The Right to Vote, and The Road toward Democracy. Kuklin excluded abuses resulting because of cultural or religious practices and showed only a sample of the "many abuses inflicted on women and children all over the world." Activists telling their own or others' stories are Li Lu (China); David Moya (Cuba); Ivana Nizich (Bosnia, Croatia and Serbia); Monique Mujawamariya (Rwanda); Ben Penglase (Brazil); Joe Ingle (U.S.A.); Jeannine Guthrie (Burma, Thailand, Nepal, India); Chanrithy Ouk (Cambodia); Michelle India Baird (Jamaica); Fatemeh Ziai (Tajikstan); and Peter Volmink (South Africa). Each first-person account is concluded with an activist's pithy advice to young readers. Usually the advice involves writing—to legislators, to national leaders, to dictators, to known violators of human rights. Often the advice is general: "Don't buy into stereotypes. Don't assume someone is evil because they are members of a certain religion, race, or ethnic group . . . Don't take for granted what everybody tells you, even your leaders . . ." (Ivana Nizich). Faces and stories are linked to the places about which Kuklin provides information, documentation, and action possibilities to her readers. Relevant articles are listed at the end along with information about human rights organizations. The opening quotation is attributed to Eleanor Roosevelt: "Where, after all, do universal human rights begin? In small places, close to home—so close and so small that they cannot be seen on any maps of the world." Such places and actions can be glimpsed in this dynamic volume. (Age 12–adult)

Kuklin, Susan. *Speaking Out: Teenagers Take on Race, Sex, and Identity.* Putnam, 1993. 165 pages. (0–399–22343–6) (pbk. 0–399–22532–3)

Susan Kuklin spent one year with students and staff at the Bayard Rustin High School for the Humanities in New York City, which has a racially, culturally, and economically diverse student body, to explore "how kids see themselves and each other." In a school environment that strives to minimize conflict and foster understanding, interviews with individual students and interactions among students of both similar and vastly differing backgrounds reveal that hurt, confusion, anger and hope all abound. In discussions about race, culture, religion, sexuality, physical appearance and many other topics, the students openly reflect upon their own lives and relate their views about themselves and one another. This profile of individuals and a school community is clearly a mirror of the larger world as well. (Age 12–adult)

Kuklin, Susan. *What Do I Do Now? Talking About Teenage Pregnancy.* Putnam, 1991. 179 pages. (0–399–21843–2, out of print)

Interviews with pregnant teens and their partners and parents, as well as with doctors, nurses and counselors, form the basis of this realistic, nonjudgmental account of the issues teens face upon finding out they're pregnant. Excellent black-and-white photographs of the people interviewed contribute a sense of intimacy to these accounts of teens making choices about their futures. (Age 10–adult)

Lewis, Barbara A. *Kids with Courage: True Stories about Young People Making a Difference.* Free Spirit (400 1st Ave. No., Suite 616, Minneapolis, MN 55401), 1992. (pbk. 0–915793–39–3)

Eighteen young social and environmental activists are featured in an unusual collection about real kids. Based on the author's interviews with the young people, the book is divided into four sections: Kids Fighting Crime, Kids Taking Social Action, Heroic Kids, and Kids Saving the Environment. Each entry includes brief biographical information about the young activist along with a photograph, in addition to a description of the contribution he or she has made to society. The young people profiled range from a 14-year-old Milwaukee boy who gave his Nikes to a shoeless pregnant woman he encountered on a city bus one winter day to a 16-year-old girl from Louisville, Kentucky, who coordinates a volunteer peer counseling group for victims of child sexual abuse that provides moral support prior to courtroom appearances. African-American, Asian-American, Latino, Native American and Euro-American youngsters from throughout the United States are featured in an engaging composite of the next generation of leaders. (Ages 8–14)

Mochizuki, Ken. *Heroes.* Illustrated by Dom Lee. Lee & Low (95 Madison Ave., New York, NY 10016), 1995. 32 pages. (1–880000–16–4) (pbk. 1–880000–50–4)

Donnie is tired of always having to pretend to be one of the bad guys when he plays with his friends. He tries to tell the other boys about his father who had fought as a soldier in Italy and France and about his uncle who was in Korea. But they continue to cast him as the enemy in their games because he is Japanese American; no matter what he says he still looks the part. His uncle tells him that real heroes don't brag, and they don't watch war shows on TV. His father suggests that the boys stop playing war. But they don't, they won't. A picture story featuring a common dilemma within an uncommon context. (Ages 6–9)

Nunes, Lygia Bojunga. *My Friend the Painter.* Translated from the Portuguese by Giovanni Pontiero. U.S edition: Harcourt Brace Jovanovich, 1991. 85 pages. (0–15–256340–7) (pbk. 0–15–200872–1, 1995)

Claudio has a special affinity with his adult friend, a painter, who tells him that, even though he's a child, he has the soul of an artist. Flattered by the painter's attention, Claudio tries hard to understand the artist's abstract linkings of emotions and colors; he faces his biggest challenge when the painter commits suicide. As Claudio slowly comes to terms with the range of emotions he feels while grieving, he begins to apply his friend's philosophy as he struggles to make the intangible visual in order to comprehend his feelings. A quiet, sensuous, and understated novel from one of Brazil's best known children's writers. (Ages 12–16)

Shea, Pegi Deitz. *The Whispering Cloth.* Illustrated by Anita Riggio. Stitched by You Yang. Boyds Mills, 1995. 32 pages. (pbk. 1–56397–623–4, 1996)

Mai, a young Hmong girl living in a refugee camp in Thailand, waits for the day she might join her cousins in the United States. To pass time, Mai listens to the women tell stories of their Laotian homeland, and she watches the stories take shape inside the beautiful borders of the *pa'ndau*, the story cloth they sew. Wanting to stitch her own *pa'ndau*, Mai finds herself remembering the death of her parents and her flight from Laos to the refugee camp with her grandmother. An important narrative about the experience of Hmong refugee people is illustrated with full-color paintings and an actual *pa'ndau* stitched for the text to tell Mai's story. An author's note provides information on Ban Vinai, the refugee camp where the story is set. (Ages 7–11)

Zak, Monica. *Save My Rainforest.* First published in the Swedish language in 1987. English version by Nancy Schimmel. Illustrated by Bengt-Arne Runnerström. U.S. edition: Volcano Press (P.O. Box 270, Volcano, CA 95689), 1992. 31 pages. (0–912078–94–4)

Eight-year-old Omar Castillo resolved to travel someday to see the rainforests in southern Mexico about which he heard from his grandfather. He became alarmed by TV news indicating that the last rainforest and its inhabitants had become endangered by excessive logging to increase grazing land for beef cattle, the changing climate, creatures such as toucans being sold as pets, and other reasons. Omar wrote to the President of Mexico but received no reply. The boy then resolved to walk from his home in Mexico City to Lacandon Rainforest. Omar's journey evolved into a 870-mile pilgrimage on foot with his father, an odyssey of survival and environmental activism for both boy and man. The full-color art illustrating every page of the unique documentary creates a fictional mood, but the color photograph of 11-year-old Omar on the final page expresses the realism of the potential impact of youth activists everywhere. (Ages 6–11)

UNDERSTANDING ONESELF AND OTHERS

Cole, Joanna. *How You Were Born.* Photographs by Margaret Miller. Revised edition: Morrow, 1993. 48 pages. (0–688–12059–8) (lib. bdg. 0–688–12060–1) (pbk. 0–688–12061–X)

"Before you were born, you grew in a special place inside your mother's body called her uterus, or womb." Written with simple, direct language, Joanna Cole's book for parents to share with children was designed to help answer the question "Where did I come from?" Cole explains the biological aspects of reproduction and fetal development with the help of simple drawings showing the union of an ovum and sperm, and remarkable photographs taken inside the womb. The happiness and excitement parents feel over a child's birth is also discussed, accompanied by photographs showing parents preparing for, and then celebrating, the arrival of a child. This newly revised and updated edition shows parents and babies of diverse racial backgrounds and firmly establishes the importance of the one special child with whom the book is being shared. (Ages 3–6)

Dwight, Laura. *We Can Do It!* Checkerboard Press (30 Vesey St., New York, NY 10007), 1992. 32 pages. (1–56288–301–1)

Captioned color photographs introduce five preschoolers with disabilities, each of whom cites several things he or she likes to do. The brief, upbeat first-person statements focus on individual personalities and accomplishments. A wonderful affirmation for all children of the many ways in which they can succeed. (Ages 3–6)

Keeshig-Tobias, Lenore. *Bineshiinh Dibaajmowin = Bird Talk.* Illustrated by Polly Keeshig-Tobias. Sister Vision/Black Women and Women of Colour Press (P.O. Box 217, Station E, Toronto, Ontario, M6H 4E2), 1991. 32 pages. (pbk. 0–920813–89–5)

After Momma and her two daughters move from an Ojibway reservation to a city, young Polly has a bad day at school when her classmates play cowboys and Indians and tease her about being an Indian. Momma manages to soothe Polly's hurt feelings and restore her sense of pride by reminding her of some of the things their grandparents taught them about their heritage. Told in first person from the point of view of Polly's older sister, the bilingual (Ojibway/English) text is accompanied by simple black-and-white line drawings. The straightforward, poignant story is based on a childhood experience of the young illustrator. (Ages 5–9)

Kidd, Diana. *Onion Tears.* Illustrated by Lucy Montgomery. U.S. edition: Orchard, 1991. 62 pages. (0–531–08470–1)

A short first-person novel details the difficulties Nam-Huong faces adjusting to her new neighborhood and school and to another culture after leaving Vietnam to live with guardians in Australia. Numb with grief and sorrow at losing her family and home, Nam-Huong rarely speaks and, as a result, is ridiculed by neighborhood children and classmates. The depth of loss she feels is communicated in a series of letters she writes to a canary, a duck and a buffalo—animals she remembers from her earlier life in Vietnam. Numerous pencil drawings accompany this sensitive story of a young girl coping with tragic loss and taking her first steps toward emotional healing. The author's sources included narratives of adolescent girls who came to Australia from Southeast Asia during the late 1970s and early 1980s. (Ages 7–10)

Moutoussamy-Ashe, Jeanne. *Daddy and Me: A Photo Story of Arthur Ashe and His Daughter Camera.* Alfred A. Knopf, 1993. 40 pages. (0–679–85096–1) (lib. bdg. 0–679–95096–6)

Jeanne Moutoussamy-Ashe's black-and-white photographs of her husband Arthur and her daughter Camera were taken in the years before Arthur died of AIDS in February, 1993, when Camera was five. The images capture a warm father-daughter relationship in which his illness, while a factor in their lives—sometimes draining his energy or hospitalizing him—is never a factor in their love. Text accompanying the photographs is written in Camera's first-person voice and describes her life with her father: "Daddy has some bad days and lots of good days . . . .On good days we go to the tennis court . . . .Or we sit in the sun and sing . . . .On Daddy's bad days, I take care of him. I give him his pills. I take his temperature. I make him wait until the thermometer beeps, just like he does for me." A remarkable portrait of a child's capacity for understanding, compassion, and love. (Ages 3–5)

Parks, Rosa with Gregory J. Reed. *Dear Mrs. Parks: A Dialogue with Today's Youth.* Lee & Low (95 Madison Ave., New York, NY 10016), 1996. 111 pages. (1–880000–45–8)

Without intending to become a moral leader during the 20th century, Mrs. Rosa Parks is that and much more to millions of people of all ages because of her civil disobedience in 1955 in Montgomery, Alabama, and the demeanor with which she has conducted her public and personal life since then. *Dear Mrs. Parks* is a uniquely designed, compact volume containing excerpts of correspondence from young people wanting to know Mrs. Parks' age (born in 1913), favorite types of movies (comedies), and favorite book (the *Bible*). They inquire whether she has bad days, and they wonder what to do when friends try to get them to do something wrong. Sixty-eight representative questions are organized within five themes: Courage and Hope, The Power of Knowledge and Education, Living with God, Pathways to Freedom, and Making a Difference. Mrs. Parks's warm, respectful replies are framed in clear prose. Her responses vary in length from a few words to more than a page. Brief information about Rosa Parks and the Civil Rights Movement opens the book, and the enterprises she supports are described at the end. Readers may send letters to Mrs. Parks at the address listed in her remarkable self-portrait. (Ages 7–16)

Zolotow, Charlotte. *The Old Dog.* Illustrated by James Ransome. Revised and newly illustrated edition: HarperCollins, 1995. 32 pages. (0–06–024409–7) (lib. bdg. 0–06–024412–7)

When Ben awakens one morning and finds that his dog doesn't respond with the usual tail wagging when he pets her, he calls his father from the breakfast table. "She's dead," his father tells him. All day long Ben thinks of his dog and the the things they used to do together. Charlotte Zolotow's outstanding text explains and comforts simultaneously while James Ransome's detailed oil paintings aptly show the sadness of a young African-American boy grieving the death of a beloved pet. (Ages 3–8)

THE ARTS

Arnold, Caroline. *Stories in Stone: Rock Art Pictures by Early Americans.* Photographs by Richard Hewett. Clarion, 1996. 48 pages. (0–395–72092–3)

Line drawings on rock walls and boulders across the Americas provide evidence of human habitation between several hundred to 6,000 (or more) years ago. Ancient artists engraved or painted human figures, abstract designs, and animals often identifiable today. Arnold's thorough explanations and Hewitt's distinctive color photographs of the astonishing petroglyphs within the Coso Range of contemporary California provide an excellent general overview of petroglyphs in the western hemisphere. Readers will find a helpful glossary, index, and listing of 13 of the North American locations where these old, permanent art forms can be seen. (Ages 9–12)

Bishop, Rudine Sims. *Presenting Walter Dean Myers.* Twayne, 1991. 123 pages. (0–8057–8214–1)

An unparalleled literary biography examines the works of Walter Dean Myers from several perspectives: Myers the humorist; Myers the realist; Myers the storyteller; Myers the war novelist; and Myers the artist. Bishop brings a strong sense of cultural authenticity to her interpretation of Myers's work, analyzing his books in the context of African-American culture in general and of African-American literature specifically. *Presenting Walter Dean Myers* can be read for inspiration and information by Myers's adolescent readers and for literary and cultural insight by adults. Other books of interest: *Presenting Rosa Guy* by Jerrie Norris (Twayne, 1988) and *Presenting Laurence Yep* by Dianne Johnson-Feelings (Twayne, 1995). (Age 11–adult)

Bryan, Ashley. *All Night, All Day: A Child's First Book of African-American Spirituals.* Atheneum, 1991. 48 pages. (0–689–31662–3, out of print)

The words and music to 20 spirituals are accompanied by luminous full-color paintings. Ashley Bryan's art provides a lush, visual interpretation of well-known songs such as "I'm Going to Eat at the Welcome Table," "Peter, Go Ring the Bells," and the title song, "All Night, All Day." This is a welcome addition to Bryan's earlier children's books interpreting this distinctive African-American contribution to music. (All ages)

Bryan, Ashley, illustrator. *What a Wonderful World.* Lyrics by George David Weiss and Bob Thiele. Atheneum, 1995. 24 pages. (0–689–80087–8)

Six children paint scenery: flowers, trees, sun, moon, stars and a rainbow. They draw, cut, and mount animal, bird, and reptile shapes. Hand puppets are costumed. Lettered signs proclaim "Puppet Show Today" and "Satchmo the Great!" The performance begins. "I see trees of green, red roses too, I see them bloom / for me and you, and I think to myself, 'What a wonderful world!' . . ." Backstage, children hold up set pieces picturing flora, fauna, and puppet people indigenous to each hemisphere. "The bright, blessed day, the dark, sacred night . . ." The hands lifting the sun and moon onto the stage vary in skin color. A trumpeter appears first as a puppet and then as a character. Bryan's inspired vision for a hopeful future is also a tribute to Louis Armstrong, whose performances of this song composed three decades ago are legendary. By addressing the young in love (". . . They'll know much more / than I'll ever know . . ."), Armstrong sang a personal testimony to goodness. That Bryan understands this song on a deep level is evident in his tempera and gouache paintings incorporating bright borders and stylized patterned shapes while expanding the meanings of the lyrics and music in this $12^{1}/4$ x $10^{1}/4$" book. (Ages 2–8)

Cha, Dia. *Dia's Story Cloth: The Hmong People's Journey to Freedom.* Story cloth stitched by Chue and Nhia Thao Cha. Denver Museum of Natural History/Lee & Low (95 Madison Ave, New York, NY 10016), 1996. 24 pages. (1–880000–34–2)

From a refugee camp in Thailand, Dia Cha's aunt and uncle, Chue and Nhia Thao Cha, sent her the story cloth that is the inspiration and the centerpiece for this important 11$^{1}/_{4}$ x 8$^{1}/_{2}$" book about the Hmong. The cloth they stitched depicts the history of the Hmong, whose culture reaches back thousands of years to China, and stretches from Asia to North America, where over 100,000 Hmong have settled in the years since the Vietnam War. Hmong means "free people," Dia writes in her introduction. "This story cloth will tell you about our life." In the text, Dia simply and skillfully threads her own story into that of the Hmong people as she tells about life farming with her family as a child in Laos, and then the violent upheaval of the Vietnam War that saw the death or displacement of thousands of Hmong in Southeast Asia. *Dia's Story Cloth* includes a discussion of Hmong history, culture, and artistic traditions by the Curator of Ethnology at the Denver Museum of Natural History. (Ages 8–11)

Curry, Barbara K. and James Michael Brodie. *Sweet Words So Brave: The Story of African American Literature.* Illustrated by Jerry Butler. Zino Press (P.O. Box 52, Madison, WI 53701), 1996. 64 pages. (1–55933–179–8)

A fictional grandfather relates the history of African Americans in North America to his granddaughter by telling her about early storytellers and writers as well as some recent literary activists. He points out that centuries ago a Black person who picked up a book and learned to read was both defiant and brave. The narrative pays homage to enslaved and oppressed people who kept their heritage alive through deed and word and to those who continue in this tradition. Thirty published writers are featured in the visually exciting, multi-dimensional presentation linking texts, photographs, varied uses of type sizes, page designs, and paintings in bold colors. The writers include Maya Angelou, James Baldwin, Amiri Baraka, Gwendolyn Brooks, Countee Cullen, Frederick Douglass, W.E.B. Du Bois, Paul Laurence Dunbar, Ralph Ellison, Olaudah Equiano, Nikki Giovanni, Lorraine Hansberry, Langston Hughes (from whose poem the title originated), Zora Neale Hurston, James Weldon Johnson, Martin Luther King, Jr., Malcolm X, Paule Marshall, Toni Morrison, Sonia Sanchez, Alice Walker, and Richard Wright. A glossary and list of selected readings accompany a volume tall in more than one way. (Ages 9–16)

Cummings, Pat, compiler. *Talking with Artists, Volume 1.* Bradbury, 1992. 96 pages. (lib. bdg. 0–02–724245–5)

Cummings, Pat, editor. *Talking with Artists, Volume 2.* Simon & Schuster, 1995. 96 pages. (0–689–80310–9)

Pat Cummings has illustrated many books for children, including *C.L.O.U.D.S.* (Lothrop, 1986), *Storm in the Night* (Harper, 1988) and *C Is for City* (HarperCollins, 1995). She also realizes that although she shares things in common with other illustrators, her studio work on any picture book is unique to who she is as an individual. In these two outstanding books, Cummings profiles picture book artists by having each respond to the same frequently asked questions, such as where ideas come from. Each artist tells about her/his childhood; this section features a childhood photograph (usually a school picture of the young artist) and a photograph of the artist today as well as one reproduction of childhood art and one or two representing their picture-book art. Among the artists profiled in Volume 1 are Pat Cummings, Leo and Diane Dillon, Tom Feelings, and Jerry Pinkney. Profiles in Volume 2 include Floyd Cooper, Sheila Hamanaka, and Brian Pinkney. Terrific organization and compelling subject matter make these unusual looks at artists' lives and careers good for general browsing and difficult to put down. (Ages 6–14)

Davol, Marguerite W. *The Heart of the Wood.* Illustrated by Sheila Hamanaka. Simon & Schuster, 1992. 32 pages. (0–671–74778–9)

Illustrations created in oil paints on bark paper celebrate the artistry and multiple procedures leading to a joyous celebration complete with ". . . music, now high, now low, / made by the fiddler with fingers and bow, / playing the fiddle created to find / the song in the heart of the wood, / shaped by the woodcarver with music in mind . . . ." The language pattern for *The House That Jack Built* serves Davol's theme of creativity, while Hamanaka's inclusive vision of community embraces all in this celebratory full-color picture book. (Ages 3–8)

Ehrlich, Amy, editor. *When I Was Your Age: Original Stories about Growing Up.* Candlewick, 1996. 156 pages. (1–56402–306–0)

Ten authors of children's and young adult books were invited to submit stories on the theme of growing up. Some responded with personal reminiscences, while others wrote a story on the theme. The authors includ Nicholasa Mohr, Walter Dean Myers, and Laurence Yep. A charming photo reproduced in black-and-white from the writer's childhood opens each writer's contribution. Brief author biographies can be found in the back. (Ages 9–16)

Field, Dorothy. *In the Street of the Temple Cloth Printers.* Pacific Educational Press (University of British Columbia, Vancouver, B.C. V6T 1Z4), 1996. 36 pages. (pbk. 1–895766–07–9)

The families who create temple cloths live and work in one section of old Ahmedabad, India. Temple cloths are associated with the worship of the Hindu Mother Goddess whose image is in the center of each hand colored assemblage of block prints. Stories unfold on cloth as readers follow the exacting work of Vaghi, Otamben, Dilip, Jagadish, Babu, Kacharaji, and others whose families before them also created drawings and block prints for the temple cloths. Folkloristic and other cultural dimensions of textile printing are explained and then shown in a variety of photographs of people at work and reproductions of their designs. This modestly produced 8$^{3}/_{8}$ x 10$^{7}/_{8}$" book printed in two colors contains a wealth of accessible information about an art. (Ages 9–14)

Gershator, David and Phillis Gershator. *Bread Is for Eating.* Illustrated by Emma Shaw Smith. Henry Holt, 1995. 28 pages. (0–8050–3173–1)

When her little boy leaves bread on his plate, Mamita says, "Bread is for eating." Gently she reminds him of the elements ripening the seeds and the people harvesting grain. She sings of these things, of millers and bakers, of family members working to earn money to buy bread, and ". . . of people around the world, dreaming of bread." Readers are invited to think in new ways because of the warm, rich colors of the ink drawings on every page and the endpages, too. Spanish and English words are provided along with a musical notation for the short title song, the Spanish language refrain of which is part of the English language text. The book's restrained energy combined with the unusual perspectives and detailed borders of the art makes it one to re-read, sing, remember. (Ages 4–8)

Greenberg, Jan and Sandra Jordan. *The American Eye: Eleven Artists of the Twentieth Century.* Delacorte, 1995. 120 pages. (0–385–32173–2)

The authors profile pioneering contemporary artists, giving examples of their art reproduced in full color, analyzing what makes each great, and suggesting why each artist is distinctively American. The back matter includes a 66-term glossary offering a virtual course in art appreciation, data about each artwork pictured, a list of where to see works by the artists, a general bibliography as well as one for each artist, and a standard index. The artists include Romare Bearden and Isamu Noguchi. A fine companion to the authors' earlier substantial works, *The Painter's Eye: Learning to Look at Contemporary American Art* (Delacorte, 1991) and *The Sculptor's Eye: Looking at Contemporary American Art* (Delacorte, 1993). (Ages 10–18)

Hartman, Karen. *Dream Catcher: The Legend, the Lady, the Woman.* Illustrated by Louise Bussiere. Weeping Heart Publications (N1634 Lakeshore Dr., Campbellsport, WI 53010), 1994. 72 pages. (0–9635204–1–5)

Hartman's book gives background information about the artistic tradition of dream catchers among the Ojibway. She describes how she herself learned to make dream catchers from an Ojibway elder years ago and relates a story the woman told her, passed down through the generations, of how dream catchers came to be made by the Ojibway people. She then provides a step-by-step account of how she makes a dream catcher, including explanations of what each part symbolizes. This treasure trove of hard-to-find information will be a welcome addition to school and public libraries. (Ages 6–13)

Hausherr, Rosmarie. *What Instrument Is This?* Scholastic, 1992. 38 pages. (0–590–44644–4, out of print)

Sixteen musical instruments are introduced one at a time with a color photograph of a boy or girl playing an instrument paired with the question forming the book's title. Upon turning the page, another photograph of someone playing the instrument is accompanied by brief information about it. The instruments include a practical mix such as recorder, saxophone, bagpipes, electric guitar, pipe organ, and trumpet. A visual symbol and phrase designate to which instrument group each one belongs. Brief details about instruments, lessons, teaching methods, practice time, joining an orchestra or band, and recitals appears at the book's end. The diversity of the children showing an interest in the instruments can encourage the natural curiosity of readers from varying backgrounds. (Ages 4–8)

Higginsen, Vy. *This Is My Song: A Collection of Gospel Music for the Family.* Illustrated by Brenda Joysmith. Crown, 1995. 95 pages. (0–517–59492–7) (lib. bdg. 0–517–59493–5)

The creator of the gospel musical "Mama, I Want to Sing" selected 30 songs from the standard gospel repertoire for this singular collection and prefaced them with a brief history of gospel music illustrated with archival photos. Each song is introduced with easy music notation and a paragraph setting it within its own Christian and/or cultural context. A full-color painting that suggests this dimension of contemporary African-American life accompanies every song. (Age 5–adult)

Hoyt-Goldsmith, Diane. *Pueblo Storyteller.* Photographs by Lawrence Migdale. Holiday House, 1991. 26 pages. (lib. bdg. 0–8234–0864–7) (pbk. 0–15–300343–X; Harcourt Brace Jovanovich, 1993) (pbk. 0–8234–1080–3, 1994)

A concise first-person text and color photographs document the day-to-day life of April Trujillo, a ten-year-old Cochiti girl who lives with her grandparents near Santa Fe, New Mexico. April is a member of a gifted family—both of her grandparents are potters and her uncle is a drum maker. She describes the step-by-step process her grandparents go through to make clay storyteller sculptures, from going out to dig up the clay they will use, to kneading and shaping it and sculpting the figure, to sanding, polishing and painting it before firing it in a kiln. A deep respect for elders and cultural traditions is apparent in April's young voice as she places everyday activities in a cultural context. (Ages 6–10)

Hudson, Wade & Cheryl Willis Hudson, selectors. *How Sweet the Sound: African-American Songs for Children.* Illustrated by Floyd Cooper. Scholastic, 1995. 48 pages. (0–590–48030–8)

The lyrics for 23 songs from African-American traditions or perspectives are printed to be read or sung with pictures of present and past African-American life for inspiration. This inviting picture book meshes the words of spirituals and modern music with other songs. Cooper's full-color illustrations were rendered in oil wash. Easy musical notations at the end take into account the African-American component of improvisation. Huddie Ledbetter, Billy Strayhorn, James Brown, Stevie Wonder, James Weldon Johnson, J. Rosamund Johnson, and Thomas A. Dorsey are among the musicians and poets represented. A brief history is provided for each song along with an eight-item list of related resources and an index. (Ages 5–12)

Hughes, Langston. *The Block.* Collage by Romare Bearden. Selected by Lowery S. Sims and Daisy Murray Voigt. Introduction by Bill Cosby. The Metropolitan Museum of Art, 1995. 32 pages. (0–670–86501–X)

Full-color reproductions from Romare Bearden's 1971 mural "The Block" are accompanied by 12 poems by Langston Hughes. In his introduction to the elegant, almost cinematic volume measuring 12¼ x 9¼", Bill Cosby relates how the mural reflects the people and events of a busy, exciting Harlem neighborhood. He comments that "it is also a universal place, a recognizable and familiar environment for many people from around the world," pointing out that while "Bearden shows us the sights, Hughes gives us the sounds." A full-page biography of each man with his photograph completes this singular book. (Age 11–adult)

Jones, K. Maurice. *Say It Loud: The Story of Rap Music.* Millbrook, 1994. 128 pages. (1–56294–386–3) (lib. bdg. 1–56294–386–3) (pbk. 1–56294–724–9, 1995)

"Rap is the voice of a population that has been ignored by mainstream leaders and institutions. It is a culture," writes the author in the first chapter of this book that is a fascinating exploration of Rap music. Jones begins by tracing the origins of rap from African societies where great value was placed on the skills of oratory—the embellished word. He continues by looking at the experience of the African in the western world, from times of bondage to the present day, always focusing on the importance of language and expression in variant forms within the culture. He then turns his attention to rap as an artistic/musical form, discussing its musical stylings, individual performers, and the very global nature of the music. Color and black-and-white photographs of performers illustrate a text dynamic in both design and content. (Ages 12–16)

La Pierre, Yvette. *Native American Rock Art: Messages from the Past.* Illustrated by Lois Sloan. Thomasson-Grant (One Morton Drive, Suite 500, Charlottesville, VA 22903; 804/977–1780), 1994. 48 pages. (1–56566–064–1)

Petroglyphs and pictographs—carvings and paintings on rocks—done by the earliest human inhabitants of North America can be found from Nova Scotia to the deserts of the Southwest. Yvette La Pierre explores what is known and how it was determined, as well as what is not known, about these ancient forms of art and communication and the people who created them. Though the illustrations and the fictionalized scenarios that open each chapter seem to assume that rock artists were always male, the unique information presented here, which includes photographs of rock art throughout North America, makes this a valuable text. (Ages 8–12)

Langstaff, John, selector and editor. *Climbing Jacob's Ladder: Heroes of the Bible in African-American Spirituals.* Illustrated by Ashley Bryan. Piano arrangements by John Andrew Ross. Margaret K. McElderry, 1991. 24 pages. (lib. bdg. 0–689–50494–2)

A triumphant tone characterizes the nine spirituals from Hebrew Scriptures (Old Testament) selected for this companion volume to *What a Morning! The Christmas Story in Black Spirituals* (Margaret K. McElderry, 1987). Ashley Bryan's original tempera paintings visually illustrate and celebrate the strength of the stories about Noah, Abraham, Jacob, Moses, Joshua, David, Ezekiel, Daniel, and Jonah. Langstaff's selections and musical notations appear chronologically; a note about each personage provides important background information; and a page at the end offers advice to adults and instrumentalists. (All ages)

Lawrence, Jacob. *The Great Migration: An American Story.* Poem by Walter Dean Myers. HarperCollins, 1993. 48 pages. (0–06–443428–1) (lib. bdg. 0–06–023038–X) (pbk. 0–06–443428–1, 1994)

According to Lawrence, his sequence of paintings, begun in 1940 when he was 22 years old, involves the "exodus of African-Americans who left their homes and farms in the South around the time of World War I and traveled to northern industrial cities in search of better lives." This book reproducing the entire series in full color was published on the occasion of the 1993 exhibition "Jacob Lawrence: The Migration Series." Images of dignity and hope are mingled with those of hard work and harsh experience created in what became panels containing an epic sweep of a people on the move. Lawrence's introduction and brief narrative accompanying the paintings offer insights into this aspect of U.S. history and his immediate family's migration experience. The closing page of this significant book contains a poem by Walter Dean Myers in which tribute is paid to the theme of the paintings and to the people. (Age 9–adult)

Littlechild, George. *This Land Is My Land.* Children's Book Press (246 First St., Suite 101, San Francisco, CA 94105), 1993. 32 pages. (0–89239–119–7)

Seventeen dazzling, thought-provoking paintings by artist George Littlechild, a member of the Plains Cree Nation, are the focus of this stunning book. In the open, engaging narrative that accompanies each vivid reproduction, most of which are full page, the artist explains the meaning and symbolism found in his paintings, making both the art and the artistic process wholly accessible to children. Describing the painting "Red Horse in a Sea of White Horses" he writes: ". . . an Indian Warrior sits atop a red horse. Not at home in his own territory, the red horse sits among the white horses, who find him different and don't understand him . . . . The red horse represents me." The artist also paints a moving portrait in words of his own life and of Native experience in this singular book that celebrates the relationship between individual, art, and culture. (Ages 9–14)

Lomas Garza, Carmen with Harriet Rohmer. *In My Family = En mi familia.* Edited by David Schecter. Translated by Francisco X. Alarcón. Children's Book Press (246 First St., Suite 101, San Francisco, CA 94105), 1996. 32 pages. (0–89239–138–3)

Brilliantly colored oil, acrylic and gouache paintings illustrate scenes from this Chicana artist's childhood in Kingsville, Texas, near the border with Mexico. She comments on growing up in her Mexican-American family in single-page narratives accompanying each work of art reproduced in the book and in the details of her paintings, as well. Children who cannot read yet can see empanadas being made, a birthday celebration complete with a barbecue and a piñata, Easter egg decoration, a healer's visit to the family, grandmother telling the story of *La Llorona*, a cousin's wedding blessing, and much more. The artist answers questions typically asked about her work in two pages at the end. The narrative passages are printed in Spanish and in English. A welcome continuation of her first book, *Family Pictures = Cuadros de familia* (Children's Book Press, 1990). (Age 5–adult)

Lyons, Mary E. *Painting Dreams: Minnie Evans, Visionary Artist.* Houghton Mifflin, 1996. 48 pages. (0–395–72032-X)

Minnie Evans always saw a world invisible to everyone else. As a child, her night dreams were filled with visions, and her days with sights and voices only she experienced. Her formal education ended after fifth grade. When she was 43 years old, Minnie Evans began recreating her dreams on scraps of paper, sometimes even on a window shade. After many years, the paintings of this longtime gate house attendant at Airlie Gardens in Wilmington, North Carolina, came to the attention of folk art experts. Today Mrs. Evans's works can be seen in the folk art collections of leading art museums. Nineteen full-color reproductions of paintings with details about which readers can marvel are included in an engrossing brief account of the unschooled but never uninformed genius of Minnie Evans, who died at age 90 in 1982. (Age 9–adult)

Medearis, Angela Shelf. *Treemonisha.* From the opera by Scott Joplin. Illustrated by Michael Bryant. Henry Holt, 1995. 37 pages. (0–8050–1748–8)

Scott Joplin created a musical autobiography in his ragtime opera *Treemonisha*, first performed in Harlem in 1915. Although the opera received a Pulitzer Prize in 1976, *Treemonisha* was first produced without costumes or scenery. Joplin choreographed that production and played the orchestral score on the piano himself. Even though he realized his work was ahead of its time, Joplin viewed this effort as a failure. He died two years later. The theme of *Treemonisha* honors African-American heritage while the story involves the daughter of freed slaves who works on behalf of her people in the post-Civil War South. Medearis's fictionalized version of the plot includes excerpts from the libretto. Rendered in watercolor and colored pencil, Bryant's many illustrations costume lively characters and stage vivid scenes in an important book to read as if it were a short novel. (Ages 9–12)

Medearis, Angela Shelf. *The Zebra-Riding Cowboy: A Folk Song from the Old West.* Illustrated by María Cristina Brusca. Henry Holt, 1992. 32 pages. (0–8050–1712–7)

Created by an unknown songwriter between 1870 and 1890, this song features an "educated fellow with jaw-breaking words" who might have been an African-American man (as he is pictured here) or a Mexican *vaquero* or one of any number of cowboys from the documented frontier history to which Medearis refers in her two-page afterword. The song lyrics read like a tall tale in verse in a humorous picture book about a city-slicker cowboy who accepted the challenge of riding Zebra Dun. An easy arrangement for the song is printed on the endpapers. (Ages 5–9)

Monceaux, Morgan. *Jazz: My Music, My People.* Foreword by Wynton Marsalis. Alfred A. Knopf, 1994. 64 pages. (0–679–85618–8)

An exciting collection of multi-media portraits and short biographies of performers who have made jazz music a vital, vibrant art form. The artwork pulsates with the color, tones, and rhythms of each performer's music, while the narratives are transformed beyond mere telling of fact by smooth, delightful descriptions of musical stylings and the author-artist's relation of his own listening experiences. Readers will discover Buddy Bolden, Leadbelly, Duke Ellington, Billie Holiday, Ethel Waters, Charlie Parker, Nat King Cole, and many others in this unique and lively history of jazz. (Age 11–adult)

Orozco, José-Luis, compiler. *De Colores and Other Latin-American Folk Songs for Children.* Selected, arranged and translated by José-Luis Orozco. Illustrated by Elisa Kleven. Dutton, 1994. 56 pages. (0–525–45260–5)

Each of the 27 Latin American songs, chants, and rhymes chosen by performer-songwriter Orozco for inclusion in this text are presented with lyrics in Spanish and English, simple musical arrangement, and explanatory notes about the song's subject and how it is traditionally sung. Kleven's brightly colored collage illustrations are lively, joyous accompaniments to the music. (Ages 5–10)

Presilla, Maricel E. and Gloria Soto. *Life around the Lake: Embroideries by the Women of Lake Pátzcuaro.* Henry Holt, 1996. 32 pages. (0–8050–3800–0)

Some of the Tarascan women of central Mexico create traditional needlework for sale at the market as one way to support themselves while the local fishing economy dwindles. A guild organized more than 14 years ago equips local women to become master embroiderers. Most of their embroideries reflect a happier time. The women honor their heritage by stitching images of life before Lake Pátzcuaro became polluted, before soil run-offs from mountains bare of trees filled the lake, before the fish began to die, before the wild ducks disappeared. Their dazzling stitchery shows an abundance of fish in Lake Pátzcuaro. It recreates Tarascan mythology and seasonal observances often still enjoyed. Full-color photographs of the women's intricately designed embroideries grace each page of this beautiful 10¼" square book about culture, economy, environment, and the art of resilient, hard working Tarascan women. (Ages 9–12)

Raschka, Chris. *Charlie Parker Played Be Bop.* Orchard, 1992. 32 pages. (0–531–05999–5) (lib. bdg. 0–531–08599–6)

Inspired upon hearing a recording of "A Night in Tunisia," the author-artist created a swinging tribute to Charlie Parker and be bop. The unified art and design elements of this 9¹/₂" square book express be bop music. The illustrations were rendered in watercolor and charcoal pencil. "Charlie Parker played be bop. / Charlie Parker played alto saxophone. / The music sounded like hip hop. / Never leave your cat / a-lone." Caution: the lyrics are contagious. (Ages 3–9)

Ringgold, Faith, Linda Freeman and Nancy Roucher. *Talking to Faith Ringgold.* Crown, 1996. 48 pages. (lib. bdg. 0–517–70914–7) (pbk. 0–517–88546–8)

Faith Ringgold burst onto the children's book scene when one of her story quilts was adapted into the award-winning picture book *Tar Beach* (Crown, 1991). Here the renowned painter, sculptor, and quilt artist takes readers on a brief gallery tour of some of her story quilts. Even more important, she engages them to think about themselves. An inspiring interactive narrative uses a variety of type sizes, color photos, pictures from family albums, and other material in new combinations and page layouts. (Ages 6–14)

Sills, Leslie. *Visions: Stories about Women Artists.* Albert Whitman, 1993. 64 pages. (lib. bdg. 0–8075–8491–6)

In a compact volume measuring 9 x 11", Sills showcases the life and art of four women: Mary Cassatt, Leonora Carrington, Betye Saar and Mary Frank. The handsome volume contains photographs of the artists as young girls as well as later in life; color photographs of selected works indicate potential child appeal about them while the text engages interest in their progressive and distinctive spirits. Only Cassatt is at all visible within other books for children. Carrington's origins in northern England exposed her to Celtic legends, Christian stories about miracles and Catholic saints and family suggestions that she raise fox terriers rather than attend art school. After learning about surrealism in art, Carrington ultimately emigrated to Mexico where she continued to "see the invisible" and create "fantasies with otherworldly creatures." Saar's early fascination with found objects extended into a career involving three-dimensional assemblages, a famous one being "The Liberation of Aunt Jemima," her response as an African-American artist to outsider notions about kitchen slaves. In recent years Saar continues to transform ordinary objects, including circuit boards, into artistic statements. Born in England, Frank was sent to the U.S. in 1940 to live with grandparents. Throughout her career sculpting and, more recently, creating monoprints, Frank explores universals: life and life experience. Detailed picture credits and bibliographies conclude Sills's second fine work about women artists, the first of which was *Inspirations* (Albert Whitman, 1989). (Ages 9–14)

Sullivan, Charles, editor. *Children of Promise: African-American Literature and Art for Young People.* Harry N. Abrams, 1991. 126 pages. (0–8109–3170–2)

A curious mix of African-American and other voices from U.S. history shows "the evidence of a country striving toward the reconciliation between the real and the ideal." The written and visual statements of a surprising range of public servants, philosophers, writers, and artists bear witness to both a proud and painful past. At the back of this anthology are poetry, title, and author indexes, as well as an alphabetical listing of the 111 contributors represented by more than 100 texts and 80 color or black-and white illustrations. Examples of the wide range of people included within *Children of Promise* are James Baldwin, Imamu Amiri Baraka, Romare Bearden, Gwendolyn Brooks, Lucille Clifton, Countee Cullen, W.E.B. DuBois, Paul Laurence Dunbar, Bob Dylan, Amos Fortune, Stephen Foster and Meta Vaux Warwick Fuller. (Age 5–adult)

Turner, Robyn Montana. *Faith Ringgold.* (Portrait of Women Artists for Children) Little, Brown, 1993. 32 pages. (0–316–85652–5)

Turner, Robyn Montana. *Frida Kahlo.* (Portrait of Women Artists for Children) Little, Brown, 1993. 32 pages. (0–316–85651–7)

Ringgold's children's books *Tar Beach* (Crown, 1991) and *Aunt Harriet's Underground Railroad in the Sky* (Crown, 1992) originated from her three-dimensional story quilts and thrust other works based on her African-American heritage into the spotlight as well. The past decade has seen new visibility for the work of Mexican artist Kahlo as well, whose dramatic, surreal paintings reveal an artistic vision rooted in her culture and female identity. Like the other 11¹/₄ x 8³/₄" books in the series, each of these concise biographies contains material documented from sources typically not tapped in children's books about artists. Each is generously illustrated with reproductions of artwork reproduced in full color. (Ages 7–12)

Williams, Neva. *Patrick DesJarlait: Conversations with a Native American Artist.* Revised edition: Runestone/Lerner, 1995. 56 pages. (0–8225–3151–8)

Patrick DesJarlait was an artist who belonged to the Red Lake Chippewa Band (Anishinabe) of northern Minnesota. More than 20 years ago, Williams tape-recorded the interviews forming the basis for this book featuring DesJarlait's life and art, along with his comments about reservation life in the 1920s, boarding school, and his development as an artist. During World War II, he worked as a film animator for the U.S. Navy and had a short stint as the art director at a relocation camp where Japanese Americans were held. His paintings employ bright, rich tones to portray the many traditions of his people. Although DesJarlait did not receive wide recognition or acclaim while alive, his career has inspired younger American Indian artists, and his paintings were pivotal in the development of contemporary American Indian art. (Ages 8–14)

Winter, Jonah. *Diego.* Illustrated by Jeanette Winter. Alfred A. Knopf, 1991. 32 pages. (0–679–85617-X)

A poetic, easy-to-read account of the childhood and early adulthood of Mexican muralist Diego Rivera is presented in a bilingual text (English/Spanish). Rivera is characterized as a visionary and dreamer who liked to draw the colors, people, and events he witnessed in his native land. The brief text of the 9¼ x 7¼" volume is accompanied throughout by bordered 3 x 3½" exquisitely stylized paintings which dramatically lead up to a wordless double-page spread of the artist at work on a mural, effectively communicating the magnitude of Rivera's art form. (Ages 5–9)

Wolf, Sylvia. *Focus: Five Women Photographers.* Albert Whitman, 1994. 64 pages. (0–8075–2531–6)

The five photographers whose lives and work are profiled span 130 years of the art of photography. Each of them has, through the style, content, and purpose of her work, made a unique and stunning contribution to photographic arts. Flor Garduño captures life, rituals, and traditions in Latin American cultures on film. Lorna Simpson pairs images with words to challenge prejudice and stereotypes as she creates art rooted in African-American history and her own experience as an African-American woman. The other artists featured are Margaret Bourke-White, Julia Margaret Cameron, and Sandy Skoglund. A fascinating documentary of five distinct approaches to art—and life—filled with photographs displaying each woman's unique perspective. (Ages 11–14)

Wood, Michele with Toyomi Igus. *Going Back Home: An Artist Returns to the South.* Children's Book Press (246 First St., Suite 101, San Francisco, CA 94105), 1996. 32 pages. (0–89239–137–5)

Michele Wood's paintings are based on her family's early 20th century sharecropping experiences in the southern U.S.A. Containing patterns reminiscent of African textiles, Ms. Wood's works are distinctive and intriguing. Toyomi Igus's interpretations of Wood's reflections on her journey home accompany 18 works reproduced in full color. Igus's comments serve as invitations to look closely at Wood's paintings. Both have appeal for and are accessible to children. (Ages 9–12)

Yamane, Linda. *Weaving a California Tradition: A Native American Basketmaker.* Photographs by Dugan Aguilar. (We Are Still Here) Lerner, 1996. 48 pages. (0–8225–2660–3) (pbk. 0–8225–9730–6)

Eleven-year-old Carly Tex, a member of the Western Mono tribe in California, is continuing the tradition of basketweaving that has been part of her family and her culture for generations. Carly enjoys learning from her aunt and mother about gathering and preparing grasses, branches, and other materials required for weaving, and about the various methods for creating baskets. With her entire family, which includes her father, a younger sister, and an older sister home from college, Carly also attends a California Indian Basketweavers Gathering, where she displays her work and continues to learn. Dugan Aguilar's color photographs accompany Linda Yamane's sensitive, informative text that also discusses the beliefs that go hand-in-hand with the Western Mono weaving tradition. (Ages 7–11)

Zhensun, Zheng, and Alice Low. *A Young Painter: The Life and Paintings of Wang Yani—China's Extraordinary Young Artist.* Photographs by Zheng Zhensun. (A Byron Preiss/New China Pictures Book) Scholastic, 1991. 80 pages. (0–590–44906–0)

The artistic genius of Wang Yani was recognized when she was only three years old and, a year later, she had her first major exhibition in Shanghai. Since that time she has created over 10,000 paintings and has had exhibitions throughout Asia, Europe, and North America. At age 16 she began a successful transition from child prodigy to adult artist who works in the *xieyi hua* (free style) school of traditional Chinese painting. An absorbing photoessay traces the growth and development of Wang Yani as an artist and as an extraordinary young woman dealing with the pressures of world attention, fame, and high expectations. Numerous color photographs of Yani at work and at home give young readers a close-up of her life in southern China. Fine, full-color reproductions of more than 50 of her paintings created from age two-and-one-half to age 16 show Yani's development as a gifted young artist. (Age 8–adult)

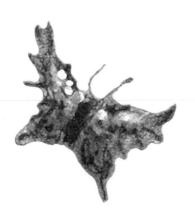

POETRY

Adedjouma, Davida, editor. *The Palm of My Heart: Poetry by African American Children.* Illustrated by Gregory Christie. Introduction by Lucille Clifton. Lee & Low (95 Madison Avenue, New York, NY 10016), 1996. 32 pages. (1–880000–41–5)

African-American children celebrate black creativity, culture, beauty, and so much more in profound and moving performance poems created during a writing workshop led by Davida Adedjouma. A brilliant and beautiful book design is distinguished in part by typeface which displays each child's poem so that it can be read in two ways: in it's entirety, or by focusing on key words that are emphasized in a contrasting boldface font: the poem within the poem. Gregorie Christie's acrylic paintings which illustrate the poems are singular, emotionally stirring works of art that resonate deeply. An introduction by Lucille Clifton and brief profiles of each child poet that emphasize interests with which young readers will relate round out this important, unparalleled volume. (Ages 7–12)

Adoff, Arnold. *In for Winter, Out for Spring.* Illustrated by Jerry Pinkney. Harcourt Brace Jovanovich, 1991. 48 pages. (0–15–238637–8)

The youngest child in a rural African-American family expresses her delight with the Earth's vivid show in the ever-changing cycle of seasons. Twenty-six poems written in a young girl's voice celebrate the beauty of nature and the security of family. Jerry Pinkney's detailed pencil, watercolor, and pastel paintings perfectly complement the child's exuberant moods within the cozy circle of her family. (Ages 5–8)

Angelou, Maya. *Life Doesn't Frighten Me.* Paintings by Jean-Michael Basquiat. Stewart, Tabori & Chang, 1993. 32 pages. (1–55670–288–4)

Maya Angelou asserts a brave voice in the face of fears both real and imagined (which are often one and the same to a child) in a bold and comforting poem for readers of many ages. Child-friendly references offer both humor and depth ("Mean old Mother Goose / Lions on the loose / . . . Panthers in the park / Strangers in the dark"), engaging young children with the images and sound and offering older readers launching points for exploration of deeper layers of meaning. Jean-Michel Basquiat's paintings are like an artist's imagination exposed, intricate and energetic, complex and colorful. Like the text, the visual images can be interpreted and embraced by younger children while offering older viewers much to contemplate. (Age 6–adult)

Begay, Shonto. *Navajo: Visions and Voices Across the Mesa.* Scholastic, 1995. 48 pages. (0–590–46153–2)

Pairing paintings and poems, Navajo artist and writer Shonto Begay takes readers on a journey through past and present from the viewpoint of a 20th century Navajo, for whom the struggle for balance—"New World" with ancient world—is constant. In his powerful introduction, which provides an important context for the poems and paintings that follow, Begay writes, "These are my personal visions and memories of voices shared." His images on page and canvas reflect spiritual beliefs, his relationship with nature, and aspects of history and contemporary life in Navajo culture. (Ages 12–15)

Berry, James. *When I Dance.* U.S. edition: Harcourt Brace Jovanovich, 1991. 120 pages. (0–15–295568–2)

"It is that when I dance / I'm costumed in a rainbow mood, / I'm okay at any angle . . ." Drawing on his experiences growing up in rural Jamaica and in a British inner city, Berry presents 59 original poems collected here for teenagers. The dreams, fears, and boundless energy of adolescents everywhere are marvelously conveyed with a Caribbean cadence. (Age 12–adult)

Bryan, Ashley. *Sing to the Sun: Poems and Pictures.* HarperCollins, 1992. 32 pages. (0–06–020829–5) (lib. bdg. 0–06–020833–3) (pbk. 0–06–443437–0, 1996)

Twenty-three original poems full of vitality and hope offer tributes to people, the arts, the past and the future. Bryan creates the exuberance of song in a range of poetic forms exploring such diverse themes as "Beaded Braids," "The Hurricane," "Grape Pickers," "Granny," "Mama's Bouquet's," "The Storyteller," and "The Artist" (". . . He knows / That to have / Anything he loves / He can have it / Fair and forever / If he paints / A picture of it . . ."). The distinguished African-American poet and artist, influenced by the arts of the world and especially by those in the Caribbean, further honors his subjects by pairing each poem with a work of full-color art reminiscent of a mosaic. (Ages 8–14)

Bruchac, Joseph. *The Circle of Thanks: Native American Poems and Songs of Thanksgiving.* Illustrated by Murv Jacob. BridgeWater, 1996. 32 pages. (lib. bdg. 0–8167–4012–7)

American Indian peoples from across the country recite poems and songs of thanks to acknowledge their gratitude for creation and the bounty of the natural world. Abenaki storyteller and writer Joseph Bruchac retells some of these thanksgiving poems in a collection illustrated with Cherokee painter Murv Jacob's singular full-color art which reflects the heritage of the people from which each poem or song has come. Reader-friendly notes at the end of the text provide additional information on the importance of each poem's subject. (Ages 7–11)

Carlson, Lori, ed. *Cool Salsa: Bilingual Poems on Growing Up Latino in the United States.* Introduction by Oscar Hijuelos. An Edge Book/Henry Holt, 1994. 123 pages. (0–8050–3135–9) (pbk. 0–449–70436–X; Fawcett, 1995)

"Life / to understand me / you have to know Spanish / feel it in the blood of your soul." (From "Learning English" by Luis Alberto Ambroggio.) In sections titled School Days, Home and Homeland, Memories, Hard Times, Time to Party, and A Promising Future, poems of 29 Latin American writers are presented in both English and Spanish. A collection rich with language and memories, events and emotions grounded in Latino experience. (Age 12–adult)

Cassedy, Sylvia and Kunihiro Suetake, translators from the Japanese. *Red Dragonfly on My Shoulder: Haiku.* Illustrated by Molly Bang. HarperCollins, 1992. 32 pages. (lib. bdg. 0–06–022625–0)

Thirteen playful haiku poems gain heightened meanings as each is superimposed upon a color photograph of a collage created from materials common to some homes and classrooms. Ingenious assemblages utilize objects such as cutout cookies, blue corn chips, a sweet potato, a shell, a feather, beads, safety pins, grains of rice, and clothespins. The presence of Bang's note on the last page listing materials used in each assemblage can encourage others to illustrate this spare poetic form similarly. The brief translators' comment suggests ways to understand and read haiku. (Ages 9–14)

Feelings, Tom, compiler and illustrator. *Soul Looks Back in Wonder.* 1993. 32 pages. (0–8037–1001–1, out of print)

In a powerful introduction the compiler-artist writes about the way African creativity has sustained the people in the past and how "it still flows—seeking, searching for new ways to connect the ancient with the new, the young with the old, the unborn with the ancestors." Feelings reminds readers about being "part of a collective that shares a common history and future." A stunning 9³⁄₄ x 10⁵⁄₈" volume melds striking art with 13 inspiring poems by Maya Angelou, Lucille Clifton, Alexis De Veaux, Mari Evans, Darryl Holmes, Langston Hughes, Rashidah Ismaili, Haki R. Madhubuti, Walter Dean Myers, Mwatabu Okantah, Eugene B. Redmond, Askia M. Touré, and Margaret Walker. Feelings's process for creating the full-color illustrations done in mixed media is explained in detail; they originated with sketches made in Ghana and Senegal, West Africa; Guyana, South America; and in the United States. Biographical paragraphs about each poet appear at the end of this splendid volume. (Age 9–adult)

Giovanni, Nikki. *The Genie in the Jar.* Illustrated by Chris Raschka. Henry Holt, 1996. 32 pages. (0–8050–4118–4)

". . . take a note / and spin it around / on the Black loom / on the Black loom / careful baby / don't prick your finger . . . ." There is comfort and warning in this strong and softly woven poem. Nikki Giovanni's imagery sends a powerful and moving message of strength and identity drawn from Black creativity. Chris Raschka's visual interpretation, rendered in oil sticks and watercolor on brown paper, shows a child enveloped in the loving, protective circle of Black community. Children can enter the music of the poem and be soothed by its cadence and sounds; but some, especially older readers, will also want to think about what the poet meant, and, more importantly, what the poem means to them. (Ages 5–10)

Giovanni, Nikki. *Shimmy Shimmy Shimmy Like My Sister Kate: Looking at the Harlem Renaissance through Poems.* Henry Holt, 1996. 186 pages. (0–8050–3494–3)

The Harlem Renaissance, a period and a place of concentrated creative expression among African-Americans that was centered in the area of New York City known as Harlem between 1917 and 1935, was not wholly contained by either time or space. That is the first thing Nikki Giovanni wants young readers of *Shimmy Shimmy Shimmy Like My Sister Kate* to know. In a unique exploration of African-American poetry of the late 19th century through today, Giovanni shares her excitement and passion for the vision and the voice of 23 poets who wrote before, during and after the Harlem Renaissance about their people's lives and dreams. The result is a collection that is as much about culture as poetry, as much about survival as celebration. Giovanni's energizing narrative is her reader-response to the poems and poets she presents; a gift of insight and ideas that will invite young readers to explore these and other poems further, to find their own truth that resonates in the words. (Age 12–adult)

Giovanni, Nikki. *The Sun Is So Quiet.* Illustrated by Ashley Bryan. Henry Holt, 1996. 31 pages. (0–8050–4119–2)

Thirteen poems by Nikki Giovanni cover a range of subjects but are unified by their celebratory feeling and the poet's delightful ability to contemplate subjects in new and unexpected ways. "Little Boys are like snowflakes" begins one poem. Stars "pirouette and boogie down" in another. The poems are illustrated by Ashley Bryan, whose bright, vivid art showing animals, flowers, and children of many racial and ethnic backgrounds, but especially those of African descent, is a joyous burst of color on every page. (Ages 5–9)

Gordon, Ruth, selector. *Time Is the Longest Distance: An Anthology of Poems.* A Charlotte Zolotow Book/HarperCollins, 1991. 74 pages. (0–06–022297–2) (lib. bdg. 0–06–022424–X)

"Sunset is always disturbing / whether theatrical or muted, / but still more disturbing / is that last desperate glow . . ." Thus begins "Afterglow" by Jorge Luis Borges, one of 61 brief poems in English offering sophisticated understandings of the life measurement called Time. A wide range of centuries, nations, and traditions are represented in the strong collection which draws its title from *The Glass Menagerie* by Tennessee Williams. Eighteen of the poems are by people of color, while the others stem from European and other sources. Four Chinese poets from the 5th through the 9th centuries and two Japanese poets from the 9th to the 11th centuries account for 14 of the translated poems in this handsomely designed volume containing many poems from the 20th century. Four poems are from American Indian traditions (Hopi, Pima, Zuni, Papago). (Age 11–adult)

Greenfield, Eloise. *Honey, I Love.* Illustrated by Jan Spivey Gilchrist. (Let's Read Aloud) HarperFestival, 1995. 16 pages. (0–694–00579–7)

The title poem from the much-loved collection, *Honey, I Love and Other Love Poems* (Crowell, 1978) serves as the complete text for an easy picture book. Jan Spivey Gilchrist's pastel paintings interpret the poems as events occurring over the course of one day. (Ages 3–6)

Greenfield, Eloise. *Night on Neighborhood Street.* Illustrated by Jan Spivey Gilchrist. Dial, 1991. 32 pages. (0–8037–0777–0) (lib. bdg. 0–8037–0778–9) (pbk. 0–14–055683–4; Puffin, 1996)

Each of the 17 poems in this collection offers a glimpse into the lives of African-American children on a single night in an urban neighborhood: Nerissa telling her parents bedtime jokes, Tonya hosting a sleepover, Darnell afraid of nighttime noises, independent Lawanda determined not to let her daddy carry her from the car to the front door even though she's very sleepy, Juma talking his daddy into letting him stay up just a little longer, and Buddy, already asleep and dreaming of impressing the world with his wonderful, amazing self. Jan Spivey Gilchrist's full-color gouache paintings evoke a perfect nighttime mood in Greenfield's celebratory tribute to African-American families and communities. (Ages 3–9)

Grimes, Nikki. *Come Sunday.* Illustrated by Michael Bryant. Eerdman's, 1996. 32 pages. (0–8028–5108–8) (pbk. 0–8028–5134)

"Now I lay me down to sleep . . ." prays a small African-American girl who has just enjoyed a satisfying day in what Grimes's poem "Lights Out" names as Paradise with her family and their church family. Bryant's full-color double page spreads evoke Sunday events in their welcoming Christian community. In addition to the title poem, the child's first-person voice radiates joy in "Blue-Haired Ladies," "Ladies' Hats," "White Gloves," "On the March," "Jubilation," "Baptism," "Esther," "My Offering," "At the Altar," Church Supper," Lady Preacher," and "Sunday Evening." (Ages 4–9)

Grimes, Nikki. *Meet Danitra Brown.* Illustrated by Floyd Cooper. Lothrop, Lee and Shepard, 1994. 32 pages. (lib. bdg. 0–688–12074–1)

Thirteen poems about the friendship of two young African-American girls living in a city neighborhood. Title character Danitra Brown has a strong sense of heritage, self, and self-respect, giving her a dynamic presence. Her best friend, Zuri Jackson, is shy and less confident, but it is her narrative voice which carries each poem, the themes of which extend from their friendship and families to growing up African American and female. Together, Nikki Grimes's free-verse text and Floyd Cooper's warm-toned paintings capture moments of joy and moments of sadness that best friends share. (Ages 7–10)

Ho, Minfong. *Hush! A Thai Lullaby.* Illustrated by Holly Meade. Orchard, 1996. 32 pages. (0–531–08850–2) (lib. bdg. 0–531–09500–2)

A worried Thai mother tries to quiet all the animals and insects that might wake her napping baby in rythmic verse graced with gentle humor. Observant readers and listeners will find delight in the supposedly sleeping baby's active endeavors while his mother appeals to each animal in turn to "Hush!" and all will enjoy the soothing pattern of the text. Cut-paper collage illustrations in warm earth tones fill each double-page spread with varied visual perspectives. (Ages 2–5)

Ho, Minfong, compiler. *Maples in the Mist: Children's Poems from the Tang Dynasty.* Translated from the Chinese by Minfong Ho. Illustrated by Jean & Mou-sien Tseng. Lothrop, Lee & Shepard, 1996. 28 pages. (lib bdg. 0–688–14723)

Lovely moments of quiet observation, wonder, and longing characterize this unique collection of poems from China's Tang Dynasty (618–907 A.D.). Minfong Ho has translated selected poems into English to introduce new generations of children outside of China to these simple and beautiful verses that have endured over a thousand years and remain a vital part of Chinese culture today for children and adults alike. Her introduction and brief biographical sketches on all the poets further inform readers about this important literary legacy. Jean and Mou-sien Tseng provide misty watercolor backdrops for each poem in this soothing volume. (Ages 6–10)

Hudson, Wade, selector. *Pass It On: African-American Poetry for Children.* Illustrated by Floyd Cooper. Scholastic, 1993. 32 pages. (0–590–45770–5)

A $10^3/_4$ x $8^5/_8$" picture-book poetry anthology ranges in theme and mood from Eloise Greenfield's light-hearted "To Catch a Fish" to "Incident" by Countee Cullen. A line from "Listen Children" by Louise Clifton suggested the title of the collection. Other poets represented by the 19 selections are Gwendolyn Brooks, Henry Dumas, Paul Laurence Dunbar, James A. Emanuel, Mari Evans, Nikki Giovanni, Nikki Grimes, Langston Hughes, Lessie Jones Little, Lindamichellebaron, and Naomi Long Madgett. The title also represents the compiler's hope that a fine heritage will be introduced to a generation for whom this African-American poetry and some of these poets are unfamiliar. Cooper's illustrations painted in oil wash appear in full color on every page. Brief information is provided about each poet. (Ages 4–9)

Hughes, Langston. *The Sweet and Sour Animal Book.* Illustrated by students from the Harlem School of the Arts. Introduction by Ben Vereen. Afterword by George P. Cunningham. Oxford, 1994. 48 pages. (0–19–509185-X)

Children from the Harlem School of the Arts created animal figures out of clay, paper, and paint to illustrate this alphabet of animal verse from the poet Langston Hughes. *The Sweet and Sour Animal Book* was written by Hughes in the 1930s but never published. This beautifully designed collaboration puts the short, sweet (sometimes bittersweet), funny poems into readers hands while inspiring the imaginations of young artists. An afterword by George P. Cunningham provides older readers with information about Hughes's career, looking at *The Sweet and Sour Animal Book* in the light of his other works, especially those for young people, and examining how even the playful rhymes in these short poems can offer much to think about in the context of African-American experience. (All ages)

Lewis, Richard. *All of You Was Singing.* Illustrated by Ed Young. Atheneum, 1991. 32 pages. (lib. bdg. 0–689–31596–1) (pbk. 0–689–71853–5; Aladdin, 1994)

A poetic retelling of an Aztec legend recounts how music came to earth. Ed Young's brightly hued paintings move gradually from an abstract to a concrete style, perfectly expressing the sky's voice recounting the universal creation story of order emerging from chaos. (Ages 5–10)

Mora, Pat. *Confetti: Poems for Children.* Illustrated by Enrique O. Sánchez. Lee & Low (95 Madison Ave., New York, NY 10016), 1996. 28 pages. (1–880000–25–3)

"Red shouts a loud, balloon-round sound . . ." (From "Colors Crackle, Colors Roar"). Children will delight in the imagery and rhythm of these 13 lively, evocative poems from writer Pat Mora. Spanish words are used throughout and are listed in a glossary at the end of the book. Enrique O. Sánchez illustrates each verse with colorful acrylic art that is filled with energy, joy and details from Latino culture. (Ages 5–8)

Mathis, Sharon Bell. *Red Dog, Blue Fly: Football Poems.* Illustrated by Jan Spivey Gilchrist. Viking, 1991. 32 pages. (0–670–83623–0) (pbk. 0–14–054337–6; Puffin, 1995)

The first-person voice of these 13 poems is a 70-pound quarterback who describes the ups and downs of a championship season. Some of the ecstasies of this youthful player are a touchdown, a playoff pizza, a coach's compliment and, of course, winning the trophy. And some of the agonies are trying to keep the signals straight at practice, playing a game against his cousin's team, and catching a glimpse of the face of a player on the losing team: "His face / grab something / from / my win . . ." The action-packed, full-color illustrations show all team members, coaches and cheerleaders as African American. (Ages 7–11)

Mora, Pat. *The Desert Is My Mother = El Desierto Es Mi Madre.* Illustrated by Daniel Lechón. Piñata/Arte Público Press (University of Houston, M.D. Anderson Library, Room 2, Houston, TX 77204), 1994. 32 pages. (1–55885–121–6)

A lovely extension of the metaphor expressed in the title, the text of this poem is a soothing recitation of the many ways in which the desert cares for the speaker: "I say feed me. / She serves red prickly pear on a spiked cactus. / I say tease me. / She sprinkles raindrops in my face on a sunny day . . . ." Each double-page spread pairs a single idea stated in both English and Spanish on the left page with the artist's full-color visual rendering of the concept on the right. (Ages 4–7)

Mora, Pat. *Listen to the Desert = Oye al Desierto.* Illustrated by Francisco X. Mora. Clarion, 1994. 24 pages. (0–395–67292–9)

"Listen to the owl hoot, whoo, whoo whoo. / Listen to the owl hoot whoo whoo whoo. = *Oye la lechuza, uuu, uuu, uuu. / Oye la lechuza uuu, uuu, uuu."* A simple, rhythmic poem in which each colorful double-paged spread invites the reader to listen to—and hear—a different desert sound expressed in both English and Spanish. The repeating pattern and rhythm of each line creates a pleasing sense of certainty, and also anticipation, about what the next page will bring, while pacing the poem to evoke a sense of having stopped for a moment to listen to the sounds of the desert—and the languages. Francisco Mora's paintings combine geometric patterns with images suggested by the text to form a pleasing backdrop. (Ages 4–7)

Moss, Thylias. *I Want To Be.* Illustrated by Jerry Pinkney. Dial, 1993. 32 pages. (0–8037–1286–3) (lib. bdg. 0–8037–1287–1)

A young African-American girl ponders the answer to the question "What do you want to be?" and her imagination is alive with possibility: "I want to be big but not so big that a mountain or a mosque or a synagogue seems small. / I want to be strong but not so strong that a kite seems weak." Each stirring dream is expressed in Moss's exquisite, sensual writing that sends the child's strands of thought soaring into a realm where anything is possible, and then tethers them to concrete images that make what can only be imagined something tangible after all. Pinkney's illustrations, grounded in the writer's images, are filled with movement, color and light. (Ages 3–6)

Myers, Walter Dean. *Brown Angels: An Album of Pictures and Verse.* HarperCollins, 1993. 40 pages. (0–06–022917–9) (lib. bdg. 0–06–022918–7) (pbk. 0–06–443455–9, 1996)

Original rhymes and poems accompany old photographs of young African-American children collected earlier by Myers. Myers comments in his brief opening statement that these were children loved in their time by the adults who prepared them for a photograph, and valued by the person behind the camera. By immortalizing these Brown Angels, Myers implies the importance of all children. In writing about them, he specifies their beauty and worth. Preschoolers will enjoy paging through the album to see other children in photographs. Older children might make up stories about them and their families or wonder about photographs kept by their family. Adults can reflect upon what can be understood by seeing the faces, little suits and dresses, ribbons and ties, bare feet and toys. This exquisitely designed and printed album of brown-toned photos is wonderfully decorated with the recurring image of a full-color bird in flight. Elegant bookmaking expresses Myers's tender respect for these children of yesterday. (Age 3–adult)

Myers, Walter Dean. *Glorious Angels: A Celebration of Children.* HarperCollins, 1995. 40 pages. (0–06–024822–X) (lib. bdg. 0–06–024823–8)

Myers, a distinguished author of novels and biographies for teen readers and stories for young children, is also a poet and collector of antique photographic portraits. In the sepia-toned portraits in *Glorious Angels*, most children will be able to find at least one old photo close to their own heritage. Children need nurturing adults to love them; two sections focus upon mothers and fathers the world around. Children require a community to nurture them, and there is a section titled Villages. Myers's first photo-poetry album, *Brown Angels* (HarperCollins, 1993), celebrated African-American children who lived almost a century ago. The elegant bookmaking of each volume underscores Myers's respect for all children of yesterday, along with his hopes for all children of tomorrow. His photos and poems are reminders that angels are in front of us today. (Age 3–adult)

Nye, Naomi Shihab, selector. *This Same Sky: A Collection of Poems from Around the World.* Four Winds, 1992. 207 pages. (lib. bdg. 0–02–768440–7) (pbk. 0–689–80630–2, Aladdin, 1996)

This outstanding global anthology is organized into themes such as Words and Silences, Dreams and Dreamers, Families, This Earth and Sky In Which We Live, Losses, and Human Mysteries. The poets represented "shared the twentieth century from many other vantage points," all being citizens of nations other than the United States. Some poems express universal emotions, others convey insights or intensities known firsthand by those who live in poverty or under political oppression. Endpaper collages of cancelled stamps from many nations and signatures in a variety of languages introduce an unparalleled collection of 129 poems. Deckled pages, a ribbon marker, and elegant production honor the commitment of the poets and the anthologist to all readers. (Age 11–adult)

Nye, Naomi Shihab. *The Tree Is Older Than You Are: A Bilingual Gathering of Poems & Stories from Mexico with Paintings by Mexican Artists.* Simon & Schuster, 1995. 110 pages. (0–689–80297–8)

Leticia Tarragó's intriguing cover art shows a scarlet fish with wheels on two fins, a propeller on the third, and a child riding on its back in a terrain inhabited by a cat, a pair of giraffes, and two moons. The inviting jacket leads readers or browsers into a handsome volume introducing more than 100 poems and other writings, including five folktales and 24 full-color art reproductions. Separate indexes of English language and Spanish language titles help readers locate poems, while a third index cites the writers and artists. Biographical information is provided for them and for the translators. The title of this lovely, unique anthology originates in the poem "The Lemon Tree" *(Árbol de limón)* by Jennifer Clement from Mexico City. ". . . Remember / the tree is older than you are / and you might find stories / in its branches." (Age 8–adult)

Nye, Naomi Shihab and Paul B. Janeczko, editors. *I Feel a Little Jumpy Around You: A Book of Her Poems & His Poems Collected in Pairs.* Simon & Schuster, 1996. 256 pages. (0–689–80518–7)

Naomi Shihab Nye and Paul B. Janeczko have paired poems from female and male writers to present readers with language-rich, eye-opening juxtapositions that explore a wide range of experiences and perceptions from the perspective of gender. Sometimes disparate, sometimes in apparent harmony, the selected pairs of poems, from poets across the United States and from other countries, are about aspects of daily life, relationships, and other acts small and large that are the seed and the soil of poem-making. Among the poets included are Francisco X. Alarcón, Lucille Clifton, Rita Dove, Li-Young Lee, Thylias Moss, Nellie Wong, and Daisy Zamora. Separate introductions by Nye and Janeczko, as well as a delightful running commentary between them on the opening and end pages of the text, lend readers insight into things the editors were considering while selecting the poems for this excellent collection which celebrates the union of language, ideas, understanding, and cultures. (Age 13–adult)

Orie, Sandra De Coteau. *Did You Hear Wind Sing Your Name? An Oneida Song of Spring.* Illustrations by Christopher Canyon. Walker, 1995. 32 pages. (0–8027–8350–3) (lib. bdg. 0–8027–8351–1) (pbk. 0–8027–7485–7, 1996)

A lyrical poem from Oneida writer Sandra De Coteau Orie celebrates the coming of spring with keen, gentle questions that invite children to observe and appreciate nature's gifts. "Did you see / the White Birch standing tall among the Darkwoods / and the greening of the Aspen saplings?" Orie, who grew up and still resides in Wisconsin, uses elements of nature significant to her Oneida culture to mark spring's arrival, explaining their meaning in an author's note. Christopher Canyon's rich, detailed paintings are filled with the small wonders of nature, as well as its expansive beauty. (Ages 4–9)

Rogasky, Barbara, selector. *Winter Poems.* Illustrated by Trina Schart Hyman. Scholastic, 1994. 40 pages. (0–590–42872–1)

Twenty-five poems evoke possibilities of the season—its weather, bird-watching, skiing, moon, deer, geese, even its germs, as well as its indoor warmth. It's the warmth that readers of this incomparable anthology can experience, the warmth resulting from reading or hearing superb classic poetry in many voices and forms, and the warmth evoked by the illustrations, which feature a mixed-race (Black/white) child and his loving extended family. Hyman's paintings, reproduced in full color on every page, were rendered in acrylics on illustration board. They contribute significantly to the excellence of the appealing volume. A poem written in Japan in the 10th century, and one by Langston Hughes, are included. (Ages 5–14)

Rosenberg, Liz, editor. *The Invisible Ladder: An Anthology of Contemporary American Poems for Young Readers.* Henry Holt, 1996. 210 pages. (0–8050–3836–1)

Forty contemporary poets write about the connections between their lives and their love of words in brief commentaries that preceed a selected poem or poems by each one. Liz Rosenberg's anthology is notable for the outstanding and diverse selection of poets and poetry it introduces as well as for the thoughtful and inspiring statements by each of the artists on their work. Two black-and-white photographs accompanying each poet's commentary, one showing her or him as a child or young adult and one as he or she looks today, add another unusual element, as does Rosenberg's brief closing chapter in which she launches ideas for creative expression from comments that many of the poets have made about writing. Featured poets of color include Rita Dove, Cornelius Eady, Martín Espada, Nikki Giovanni, Li-Young Lee, Kyoko Mori, and Alice Walker. (Age 12–adult)

Shange, Ntozake. *i live in music.* Paintings by Romare Bearden. Welcome Enterprises/ Stewart, Tabori & Chang, 1994. 32 pages. (1–55670–372–4, out of print)

Twenty-one paintings from the celebrated African-American artist Romare Bearden are perfectly matched with lines from Ntozake Shange's poem "i live in music" to render a tribute to the power of words, images, and sound. The poem is soothing ("sound / falls around me like rain on other folks") and smiling ("i got 15 trumpets where other women got hips") and washed with the many moods that music can evoke. Bearden's art reflects the emotions and poetic images with such startling clarity that it could have been created to exist side by side with Shange's words. A stunning marriage of creative forms that students studying writing, art, or music all will find greatly inspiring. (Age 12–adult).

Shannon, George. *Spring: A Haiku Story.* Translated from the Japanese. Illustrated by Malcah Zeldis. Greenwillow, 1996. 32 pages. (0–688–13888–8)

"Each haiku poem evokes a moment of 'Ah!'—a sensation of seeing something for the first time." George Shannon's helpful introduction gives readers a meaningful entry into the world of haiku poetry and the 14 specific poems that comprise this book. Arranged by Shannon to suggest an early spring walk, the poems, appearing in translation, represent the work of some of the most outstanding Japanese haiku writers stretchng back for several centuries. Malcah Zeldis's vibrant gouache paintings are visual celebrations of revealing moments and quiet observations captured by the poems as the season unfolds. The featured poets include Bakusi, Basho, Chiyo, Issa, Ryunosuke, Shiki, Shumpa, Shun' ichi, and Teitoku. (Ages 8–11)

Slier, Deborah, editor. *Make a Joyful Sound: Poems for Children by African-American Poets.* Illustrated by Cornelius Van Wright and Ying-Hwa Hu. Checkerboard Press (30 Vesey St., New York, NY 10007), 1991. 97 pages. (1–56288–000–4) (0–590–67432–3; Cartwheel/Scholastic, 1996)

A thick volume, generously illustrated, pulls together 75 poems from diverse sources by well-known poets (Lucille Clifton, Countee Cullen, Eloise Greenfield, Langston Hughes), as well as others who rarely appear in children's poetry anthologies (Kali Grosvenor, Nanette Mellage, Useni Eugene Perkins, Quincy Troupe). These poems for young children touch on such topics as family, friends, playing outside, and school, in addition to expressing cultural pride in African-American heritage. The overall effect of this marvelously rich anthology is best expressed by one of the selections by Mari Evans: "Who / can be born black / and not / sing / the wonder of it / the joy / the challenge . . ." (Ages 4–12)

Soto, Gary. *Canto Familiar.* Illustrated by Annika Nelson. Harcourt Brace, 1995. 79 pages. (0–15–200067–4)

Gary Soto offers 25 original poems in a collection that is rich with the sounds and images of Mexican-American culture and brims with experiences of childhood. Little brothers, sarapes, lost eyeglasses, tortillas, dish washing, math tests, and other familiar events and objects are depicted in poems that weave Spanish words, like touchstones, into their fabric. Colorful full-page prints by Annika Nelson accompany some poems. (Ages 9–12)

Soto, Gary. *A Fire in My Hands: A Book of Poems.* Scholastic, 1991. 63 pages. (pbk. 0–590–44579–0, 1992)

In his introduction to this collection of 23 poems, Gary Soto tells his readers that he thinks of his poems as a "working life, by which I mean that my poems are about commonplace, everyday things . . . ." Arranged in chronological order beginning with childhood and moving up through adolescence and young adulthood, the poems celebrate small, significant moments in the life of a working-class Chicano male. Each poem is introduced with a brief anecdote that places it in the context of Soto's life. In a four-page section at the book's end, he answers some of the questions young people have about poetry. (Age 11–adult)

Soto, Gary. *Neighborhood Odes.* Illustrated by David Diaz. Harcourt Brace Jovanovich, 1992. 68 pages. (0–15–256879–4) (pbk. 0–590–47335–2; Scholastic, 1994)

Twenty-one poems reflect pleasures, loves, joys, regrets, and fears experienced growing up in a Chicano neighborhood in California. The poet hones in on the small details of ordinary places (the park, the library) and ordinary things (a sprinkler, Pablo's tennis shoes) with such extraordinary clarity of vision that each ode packs an emotional punch, taking the reader by surprise. The poems are accompanied by striking black-and-white illustrations. (Age 8–adult)

Steele, Susanna and Morag Styles, editors. *Mother Gave a Shout: Poems by Women and Girls.* Illustrated by Jane Ray. U.S. edition: Volcano Press (P.O. Box 270, Volcano, CA 95689), 1991. 126 pages. (0–912078–90–1)

One hundred poems about identity, nature, women's work, dreaming, grandmothers, mothers, and daughters are gathered from a wide range of traditional and contemporary sources, featuring poets such as Maya Angelou, Gwendolyn Brooks, Nikki Giovanni, and Alice Walker. Exquisite black-and-white vignettes reinforce the multicultural focus and enhance the celebratory tone. (Ages 9–13)

Strickland, Dorothy S. and Michael R. Strickland, selectors. *Families: Poems Celebrating the African American Experience.* Illustrated by John Ward. Wordsong/Boyds Mills, 1994. 31 pages. (1–56397–288–3)

Naomi F. Faust writes ". . . Your world's wide open, child. / Walk right in." Children who have the opportunity to see the full-color paintings of families on every page and to hear the poems in this fine picture book collection will feel certain their world is wide open to them. The other poets with one or more works selected by the mother and son who edited this picture-book collection are Arnold Adoff, Gwendolyn Brooks, Lucille Clifton, Julia Fields, E. Alma Flagg, Nikki Giovanni, Eloise Greenfield, Langston Hughes and Lindamichellebaron. (Ages 3–9)

Thomas, Joyce Carol. *Brown Honey in Broomwheat Tea.* Illustrated by Floyd Cooper. HarperCollins, 1993. 32 pages. (0–06–021087–7) (lib. bdg. 0–06–021088–5) (pbk. 0–06–443439–7, 1996)

African-American experience is depicted in 12 original poems that exquisitely express feelings of pride, joy, love, wonder, sorrow, and hope, and delicately extract and magnify moments imbedded in everyday life. "I spring up from mother earth / She clothed me in her own colors / I was nourished by father sun / He glazed the pottery of my skin . . ." begins the affirming opening poem, "Cherish Me." The simplest gestures take on the significance of ritual in "Mama" (". . . She bows to the plant for permission / Prunes a small twig / Carries it like a healing flower / Over and over the rising road . . ."). "Family Tree" mourns losses of the past, while the title poem, speaking of the present, cautions, "There are those who / Have brewed a / Bitter potion for / Children kissed long by the sun." The final offering, "Becoming the Tea," assures that ". . . like the steeping brew / The longer I stand/ The stronger I stay." Floyd Cooper's intimate paintings warmly reflect and extend the theme of the text. Steeped in tones of brown, rust, and gold, they are themselves a celebration of African-American life. (Ages 5–10)

Wong, Janet S. *Good Luck Gold and Other Poems.* Margaret K. McElderry, 1994. 42 pages. (0–689–50617–1)

Poems for young readers draw on the author's experiences as a child of Chinese and Korean ancestry growing up in the United States. Janet Wong writes with respect and fondess for family and culture in some poems, while examining in others the difficulties and pain that children who don't look like white America often endure. Throughout, young readers will be able to identify with the emotions of the experiences, both pleasant and painful, allowing them to make connections and create a meaningful context for the words, whether or not specific cultural references are familiar to them. (Ages 8–10)

NEW EDITIONS OF CLASSIC LITERATURE

Adoff, Arnold, editor. *My Black Me: A Beginning Book of Black Poetry.* Revised edition: Dutton, 1994. 83 pages. (0–525–45216–8) (pbk. 0–14–037443–4; Puffin, 1995)

The compiler's new introduction to the 20th anniversary edition of his important fifty-poem anthology encourages youth to "use these poems for power and love" and to "Stay strong for yourself. Strong for the people." He suggests that the poems are "for *all* sisters and brothers. Of every race. Every open face." The 26 poets represented include Imamu Amiri Baraka, Sam Cornish, Lucille Clifton, Julia Fields, Nikki Giovanni, Langston Hughes, Ray Patterson, and Sonia Sanchez. (Ages 11–16)

Douglass, Frederick. *Escape from Slavery: The Boyhood of Frederick Douglass in His Own Words.* Edited and illustrated by Michael McCurdy. Foreword by Coretta Scott King. Alfred A. Knopf, 1994. 63 pages. (0–679–84652–2) (pbk. 0–679–84651–4, 1994)

This handsomely designed edition is a shortened version of *Narrative of the Life of Frederick Douglass, An American Slave, Written by Himself.* Initially published in Boston by the Anti-Slavery Office in 1845, it was the first of Frederick Douglass's three autobiographies. In this edition, the action and events of the longer work are emphasized for young readers. Although the editor reports separating some of Douglass's paragraphs and chapters for clarity in modern times, he says the author's own words, spelling, and distinctive punctuation were retained. A helpful introduction provides the context for each section. Eleven black-and-white drawings by McCurdy are interspersed among Douglass's inspiring passages. (Ages 11–16)

Hughes, Langston. *The Dream Keeper and Other Poems.* Illustrated by Brian Pinkney. Introduction by Lee Bennett Hopkins. Alfred A. Knopf, 1994. 83 pages. (0–679–84421-X) (lib. bdg. 0–679–94421–4)

This handsome volume features Brian Pinkney's dignified scratchboard artwork accompanying Hughes's 66 poems for youth, 59 of which appeared in an earlier edition. The splendid layout and design, choice of paper, and judicious use of two colors for the text add elegance to this tribute to an important poet who wrote both in dialect and in standard English. (Ages 11–16)

Jiménez, Juan Ramón. *Platero y Yo = Platero and I.* Selected, translated and adapted from the Spanish by Myra Cohn Livingston and Joseph F. Domínguez. Illustrations by Antonio Frasconi. Text ©1957. Translation and illustrations ©1994. Clarion, 1994. 47 pages. (0–685–71523–X)

Designed to introduce today's youth to the winner of the 1956 Nobel Prize for Literature and to introduce a classic known to most children in the Spanish-speaking world, this intriguing volume captures the essence of a place and time: Moguer, an Andalusian village in the South of Spain, in 1914. Readers are invited to consider the universals within a man's specific musings as he travels by donkey, enjoying the festivals and people of the countryside and yet understanding their poverty and loss. Nineteen one-page passages from Jiménez's longer work of 138 chapters appear side-by-side in Spanish and the English translation. The excerpts are illustrated with superb full-color images created in woodcuts and mixed media by Uruguayan-born Antonio Frasconi. (Ages 9–12)

Johnson, James Weldon. *The Creation.* Illustrated by James E. Ransome. Holiday House, 1994. 32 pages. (lib. bdg. 0–8234–1069–2) (pbk. 0–8234–1207–5, 1995)

Ransome's paintings accompanying Johnson's poem alternate between two types of images, one being a contemporary male storyteller under a large shade tree with five African-American children. The other images show some of the landscapes and creatures named in this poem about the beginning of the universe according to a story in *Genesis*. Excerpted from Johnson's poetic sermon *God's Trombones*, this full-color picture book can be an inspiration as well as an introduction to the works of an achiever of the past century. (Ages 4–9)

Johnson, James Weldon. *Lift Ev'ry Voice and Sing.* Illustrated by Jan Spivey Gilchrist. Scholastic, 1995. 32 pages. (0–590–46982–7)

Gilchrist's powerful Afro-centric images offer an emotional match for the classic words of Johnson's famous anthem. Her watercolor paintings suggest a painful history and the pride of heritage while celebrating African-American struggle and survival. The jacket art features children looking forward and up, while the title page offers a personified image of continental Africa, weeping into the ocean. Water becomes a life force in illustrations picturing elders from past centuries next to their descendants today. Hope is offered through images of a rooted tree and liberation by flying. Although the artistic concepts are sophisticated, all family members can appreciate this important $12^{1}/_{4}$ x $9^{1}/_{4}$" book in one or more ways. (Age 3–adult)

Lee, Jeanne M. *The Song of Mu Lan.* Translated from the Chinese. Original calligraphy by Chan Bo Wan. U.S. edition: Front Street, 1995. 32 pages. (1–886910–00–6)

"Click, click. Click, click. / Mu Lan is at her loom. / We no longer hear her weave. / Now we only hear her sigh. / Why does Mu Lan sigh? / Why is Mu Lan sad?" Mu Lan claims she does not sigh and is not sad. Instead, she wishes to take her father's place in response to the Emperor's recent call to arms. She does, dressed as a man. Young readers can always spot the uniformed Mu Lan seated on her white horse in the thick of combat. During ten years of battles, she becomes famous, but she reveals her identity only after returning to her village and family. Lee's watercolor compositions suggest traditional forms and include a contemporary Chinese text. Notes indicate that *The Song of Mu Lan* is thought to be a folk poem that originated during the Northern and Southern Dynasties, 420–589 C.E., and recorded in court anthologies as early as the Tang Dynasty. Versions in Chinese from the Sung and Ming Dynasties are reproduced on the endpages. Children in China still learn this story, which occasionally appears in Chinese operas. (Ages 5–9)

Lester, Julius. *Othello.* Scholastic, 1995. 151 pages. (0–590–41967–6)

A fictionalized version of Shakespeare's drama offers engrossing reading because of its lyrical language and new vision of the classic tragedy. In his reinterpretation of the racial identities of Iago and Emilia, Lester provides a provocative exploration of racism. Lines from the play are incorporated into the novel along with modern English in this eloquent rendering of the story of a Black African general's downfall and the playing out of jealousy, deception, and revenge. (Ages 12–17)

Rollins, Charlemae Hill, compiler. *Christmas Gif': An Anthology of Christmas Poems, Songs, and Stories Written by and about African-Americans.* Illustrated by Ashley Bryan. Revised edition: Morrow, 1993. 106 pages. (0–688–11667–1)

The long-standing tradition of Christmas Gif' and other African-American Christmas practices and writings were detailed three decades ago in the original edition of this classic anthology. From Christian to secular in theme, the assemblage of Christmas stories, poems, memories, spirituals, and recipes reflects a rich cultural heritage. The anthology includes writings by Gwendolyn Brooks, Countee Cullen, Frederick Douglass, Paul Laurence Dunbar, Lorenz Graham, Langston Hughes, Zora Neale Hurston, and Gabriela Mistral. In the introduction, Mrs. Augusta Baker comments on the scarcity of culturally authentic Christmas selections before Librarian Charlemae Hill Rollins collected such material with children and families in her Chicago community in mind. Artist Ashley Bryan provides more than five dozen original black-and-white linoleum prints to illustrate or decorate every page spread, complementing the multiple moods within this elegant and appealing new edition. (All ages)

Tagore, Rabindranath. *Paper Boats.* Illustrated by Grayce Bochak. Caroline House, 1992. 32 pages. (1–878093–12–6)

A child launches paper boats on a string in the hope that someone in a village "in some strange land will find them and know who I am." Full-color paper assemblages offer a strikingly suitable medium to illustrate a selection first published in 1913 within one of Tagore's longer works, *Crescent Moon*. Written by the essayist, poet, and playwright from India who won the Nobel Prize for Literature that year, this quiet edition echoes Tagore's belief that teaching and nature should blend together. (Age 5–adult)

APPENDIX I

Authors and Illustrators of Color

This appendix provides the racial background of some of the people of color who created the books included in this bibliography. While a particular racial background is not necessary for the creation of a children's book on a particular theme or topic, the CCBC often receives frequent requests for this type of information about book creators. For this reason the following listing has been compiled. The information in this appendix is not complete or exhaustive; we were not able to determine this information for all book creators. Errors of any kind are unintentional. The compilers accept responsibility for any mistakes and welcome additions and corrections to this partial listing.

This partial listing cites many of the authors, illustrators, and compilers of books included in this bibliography. Translators, individuals whose works are part of an anthology, or those who wrote a foreword, introduction or similar commentary are not cited below. Individuals who identify themselves as belonging to more than one racial group are cited in more than one list.

African/Afro Caribbean/ African American

Adedjouma, Davida
Angelou, Maya
Barber, Barbara E.
Basquiat, Jean-Michael
Bearden, Romare
Belton, Sandra
Berry, James
Bishop, Rudine Sims
Boyd, Candy Dawson
Brodie, James Michael
Bryan, Ashley
Bryant, Michael
Burden-Patmon, Denise
Burrowes, Adjoa J.
Butler, Jerry
Byard, Carole
Byrd, Samuel
Carter, Gail Gordon
Case, Dianne
Chocolate, Deborah M. Newton
Christie, Gregory
Clay, Wil
Clifton, Lucille
Cooper, Floyd
Cox, Clinton
Crews, Donald
Crews, Nina
Cummings, Pat
Curry, Barbara K.
Curtis, Christopher Paul
Davis, Ossie
Dee, Ruby
DeGross, Monalisa
Dillon, Leo
Douglass, Frederick
Draper, Sharon M.
Ellis, Veronica Freeman
Feelings, Tom
Flournoy, Valerie
Flournoy, Vanessa
Ford, George

Gilchrist, Jan Spivey
Giovanni, Nikki
Goss, Clay
Goss, Lynda
Green, Jonathan
Greenfield, Eloise
Greenfield, Monica
Grimes, Nikki
Guy, Rosa
Hamilton, Virginia
Hanna, Cheryl
Hansen, Joyce
Haskins, James
Higginsen, Vy
Hodge, Merle
Howard, Elizabeth Fitzgerald
Hru, Dakari
Hudson, Cheryl Willis
Hudson, Wade
Hughes, Langston
Igus, Toyomi
Jameson, Marcia
Johnson, Angela
Johnson, Dolores
Johnson, James Weldon
Johnson, Larry
Joplin, Scott
Joseph, Lynn
Joysmith, Brenda
Kim, Jody
Lawrence, Jacob
Lester, Julius
Lucas, Cedric
McKissack, Patricia C.
McKissack, Fredrick, Jr.
McKissack, Fredrick L.
Marshall, Felicia
Massey, Cal
Mathis, Sharon Bell
Medearis, Angela Shelf
Miles, Calvin
Mitchell, Margaree King
Mitchell, Rhonda
Mollel, Tololwa M.

Monceaux, Morgan
Moore, Yvette
Morninghouse, Sundaira
Moss, Thylias
Moutoussamy-Ashe, Jeanne
Myers, Walter Dean
Olaleye, Isaac
Onyefulu, Ifeoma
Parks, Rosa
Patrick, Diane
Pinkney, Andrea Davis
Pinkney, Brian
Pinkney, Gloria Jean
Pinkney, Jerry
Porter, A. P.
Ransome, James E.
Rich, Anna
Ringgold, Faith
Robinson, Aminah Brenda Lynn
Rochelle, Belinda
Rollins, Charlemae Hill
Rosales, Melodye
Ruffins, Reynold
Saint James, Synthia
Sandoval, Dolores
Smalls-Hector, Irene
Smothers, Ethel Footman
Strickland, Dorothy S.
Strickland, Michael R.
Stroud, Bettye
Tate, Eleanora E.
Taylor, Mildred D.
Thomas, Joyce Carol
Turner, Glennette Tilley
Van Wright, Cornelius
Walter, Mildred Pitts
Ward, John
Wells, Daryl
Wesley, Valerie Wilson
Williams, Lorraine
Williams, Sherley Anne
Williams-Garcia, Rita
Woodson, Jacqueline
Wright, Richard

American Indian

Afraid of Hawk, Wanbli Numpa
Allen, Joe
Aguilar, Dugan
Allen, Paula Gunn
Bad Heart Bull, Amos
Begay, Shonto
Braine, Susan
Bruchac, Joseph
Canyon, Christopher
Cooper, Floyd
Dorris, Michael
Echo-Hawk, Roger C.
Echo-Hawk, Walter R.
Fadden, David Kanietakeron
Fadden, John Kahionhes
Hartman, Karen
Hunter, Sally M.
Jacob, Murv
Kakkak, Dale
Keeshig-Tobias, Lenore
Keeshig-Tobias, Polly
King, Sandra
Littlechild, George
Orie, Sandra De Coteau
Peters, Russell M.
Plain, Ferguson
Printup, Erwin Jr.
Regguinti, Gordon
Rendon, Marcie R.
Roessel, Monty
Ross, Gayle
Singer, Beverly R.
Swamp, Chief Jake
Swentzell, Rina
Taylor, C. J.
Whipple, Catherine
Wittstock, Laura
Yamane, Linda
Yerxa, Leo

Asian/Asian Pacific/ Asian American

Balgassi, Haemi
Cha, Chue
Cha, Dia
Cha, Nhia Thao
Chang, Ina
Chinn, Karen
Choi, Sook Nyul
Hamanaka, Sheila
Hayashi, Akiko
Heo, Yumi
Ho, Minfong
Hong, Lily Toy
Hu, Ying-Hwa
Igus, Toyomi
Jordan-Wong, Jennifer
Kim, Helen
Lee, Dom
Lee, Huy Voun
Lee, Jeanne M.
Lee, Marie G.
Mai, Vo-Dinh
Miyake, Yoshi
Mochizuki, Ken
Mori, Kyoko
Namioka, Lensey
Narahashi, Keiko
Nunes, Susan Miho
Pinto, Venantius J.
Russell, Ching Yeung
Saito, Manabu
Say, Allen
Soentpiet, Chris K.
Sogabe, Aki
Suetake, Kunihiro
Sun, Chyng Feng
Tagore, Rabindranath
Tseng, Jean
Tseng, Mou-Sien
Uchida, Yoshiko
Vuong, Lynette Dyer
Wan, Chan Bo
Watkins, Yoko Kawashima
Yang, You
Yen, Clara
Yep, Laurence
Yoshida, Hideo C.
Young, Ed
Yumoto, Kazumi
Zhang, Christopher Zhong-Yuan
Zhensun, Zheng

Latino/Latina

Ada, Alma Flor
Alarcón, Francisco X.
Aldana, Patricia
Ancona, George
Anzaldúa, Gloria
Arroyo, Andrea
Barbot, Daniel
Blanco, Alberto
Brusca, María Cristina
Casilla, Robert
Casteñeda, Omar S.
Cisneros, Sandra
Cofer, Judith Ortiz
Crespo, George
Cruz Martinez, Alejandro
Cubias, Daisy
Delacre, Lulu
Diaz, David
Fuenmayor, Morella
Garay, Luis
González, Lucía
Guevara, Susan
Herrera, Juan Felipe
Jaramillo, Nelly Palacio
Jenkins, Lyll Becerra de
Lechón, Daniel
Lee, Hector Viveros
Lomas Garza, Carmen
Martinez, Victor
Martorell, Antonio
Mohr, Nicholasa
Mora, Francisco X.
Mora, Pat
Morales, Rodolfo
Nodar, Carmen Santiago
Nunes, Lygia Bojunga
Olivera, Fernando
Ordóñez, María Antonia
Orozco, José-Luis
Picó, Fernando
Presilla, Maricel E.
Sánchez, Enrique O.
Smith, Patricia Clark
Soto, Gary
Soto, Gloria
Velasquez, Eric
Vidal, Beatriz
Zubizarreta, Rosalma

APPENDIX II

Ethnic/Cultural Groups

Most of the titles in this bibliography deal with the history, culture, and/or contemporary lives of people of color in the Americas, Africa, and Asia. The following is a list of titles categorized by the nation and ethnic or cultural group represented in the content of each book. Books which depict a variety of racial or ethnic backgrounds are listed as "multiethnic." The page number indicates location of annotated entry.

Australia
Aboriginal
Dreamtime 56
Wandering Girl 58

Africa
Against All Opposition 49
Ajeemah and His Son 25
Captive 49
Great Women in the Struggle 55
Middle Passage 49
Now Is Your Time! 51
Our People 51
Botswana
South and North, East and West 45
Egypt
Quilted Landscape 63
Ethiopia
Day of Delight 36
Fire on the Mountain 44
Pulling the Lion's Tale 44
Quilted Landscape 63
Ghana
Kofi and His Magic 59
Royal Kingdoms of Ghana, Mali, and Songhay 51
Tower to Heaven 41
Mali
Royal Kingdoms of Ghana, Mali, and Songhay 51
South and North, East and West 45
Masai
Lonely Lioness and the Ostrich Chicks 39
Orphan Boy 45
Nigeria
A is for Africa 62
Bitter Bananas 14
Ogbo 62
Story of Lightning & Thunder 40
Igala
Emeka's Gift 62
Yoruba
Singing Man 45
Rwanda
Irrepressible Spirit 65
Sierra Leone
Be Patient, Abdul 63

Songhay
Royal Kingdoms of Ghana, Mali, and Songhay 51
South Africa
92 Queens Road 21
Day Gogo Went to Vote 52
Irrepressible Spirit 65
Ndebele
My Painted House, My Friendly Chicken and Me 59
Sudan
Royal Kingdoms of Ghana, Mali, and Songhay 51

Asia
Bangladesh
Quilted Landscape 63
Burma
Irrepressible Spirit 65
Cambodia
Irrepressible Spirit 65
Little Brother 25
China
First Apple 19
Golden Carp and Other Tales from Vietnam 47
How the Ox Star Fell from Heaven 43
Irrepressible Spirit 65
Maples in the Mist 77
Quilted Landscape 63
Song of Mu Lan 82
Time Is the Longest Distance 76
Why Rat Comes First 47
Young Painter 74
India
Aani and the Tree Huggers 64
In the Heart of the Village 59
In the Street of the Temple Cloth Printers 69
Irrepressible Spirit 65
Little Lama of Tibet 62
Paper Boats 80
Indonesia
South and North, East and West 45
Japan
Aki and the Fox 11
Chibi 18
Friends 24
Girl Who Loved Caterpillars 45

Grandfather's Journey 52
Kodomo 62
Loyal Cat 45
My Brother, My Sister, and I 29
On the Wings of Peace 65
One Bird 28
Red Dragonfly on My Shoulder 76
Sadako 48
Screen of Frogs 42
Shizuko's Daughter 28
Spring 80
Terrible Eek 40
Time Is the Longest Distance 76
Tree of Cranes 36
Korea
Girl-Son 56
Green Frogs 43
Long Season of Rain 27
Peacebound Trains 48
Rabbit's Escape 43
South and North, East and West 45
Year of Impossible Goodbyes 26
Laos (Hmong)
Dia's Story Cloth 69
Whispering Cloth 66
Nepal
Irrepressible Spirit 65
South and North, East and West 45
Philippines
Eagle 7
Quilted Landscape 63
Tajikstan
Irrepressible Spirit 65
Thailand
Dia's Story Cloth 69
Hush! 77
Irrepressible Spirit 65
Quilted Landscape 63
Whispering Cloth 66
Tibet
Little Lama of Tibet 62
Vietnam
Golden Carp and Other Tales from Vietnam 47
Goodbye, Vietnam 24
Hoang Anh 61
Onion Tears 67
Sky Legends of Vietnam 47
South and North, East and West 45
Two Lands, One Heart 63
Why Ducks Sleep on One Leg 41

APPENDIX III

Resources and Awards

You are invited to consult one or several of the professional resources listed here to reflect upon multicultural literature issues and/or to locate books about many cultural groups in the U.S.A. and beyond. Resources were selected with recent book publishing in mind. The resources bearing older copyright dates reflect materials with valuable content for which there is no later replacement.

- The cultural terminology in each annotation represents the language used in each particular reference resource.
- The annotations indicate the emphasis of each resource.
- Phone numbers accompany each citation for convenience in acquiring up-to-date information about availability and cost.
- Most of these publications can be examined or borrowed at/from one or more of the following places:
  1. your school library media center;
  2. your school district professional resource center;
  3. your public library (either locally or via interlibrary loan); or
  4. a nearby college or university library.

This appendix is divided into two sections: General Resources and Multicultural Children's and Young Adult Literature Awards

General Resources

Ada, Alma Flor, Violet J. Harris and Lee Bennett Hopkins, eds. *A Chorus of Cultures: Developing Literacy Through Multicultural Poetry.* Illustrated by Morissa Lipstein, Jane McCreary, Christine McNamara and DJ Simison. Hampton-Brown Books, 1993. 303 pages. (spiral-bound pbk. 1–56334–325–8) Telephone: 800–333–3510.

A practical seasonal poetry anthology organized according to months and days includes a black-and-white camera-ready poem for each day (some written by children) along with brief across-the-curriculum activities; first-person introductions to poets; information on infusing multiculturalism into the classroom (through themes, holidays, authors, activities, classroom visitors, and the physical classroom environment); and material about selecting and presenting poetry. Typical indexes aid in finding poems easily, while unique indexes provide access to poems for ESL instruction, genres of poems and themes in poems. A singular appendix contains explains the Gregorian calendar around which the book is organized as well as other calendars (Chinese, Hebrew, Islamic), includes charts about holidays important in calendars for the years 1993–2003. The Poetry Consultants were Arnold Adoff, Luis Kong, Amy Ling and Barry Wallenstein along with staff from the Cooperative Children's Book Center; Judah L. Magnes Museum; and Network of Educators on the Americas. Members of the Multicultural Review Board were Susan Matoba Adler, María Acosta, Christine Duthie and Ellie Zimet, Darwin L. Henderson, Amadita R. Muñiz, Lupe Soltero-Nava, Doris Seale and Beverly Slapin, and Tou Meksavahn. Cultural and Linguistic Consultants were Yvonne Beamer, Joseph Bruchac, Amy Catlin, Dan Duffy, Kelli Gary, Joan Gilmore, Angele Guerbidjian, Shabbir Mansuri, Kevin Minkoff, Kim-Ahn Nguyen Phan, and Isabel Schon, along with staff from Arab World and Islamic Resources; Bishop Museum; Congregation Beth Israel in Carmel, California, and the Defense Language Institute. Classroom teachers who participated in developing material for the book were Linda Ben-Zvi, Mary Boxley and Claudia Schulte, Mary Carden, Paul D. Christiansen, Debra Green, Carolyn Lau, Paul Nava, Julie Patton, Robin Roy, Barbara VandeCreek, and Deborah Wei. Although it is part of a set of materials about cultures and poetry, this resource book can be purchased separately. (Emphasis: practice, book titles)

Bishop, Rudine Sims, ed., and the Multicultural Booklist Committee of the National Council of Teachers of English. *Kaleidoscope: A Multicultural Booklist for Grades K–8.* National Council of Teachers of English, 1994. 169 pages. (pbk. 0–8141–2543–3) Telephone: 800–369-NCTE.

An annotated bibliography of 400 books carefully selected and recommended by content specialists features books published between 1990 and 1992. U.S. peoples of color are emphasized with some books set in other nations included. The books are organized by genre or theme: Poetry and Verse; The Arts; Ceremonies and Celebrations; People to Know and Places to Go; Concepts and Other Useful Information; Biography-Individuals Who Made a Difference; Immigrants and Immigrations: Coming to America; Folktales, Myths, and Legends: Old and New; Books for the Very Young; Picture Books: Primary and Beyond; Fiction for Middle Readers; Novels for Older Readers; Anthologies: Gatherings of Poems and Stories; and A Potpourri of Resources. The section Award-Winning Books is organized by book, rather than award. Index access is available separately according to author, illustrator, subject and title. A Directory of Publishers is included. In addition to the editor, the content specialists were Rosalinda Barrera, Barbara M. Flores, Patricia Grasty Gaines, Consuelo W. Harris, Violet J. Harris, Mary B.

Howard, Michael Lacapa, Junko Yokota, Terry Li, Sonia Nieto, Ngoc-Diep Nguyen, and Veran Tullie. The editor wrote the seminal work published in 1982 by the National Council of Teachers of English, *Shadow & Substance: Afro-American Experience in Contemporary Children's Fiction;* because *Shadow & Substance* is now out-of-print, look for this important study in libraries. (Emphasis: book titles)

Derman-Sparks, Louise and the A.B.C. Task Force. *Anti-Bias Curriculum: Tools for Empowering Young Children.* National Association for the Education of Young Children, 1989. 149 pages. (pbk. 0–935989–20–X) Telephone: 800–424–2460.

This manual features activities and approaches that can create an inclusive, non-racist environment for young children. Chapter topics include working with 2-year-olds; learning about racial differences and similarities, disabilities, gender identity and cultural differences and similarities; and learning to resist stereotyping and discriminatory behavior. Print and nonprint media and toys are discussed in many of the chapters. A resource bibliography and a stereotypes worksheet are included. The early childhood educators who developed the book were ReGena Booze, Cory Gann, Cheryl Greer, María Gutiérrez, Francois Polifroni, Lissa Peterson Samuel, Mary E.D. Scudder, Marjorie Shore, Bill Sparks, Sharon R. Stine, Kay Taus, and Mae Varon. (Emphasis: theory, issues, practice)

De Usabel, Frances and Jane A. Roeber. *American Indian Resource Manual for Public Libraries.* Wisconsin Department of Public Instruction, 1992. 147 pages. (pbk: no ISBN) Telephone: 800–243–8782.

American Indian educators, subject specialists, and materials specialists from Wisconsin reviewed the print materials and non-print media for children and adults recommended in this publication created for public libraries but equally useful for schools at all levels and in higher education. First-pick books are designated and books from Indian-owned-and-managed publishers are included. The first section includes information about evaluation issues. Although there is a Wisconsin emphasis, most of the information is essential for educators in all parts of the U.S.A. and Canada. Individuals involved in shaping the manual were Joan Airoldi, Janice Beaudin, Algene Carrier, Judy Cornelius, Rose Mary Leaver, Jackie Lohr, Marcia Nagy, Ida Nemec, Linda Orcutt, and Mary Tlusty, while the subject area specialists were Kimberly Blaeser, Dorothy Davids, Ruth Gudinas, Kathleen T. Horning, and David Wrone. (Emphasis: issues, book titles, other materials)

Harris, Violet J, ed. *Using Multiethnic Literature in the K–8 Classroom.* Foreword by Carl A. Grant. Christopher-Gordon, 1997. 300 pages. (pbk. 0–926842–60–9) Telephone: 800–934–8322.

In addition to an important chapter by Daniel D. Hade on Reading Multiculturally, this collection of essays and articles includes: Selecting Literature for a Multicultural Curriculum by Rudine Sims Bishop; Children's Literature Depicting Blacks by the editor; We Have Stories to Tell: Puerto Ricans in Children's Books by Sonia Nieto; one publisher's perspective-Asian Pacific American Children's Literature: Expanding Perceptions about Who Americans Are by Sandra S. Yamate; Mexican American Children's Literature in the 1990s: Toward Authenticity by Rosalinda B. Barrera and Oralia Garza de Cortes; Native Americans in Children's Literature by Debbie Reese and Naomi Caldwell-Wood; an academic analysis-The Baby-sitters Club and Cultural Diversity: or Book #X: Jessi and Claudia Get Lost by Christine A. Jenkins; Creating Good Books for Children: A Black Publisher's Perspective by Cheryl Willis Hudson; and Developing a Multicultural Perspective by Dierdre Glenn-Paul. The accompanying bibliographies vary in type: some document all books discussed in the chapter, while others list recommended children's books. Indexes provide access to subjects, titles, authors, and illustrators. Dr. Harris also edited *Teaching Multicultural Literature in Grades K–8* (Christopher-Gordon, 1992; 0–2926842–13–7). (Emphasis: issues, evaluation, book titles)

Hayden, Carla D., ed. *Venture into Cultures: A Resource Book of Multicultural Materials & Programs.* American Library Association, 1992. 165 pages. (pbk. 0–8389–0579–X) Telephone: ALA, 800–545–2433, press 7 (order dept.)

Eight chapters provide annotated bibliographies and suggestions for library programming and activities from the cultural perspectives of seven groups found in significant numbers in the U.S.A. The recommended books were chosen according to typical critical criteria (distinctive language and appropriate dialogue, style, relevance and potential interest, clear-cut plots, and believable characterizations). Guidelines for book selection also called for an examination of a "quality of reality"; the author's commitment to accuracy; avoidance of the "sensational, enumeration of unusual customs, and the practice of reverse stereotyping"; and sensitivity to a balance between cultural differences and similarities. The chapters are: African-American by Martha R. Ruff; Arabic by Julie Corsaro; Asian by Ginny Lee, Suzanne Lo and Susan Ma; Hispanic by Oralia Garza de Cortes and Louise Yarian Zwick; Jewish by Enid Davis; Native American by Elaine Goley; and Persian by Shala Sohail Ghadrboland. There is a selected bibliography of other resources. The book index is organized according to the seven cultural groups. (Emphasis: book titles, practice, activities)

Helbig, Alethea K. and Agnes Regan Perkins. *This Land Is Our Land: A Guide to Multicultural Literature for Children and Young Adults.* Greenwood Press, 1994. 401 pages. (0–313–28742–2) Telephone: 800–225–5800.

Annotations with plot summaries and critical comments follow entries for 599 recommended books of fiction, oral tradition, and poetry published between 1985 and 1993. The entries include age and grade level designations, (including those for 194 books largely published initially for adult readers and recommended here for grades 9 and/or 10 and older). All of the books were written by Americans or U.S. residents. Four general cultural groups are featured: African Americans, Asian Americans, Hispanic Americans, and Native American Indians. The board of advisors included Lorraine Boomer,

Naomi Caldwell-Wood, Oralia Garza de Cortes, Opal Moore, Jacqueline K. Sasaki, and Karen Patricia Smith. Cross-references within the annotations cite other entries, and additional works by the same author are often noted. In addition to the grade level index, books are indexed by subject, writer, illustrator, and title. (Emphasis: book titles)

Johnson, Dianne. *Telling Tales: The Pedagogy and Promise of African American Literature for Youth.* Greenwood Press, 1990. 166 pages. (0–313–27206–9) Telephone: 800–225–5800.

This important academic analysis is divided into three sections: The Pedagogy and the Promise of Du Bois' *The Brownies' Book* Magazine; The Langston Hughes, Arna Bontemps Legacy: Historical Fiction, Realistic Fiction, and the American Dream; and Attending to Family, Attending to Community: The Picture Books of Lucille Clifton. An appendix cites the Coretta Scott King Award winners and Honor Books between 1970 and 1989. Extensive notes, a bibliography of primary and secondary sources, and an index complete this important scholarly study. (Emphasis: criticism)

Kruse, Ginny Moore and Kathleen T. Horning. *Multicultural Literature for Children and Young Adults, Volume One: 1980–1990.* Third edition. Cooperative Children's Book Center, School of Education, University of Wisconsin–Madison / Wisconsin Department of Public Instruction, 1991. 78 pages. (pbk: no ISBN) Telephone: 800–243–8782.

A companion to *Multicultural Literature for Children and Young Adults, Volume Two: 1991–1996,* the first volume includes selected books by and about American Indians, African-Americans, Asian-Americans, and Latinos along with inclusive or multi-ethnic books. The more than 475 recommended books published for children and young adults between 1980 and 1990 include picture books, fiction, poetry, and biographies. A unique commentary on children's book publishing provides a retrospective context. In addition to a standard index, there are three appendices: authors and artists of color, ethnic/cultural groups, and related resources. (Emphasis: book titles, commentary)

Kuipers, Barbara J. *American Indian Reference Books for Children and Young Adults.* Second edition. Libraries Unlimited, 1995. 230 pages. (1–56308–258–6) Telephone: 800–237–6124.

Kuipers' first study of the multiplicity of published books of information (nonfiction books) "about" American Indians led to this new edition of an important resource book. The valuable 64-page opening section contains a discussion of Kuipers' criteria and evaluation instrument and information about the publishing of American Indian books, including local publishing of tribal culture. A section on incorporating American Indian resource materials into the curriculum includes social sciences, American Indian languages, mathematics, computer literacy, science, fine arts, physical education and health, home economics, English and language arts, and technology. Reference resources can be found in Part One along with selected American Indian bibliographies. Part Two contains an annotated listing of 239 recommended books for children and teenagers organized by Dewey Decimal classification numbers, a list of publishers, and indexes. The overall title may be misleading in that the books are standard trade books, not encyclopedias or other standard reference books. (Emphasis: issues, book titles)

Lindgren, Merri V., ed. *The Multicolored Mirror: Cultural Substance in Literature for Children and Young Adults.* Cooperative Children's Book Center and Highsmith Press, 1991. 195 pages. (pbk. 0–917846–05–2) Telephone: 800–558–2110.

Presenters for some sessions of a conference on multicultural literature held at the University of Wisconsin–Madison in 1991 were invited to expand their speeches for this publication. The chapters include essays on the development of self-esteem in children of color by educator Virginia Henderson; evaluating books by and about African-Americans by critic/educator Rudine Sims Bishop; comments on transcending the form by artist Tom Feelings; remarks about going around the block by photographer George Ancona; a small press publisher's perspective by Cheryl and Wade Hudson; the perspective of an editor from a large children's book publishing house by Phoebe Yeh; writers' perspectives by Elizabeth Fitzgerald Howard and Walter Dean Myers; and an American Indian perspective on 1492 to 1992 by Doris Seale. In-depth content commentaries for 16 varied books for preschoolers, children, and young teenagers were written by Ana Nuncio, June K. Inuzuka, Yai Lee, Henrietta M. Smith, Cathy Caldwell, Dorothy Davids, and Ruth Gudinas. An annotated bibliography of 101 recommended books for children and young adults developed by Kathleen T. Horning and Ginny Moore Kruse cite books published during 1990 and 1991. Brief information is provided about a parallel institute held in conjunction with the conference that week for 20 unpublished writers and artists of color. One of those artists was Michael Bryant, whose illustrations from *Bein' with You This Way* are featured on the cover and inside *Multicultural Literature for Children and Young Adults,* Volume Two). (Emphasis: issues, book titles)

Manna, Anthony L. and Carolyn S. Brodie, eds. *Many Faces, Many Voices: Multicultural Literary Experiences for Youth.* Highsmith Press, 1992. 183 pages. (pbk. 0–917846–12–5) Telephone: 800–558–2110.

Eleven published speeches originating at the Virginia Hamilton Conferences at Kent State University between 1985 and 1992 form the core of this book. The experts representing a variety of ethnic, parallel culture communities include Arnold Adoff, Marcella F. Anderson, Ashley Bryan, Barbara Juster Esbensen, Sheila Hamanaka, Virginia Hamilton, Darwin L. Henderson, Esther Cohen Hexter, Arlene Harris Mitchell, Patricia and Fredrick McKissack, Nicholasa Mohr, and Gary D. Schmidt. A selected, annotated bibliography of multicultural trade books for children and young adults represents favorite books of Virginia Hamilton Advisory Board members. Publisher sources of multicultural materials and information about the Virginia Hamilton Manuscript Collection at Kent State University precede the index. (Emphasis: issues, book titles)

Miller-Lachmann, Lyn, ed. *Our Family Our Friends Our World: An Annotated Guide to Significant Multicultural Books for Children and Teenagers.* R. R. Bowker, 1992. 710 pages. (0–8352–3025–2) Telephone: 800–521–8110.

This annotated bibliographic guide is organized according to a national and multinational organizational structure. Chapters focus upon U.S. cultural groups, Mexico and the Caribbean, Central and South America, and regions of Africa and Asia. Each chapter contains opening commentary and covers books for preschool-grade 3, grades 4–6, grades 7–9, and grades 9–12. The wide scope of the book is both its strength and weakness in that a large number of written-to-formula series books are listed. The authors include Oralia Garza de Cortes, Suzanne Lo, and Michael Afolayan. (Emphasis: book titles)

Naidoo, Beverley. *Through Whose Eyes? Exploring Racism: Reader, Text and Context.* Trentham Books, 1992. 160 pages. (pbk. 0–948080–67–1) Telephone: 0782–745567 (England)

Can a book change one's life? One's perspective? Naidoo's interest in developing a study of attitude change stems from her personal awareness of the limitations of the education available to young whites in South Africa before 1965. In 1988 Naidoo conducted a scholarly study of the teaching of four novels concerning racism to a literature class of 13/14 year old white students in an English secondary school. Her description of the project cites the work of Louise Rosenblatt, Margaret Meek, James Squire, Terry Eagleton and Sara Goodman Zimet, and others. The study involved four novels: *Buddy* by Nigel Hinton; *Friedrich* by Hans Peter Richter; *Roll of Thunder, Hear My Cry* by Mildred Taylor; and *Waiting for the Rain* by Sheila Gordon. Naidoo is the author of three novels for young readers: *Journey to Jo'burg, Chain of Fire* and *No Turning Back.* (Emphasis: theory, practice)

Rochman, Hazel. *Against Borders: Promoting Books for a Multicultural World.* Booklist Publications / ALA Books, 1993. 288 pages. (pbk. 0–8389–0601-X) Telephone: 800–545–2433, press 7 (order dept.)

The book opens with Rochman's essay, An Immigrant's Journey, in which she relates how she and her husband once buried books from their personal library in their backyard. The books were among those banned at the time by the apartheid government of South Africa, a government that had created physical and intellectual barriers and borders between peoples. As a white person who grew to adulthood in South Africa, Rochman knows that "...books matter. The apartheid government with its rigorous censorship was right about that..." The book is organized into two sections: Themes and Resources. The thematic first part is titled Journeys across Cultures and is organized as follows: Journeys across Cultures-The Perilous Journey; The Hero and the Monster; Outsiders; Friends and Enemies; Lovers and Strangers; Family Matters; and Finding the Way Home. Forty-nine indexed themes can be found in those lengthy, compelling book commentaries. The second half of the book is devoted to briefly annotated recommended books arranged under three headings: 1) Racial Oppression (The Holocaust, Apartheid); 2) Ethnic U.S.A. (African Americans, Asian Americans, Jewish Americans, Latinos, Native Americans); and 3) The Widening World. The volume emphasizes recommended books designated for readers in grades six to adulthood, including books published for adults. (Emphasis: themes, book titles)

Rollock, Barbara. *Black Authors & Illustrators of Children's Books: A Biographical Dictionary.* Second edition. Garland Publishing, 1992. 234 pages. (0–8240–7078-X) Telephone: 212–731–7447.

The intention of this dictionary is "to provide those ill-informed or curious about the subject with a single reference volume in which the works of Black authors and artists are recognized in relation to their particular contributions to children's literature." Approximately 500 titles are listed in the index, representing the works of 150 Black book creators. The dictionary is organized alphabetically by last name. Each entry contains a brief biographical sketch and a selective bibliography. Black-and-white photographs of each person are included. Appendices cite publishers, publishers' series, bookstores, and distributors. Award-winning books involving themes and topics concerning the Black experience are cited through 1991. (Emphasis: biographies, book titles)

Schon, Isabel. *The Best of the Latino Heritage: A Guide to the Best Juvenile Books about Latino People and Cultures.* Scarecrow Press, 1997. 285 pages. (0–8108–3221–6) Telephone: 800–462–6420.

This accumulated version of Schon's five earlier volumes includes what she calls "the best titles from my previous books plus additional titles which have come to my attention since their publication." The briefly annotated books are organized according to nation and culture, and there is one general chapter each on Central and Latin America. A chapter on books about Spain is included. Grade level designations range from kindergarten through high school and are intended to be guides rather than prescriptions. Three indexes provide access to the books: author, title, and subject. (Emphasis: book titles)

Slapin, Beverly, Doris Seale and Rosemary Gonzales. *How to Tell the Difference: A Guide to Evaluating Children's Books for Anti-Indian Bias.* Illustrated by John K. Fadden. Oyate, 1996. 32 pages. (pbk. 0–96625175–5–0) Telephone: 510–848–6700.

Dynamic visual and written examples of stereotypes in published children's books are extracted from *Through Indian Eyes* (see below). This brief primer on anti-Indian bias is useful for inservices, higher education, and for teaching older children, as well. (Emphasis: issues, evaluation)

Slapin, Beverly and Doris Seale. *Through Indian Eyes: The Native Experience in Books for Children.* New Society Publishers, 1992. 336 pages. (0–86571–213–1; pbk. 0–86571–212–3) Out of print.

An invaluable collection of articles offers opportunities for outsiders to grow in understanding the characteristics of a reliable book about American Indian themes and topics. The articles include The Bloody Trail of Columbus Day by the editors; Why I'm Not Thankful for Thanksgiving and I Is Not for Indian both by Michael A. Dorris; Notes from an Indian Teacher by Rosemary Gonzales; Thanking the Birds: Native American Upbringing and the Natural World and Storytelling and the Sacred: On the uses of Native American Stories both by Joseph Bruchac; Not Just Entertainment by Lenore Keeshig-Tobias; and Grandmothers of a New World by Beth Brant. A collection of poems by native poets precedes a 124-page sequence of orginial book reviews and commentaries. The reviews unabashedly criticize a large number of frequently taught and used books "about Indians" because they contain misinformation and/or visual images reinforcing stereotypes. The section titled How to Tell The Difference offers dynamic visual and written excerpts from published children's books as examples of typical errors and stereotypes. Two bibliographies of recommended books and a compendium of Native sources of reliable materials complete the volume. An annotated bibliography cites recommended books by Native authors and a selective bibliography without annotations lists additional recommended books. (Emphasis: issues, evaluations, book titles)

Smith, Henrietta M., ed. *The Coretta Scott King Awards Book: From Vision to Reality.* ALA Editions, 1994. 115 pages. (pbk. 0–8389–3441–2) Telephone: ALA, 800–545–2433, press 7 (order dept.) or ext. 4294 (OLOS).

The opening section contains the editor's history of the founding and development of these awards honoring African American authors and illustrators of books published for children and young adults. The Author awards began in 1970, and the Illustrator awards were launched in 1974. Children's and young adult books that won the Coretta Scott King Book Awards or were given Honor Book status for an Author Award are listed chronologically with extensive summaries and commentaries for books published through 1993. A similar section follows regarding the books winning Illustrator award or honor book status. Rudine Sims Bishop's in-depth interviews of artist Pat Cummings and Patricia McKissack add perspective to the significance of the awards. Biographical information and black-and-white photos of the authors and illustrators complete the volume that contains 17 full-color and two black-and-white reproductions of art from some of the honored books. (Emphasis: award history, book titles)

Smith, Karen Patricia, ed. *African-American Voices in Young Adult Literature: Tradition, Transition, Transformation.* Scarecrow Press, 1994. 405 pages. (0–8108–2907-X) Telephone: 800–462–6420.

The editor's intention is for this unique collection to inform teachers, librarians and other professionals working with young people about African-American young adult literature; to dispel "some previously held notions not only about the literature, but about the people of whom it speaks"; and to consider this literature as a genre that is a "living and dynamic entity...that like all literature... holds the promise of exciting discovery." The fourteen chapters are: African-American Young Adult Biography: In Search of the Self by Carol Jones Collins; And Bid *Her* Sing: A White Feminist Reads African-American Female Poets by Kay E. Vandergrift; Feminist Theories and the Voices of Mothers and Daughters in Selected African-American Literature for Young Adults by Hilary Crew; Periodical Literature for African-American Young Adults: A Neglected Resource by Lynn S. Cockett and Janet R. Kleinberg; The New Seed: Depictions of the Middle Class in Recent African-American Young Adult Literature by Dianne Johnson-Feelings; Color and Class: An Exploration of Responses in Four African-American Coming-of-Age Novels by Linda J. Zoppa; Man to Man: Portraits of the Male Adolescent in the Novels of Walter Dean Myers by Dennis Vellucci; Through a Glass Clearly: Positive Images of African-American Fathers in Young Adult Literature by Marcia Baghban; A Chronicle of Family Honor: Balancing Rage and Triumph in the Novels of Mildred D. Taylor by the editor; Children of the Diaspora: Four Novels about the African-Caribbean Journey by Lucille H. Gregory; Virginia Hamilton's Justice Trilogy: Exploring the Frontiers of Consciousness by Millicent Lenz; Octavia E. Butler: New Designs for a Challenging Future by Janice Antczak; Voodoo Visions: Supernatural African Themes in Horror Literature by Cosette Kies; and An Exploratory Study: Using On-Line Databases to Analyze the Dispersion of Contemporary African-American Young Adult Literature by Edna Reid. (Emphasis: analysis)

Williams, Helen E. *Books by African-American Authors and Illustrators for Children and Young Adults.* American Library Association, 1991. 270 pages. (0–8389–0570–6) Telephone: 800–545–2433, press 7 (order dept.)

Williams emphasizes a Black perspective due to her observation of a lack of promotion of Black writers and illustrators within the greater children's and young adult book industry and also because "by and about" bibliographies "provide references to books about Black experiences from other ethnic perspectives, some of which distort, trivialize, or otherwise misrepresent the cultural essence upon which the stories are based." The annotated bibliographies in the first three chapters are organized by age: Very Young Children, Intermediate Readers, and Young Adult Readers. A fourth chapter, Black Illustrators and Their Works, contains descriptions of the style, typical media, "color language," and composition of 53 Black artists. One appendix includes a comprehensive list of book awards and prizes for books by Black authors and illustrators through 1988, and the other provides a glossary of Art Terms used elsewhere in the book. (Emphasis: book titles)

Multicultural Children's and Young Adult Literature Awards

The Américas Awards. Given in recognition of a U.S. picture book and work of fiction published in the previous year in English or Spanish which authentically and engagingly present the experience of individuals in Latin America or the Caribbean, or of Latinos in the United States.
Awarded by: the Consortium of Latin American Studies Programs (CLASP) Committee on Teaching and Outreach, The Center for Latin America, University of Wisconsin–Milwaukee.
First presented: 1993
Timetable: announced annually in March or April
For a complimentary list of the most current winner(s) and commended books: telephone UW–Milwaukee, Center for Latin America 414–229–5986; or write to CLASP, Center for Latin America, UW–Milwaukee, P.O. Box 413, Milwaukee, WI 53201.

Carter G. Woodson Book Awards. Cites the most distinguished social science books for elementary and secondary levels appropriate for young readers which depict ethnicity in the United States. The award is intended "to encourage the writing, publishing, and dissemination of outstanding social studies books for young readers which treat topics related to ethnic minorities and race relations sensitively and accurately."
Awarded by: The National Council for the Social Studies.
First presented: 1974
Timetable: announced at the NCSS annual conference in November
For a complimentary list of current and past winner(s) and honor books: telephone NCSS 202–966–7840 or write to NCSS, 3501 Newark Street, NW, Washington, D.C., 20016–3167.

Coretta Scott King Awards. Three awards honor an African American author of outstanding writing for children or young adults, an African American illustrator for outstanding for children or young adults, and to a promising new African American author or illustrator of a book for children or young adults.
Awarded by: the Coretta Scott King Task Force, Social Responsibilities Round Table, Office for Literacy and Outreach Services (OLOS), American Library Association.
First presented: Author–1970; Illustrator–1974; Genesis Award–1995
Timetable: announced annually in mid-to-late January or early February at the Midwinter Conference of the American Library Association
To purchase seals and/or a quantity of brochures, or to request single complimentary copy of the current full-color brochure listing winner(s) and honor books: telephone ALA 800–545–2433, ext. 4294 (OLOS) for information.

Image Award. Given for an outstanding book written or illustrated for young people by a Black author or artist.
Awarded by: the NAACP (National Association for the Advancement of Colored People)
First presented: 1968
Timetable: each fall five nominees are announced after which one book is honored during the annual Image Awards ceremony
For information: telephone the NAACP 410–358–8900.

Pura Belpré Awards. Given biennially for writing and illustration for outstanding works published in the U.S.A. for children by a Latino author and/or illustrator and which affirm Chicano/Latino/Hispanic ethnicity, heritage, and experiences in the United States.
Awarded by: Two groups within the American Library Association-REFORMA (National Association to Promote Library Services to the Spanish-Speaking, an affiliate of the ALA Office for Literacy and Outreach Services) and ALSC (ALA Association for Library Services to Children)
First presented: 1996
Timetable: announced in alternate years
For winner(s) and honor books: telephone ALA/ALSC 800–545–2433, ext. 2163. Request a complimentary list of winners.

BACKGROUND INFORMATION

About the Cooperative Children's Book Center

Vision Statement

All children and young adults deserve excellent literature which reflects their own experience and encourages them to imagine experiences beyond their own, which satisfies their innate curiosity, and which invites them to dream. We believe such literature fosters a fundamental understanding of themselves and one another, stimulates their creativity, and, most important, enriches their lives.

At the Cooperative Children's Book Center (CCBC), a library of the School of Education at the University of Wisconsin–Madison, we are committed to identifying excellent literature for children and adolescents and bringing this literature to the attention of those adults who have an academic, professional, or career interest in connecting young readers with books. The identity of the Cooperative Children's Book Center is grounded in literature for children and young adults. This is reflected in its collections, its role as a book examination center and research library, and its staff expertise in book arts, book evaluation, multicultural literature, alternative press publishing, and intellectual freedom. Within each of these areas, the CCBC is acknowledged as a leader and a catalyst for change. We are committed to fulfilling these roles by advocating and actively modeling a philosophy that embraces diversity, promotes understanding, and respects the rights of the individual child.

The concepts of access and inclusiveness are vital to the discussion and evaluation of literature for children and young adults. These elements are also central to any discussion of the CCBC itself with regard to its collections and information services. Therefore, the CCBC seeks to expand both the means by which CCBC information is made available and the types of information to which users have access. We will be at the forefront in:

- collecting a wide range of contemporary and historical literature for children and young adults, including literature published by alternative presses and literature created by current and former Wisconsin residents;
- encouraging awareness and discussion of issues essential to literature for children and young adults;
- advocating the First Amendment rights of children and young adults by: 1) providing Wisconsin teachers and librarians with in-depth information on literature whenever a minor's access to books is questioned, and 2) preparing Wisconsin teachers and librarians to respond to challenges to intellectual freedom;
- providing educational support for students in higher education and individuals with an interest in literature for children and young adults;
- shaping electronic means of access to and dissemination of information about literature for children and young adults, within the School of Education, across the university, throughout the state of Wisconsin, and beyond; and
- networking nationally and internationally with colleagues in related fields to create coalitions which recognize the importance of high quality materials for all children and young adults.

The CCBC is a unique and vital gathering place for books, ideas, and expertise. The CCBC vision for the future is the continued pursuit of excellence in literature for children and young adults by whatever resources are available, unwavering commitment to the First Amendment rights of children and young adults, and the establishment of a national and international network to connect all who share the belief that excellent literature can insure a brighter future for the world's children.

Purpose

The Cooperative Children's Book Center (CCBC) of the School of Education at the University of Wisconsin–Madison is a noncirculating examination, study and research children's and young adult literature library for adults. The purposes of the CCBC are: 1) to provide adults with a collection of current, retrospective and historical books for children and young adults; 2) to provide Wisconsin librarians, teachers, students, and others informational and educational services based on the collection; and 3) to support teaching, learning, and research needs related to children's and young adult literature. The CCBC collections are noncirculating.

The CCBC is funded for these purposes by the UW–Madison School of Education and by a contract from the Wisconsin Department of Public Instruction/Division for Libraries and Community Learning. The CCBC was established in 1963.

Collections

The library collection contains review copies of newly published juvenile trade books; recommended children's and young adult trade books; historical children's books; contemporary and historical reference materials related to children's and young adult literature; children' and young adult books by Wisconsin authors and illustrators; and alternative press books for children.

Services

Reference assistance from student employees is available to anyone on a walk-in basis. Reference assistance from a professional librarian/children's literature specialist is available to university students and faculty and Wisconsin librarians and teachers, usually by advance arrangement. Specialized reference assistance and children's literature consultation is also available by mail and phone to the above constituents anywhere in the state. Intellectual freedom information services are available to anyone serving minors in Wisconsin libraries and schools.

Continuing education courses are taught throughout the year by the CCBC professional staff. As possible, the CCBC participates in statewide and regional conferences through the provision of book examination exhibits and/or leadership in scheduled sessions. The CCBC often co-sponsors conferences and workshops with UW–Madison Extension Programs.

The CCBC invites any adult with an academic, professional, or career interest in literature for children and young adults to visit the library. In addition to the collections, children's and young adult literature displays can be seen by walk-in library users. Monthly book discussions and annual book award discussions apply literary standards and book evaluation techniques to new books and are open to any student, faculty member, librarian, teacher, or other interested adult who reads some of the scheduled books in advance.

CCBC-NET is an electronic forum of the CCBC and the School of Education at the University of Wisconsin–Madison designed to encourage awareness and discussion of ideas and issues essential to literature for children and young adults. *CCBC-NET* is a community of individuals with an interest in children's and young adult literature extending across Wisconsin, the nation, North America, and beyond. *CCBC-NET* provides opportunities for spontaneous as well as guided discussions of contemporary children's and young adult literature, including multicultural literature, translated books, outstanding and award-winning books, and equity themes and topics in literature. To find out how to subscribe to *CCBC-NET*, inquire at the CCBC or send e-mail (cdowling@ccbc.soemadison.wisc.edu).

For more information on CCBC resources and services, contact the CCBC at 4290 Helen C. White Hall, 600 N. Park St., Madison, Wisconsin 53706; 608–263–3720 (ccbcinfo@mail.soemadison.wisc.edu). If you write to the CCBC for a current list of program information and/or a list of CCBC publications, please enclose a stamped, self-addressed business-size envelope.

Learn more about the CCBC at http://www.soemadison.wisc.edu/ccbc/ on the World Wide Web. When you visit the "Virtual CCBC" you will find information about new books as well as a listing of small press children's book publishers of color and helpful links to other resources relating to multicultural literature.

About the University of Wisconsin–Madison and the UW–Madison School of Education

Founded in 1849, the University of Wisconsin–Madison is one of the nation's largest and most productive institutions of higher learning. UW–Madison enrolls more than 40,000 students in 150 undergraduate majors, 182 master's, and 125 doctoral degree programs.

As one of the nation's first land-grant universities, UW–Madison maintains a strong research emphasis in agricultural and life sciences. Award-winning research spanning the academic disciplines, however, has earned UW–Madison a place among the world's elite institutions of higher education. UW–Madison graduate and undergraduate programs consistently score high marks in national rankings.

As the flagship campus of the state UW System, UW–Madison has always sought to serve the public with activities that benefit the community, the state and the region.

The University of Wisconsin–Madison has adopted the following non-discrimination statement:

True learning requires free and open debate, civil discourse, and tolerance of many different individuals and ideas. We are preparing students to live and work in a world that speaks with many voices and from many cultures. Tolerance is not only essential to learning, it is an essential to be learned. The University of Wisconsin–Madison is built upon these values and will act vigorously to defend them. We will maintain an environment conducive to teaching and learning that is free from intimidation for all.

In its resolve to create this positive environment, the UW–Madison will ensure compliance with federal and state laws protecting against discrimination. In addition, the UW–Madison has adopted policies that both emphasize these existing protections and supplement them with protections against discrimination that are not available under either federal or state law. Federal and state laws provide separate prohibitions against discrimination that is based on race, color, creed, religion, sex, national origin, or ancestry, age, or disability. State law additionally prohibits discrimination that is based on sexual orientation, arrest or conviction record, marital status, pregnancy, parental status, military status, or veteran status. The application of specific state prohibitions on discrimination may be influenced by an individual's status as an employee or student.

University policies create additional protections that prohibit harassment on the basis of cultural background and ethnicity.

Inquiries concerning this policy may be directed to the appropriate campus admitting or employing unit or to the Equity and Diversity Resource Center, 179-A Bascom Hall, University of Wisconsin–Madison, Madison, Wisconsin 53706–1380 (608–263–2378; TTY 608–263–2473).

For prospective undergraduate students, the UW–Madison Office of Admissions, 750 University Ave., Madison, Wisconsin 53706 USA (608–262–3961) provides academic program information and publications. Details about graduate study are available at: Graduate School Admissions, 228 Bascom Hall, 500 Lincoln Drive, Madison, Wisconsin USA (608–262–3961).

More information about the University and its programs can also be found at http://www.wisc.edu/ on the World Wide Web.

The School of Education at the University of Wisconsin–Madison consistently ranks among the top five educational programs in the nation. A national survey published in 1995 ranked the school number one. The School has traveled far beyond the traditional role of a teacher training institution, yet it continues to fulfill that mission for the state and nation. An important part of the UW–Madison campus instructional program, the School's nine academic departments provide courses to students in a wide variety of disciplines and offer many noninstructional services both on and off campus. Its research programs have worldwide impact. The Cooperative Children's Book Center (CCBC) is a library of the School of Education.

About the Wisconsin Department of Public Instruction's Division for Libraries and Community Learning

The Division for Libraries and Community Learning (DLCL) of the Wisconsin Department of Public Instruction (DPI) is one of four DPI divisions. It is responsible for administering programs relating to public and school library development, interlibrary cooperation and resource sharing, information and instructional technology, early childhood development, family and community involvement in education, and educational information.

The DLCL serves as the state library agency for Wisconsin. The DLCL administers the state aid program for Wisconsin's 17 federated public library systems and the federal Library Services and Construction Act. The DLCL provides interlibrary loan and reference services to the state's libraries and maintains an electronic union catalog of statewide library holdings. The public librarian certification program is administered by the DLCL.

The DLCL collects and disseminates education and library statistics; administers an educational publications program; distributes information to the public and the media relating to education; and administers the federal Learn and Serve America program and the Nutrition Education Training program. The DLCL also administers the data processing and information technology support functions of the Wisconsin Department of Public Instruction.

According to the Wisconsin Department of Public Instruction,

> The DPI does not discriminate on the basis of sex, race, religion, age, national origin, ancestry, creed, pregnancy, marital or parental status, sexual orientation, or mental, emotional or learning disability.

Inquiries concerning this policy should be directed to the Wisconsin Department of Public Instruction, Division for Libraries and Community Learning, P.O. Box 7841, Madison, Wisconsin 53707–7841 USA.

About the Friends of the CCBC, Inc.

This membership organization sponsors programs to develop public appreciation for children's and young adult literature and supports special projects at the CCBC.

Friends receive invitations to events open only to the membership and to other opportunities for adults who share an interest in children's and young adult literature. Members receive a membership newsletter with children's and young adult literature information as well as advance announcements about CCBC publications and information services.

The Friends provide volunteer assistance at the CCBC. Friends also provide volunteer service on behalf of the CCBC, such as promotion and distribution of selected CCBC and Friends publications.

Annual membership benefits include a copy of *CCBC Choices*, an annual publication of recommended books of the year that is funded by the Friends of the CCBC, Inc.

Membership is open to all. The membership year is January through December. Dues paid after October 1 each year apply to membership for the next year. Membership dues are tax deductible to the fullest extent of the law. Individual memberships are: personal–$18; sustaining: $30; supporting: $50; patron: $100; and student: $9. Group memberships are: honor (2–5 individuals): $75; award (6–10 individuals): $150; distinguished (11–15 individuals): $250. To join the Friends, send a check payable to Friends of the CCBC, Inc., to: Treasurer, Friends of the CCBC, Inc., Box 5288, Madison, WI 53705–0288 USA.

About the Compilers

Kathleen T. Horning is a librarian and coordinator of Special Collections at the Cooperative Children's Book Center of the School of Education at the University of Wisconsin–Madison. She is the author of *From Cover to Cover: Evaluating and Reviewing Children's Books* (HarperCollins, 1997). She edited *Alternative Press Publishers of Children's Books: A Directory* and, with Ginny Moore Kruse, she co-authored *Multicultural Literature for Children and Young Adults, Volume One: 1980–1990*. She was also a contributor to *The Multicolored Mirror: Cultural Substance in Literature for Children and Young Adults*. Katy chaired ALA/ALSC's 1995 John Newbery Committee, the 1997 ALA/ALSC Mildred Batchelder Award Committee, and served on ALA/ALSC's Notable Children's Books Committee and an earlier Newbery Award Committee. She chaired USBBY's Hans Christian Andersen Award Committee which selected U.S. nominees for the international award in 1992. She served on the ALA/SRRT Coretta Scott King Award Committee, and as chair of ALA/ALSC's first Committee on Social Issues in Relationship to Materials and Services for Children she provided leadership in developing a recommended list of multicultural literature. She was a children's librarian at Madison Public Library between 1989 and 1997. She is a member of the 1997–99 Américas Award jury. Katy frequently lectures to librarians and teachers on issues in evaluating literature for children and young adults. She has a B.A. in Linguistics and a Master's Degree in Library and Information Studies, both from the University of Wisconsin–Madison.

Ginny Moore Kruse is director of the Cooperative Children's Book Center of the School of Education at the University of Wisconsin–Madison and a teacher of undergraduate children's literature and adult continuing education courses on and off campus and by means of distance learning. She is a former public school teacher, school librarian, and public librarian. Ginny founded the award-winning CCBC Intellectual Freedom Information Services. She has chaired or served on many national children's literature award and distinction committees including the John Newbery, Randolph Caldecott, Mildred L. Batchelder, May Hill Arbuthnot, Laura Ingalls Wilder, Coretta Scott King, Boston Globe-Horn Book, Jane Addams, and Teachers' Choices committees. She chaired the *Book Links* Editorial Advisory Board and served on the Freedom to Read Foundation Board, the ALA Intellectual Freedom Committee, and the USBBY Board. Ginny is co-author with Katy of *Multicultural Literature for Children and Young Adults, Volume One: 1980–1990* and a contributor to *The Multicolored Mirror: Cultural Substance in Literature for Children and Young Adults.* During 1996 Ginny received four formal acknowledgments of her professional leadership: Award of Excellence (Wisconsin Educational Media Association), Alumna of the Year Award (School of Library and Information Studies, UW–Madison), Distinguished Service Award (Association for Library Service to Children, ALA), and the Intellectual Freedom Award (Wisconsin Library Association-SIRS). In 1997, she was the recipient of the ALA/AASL-SIRS Intellectual Freedom Award and the Hope S. Dean Memorial Award (Foundation for Children's Books). Ginny has a B.S. Degree in Education from UW–Oshkosh and a Master's Degree in Library Science from the University of Wisconsin–Madison.

Megan Schliesman is a librarian and administrator of the Cooperative Children's Book Center of the School of Education at the University of Wisconsin–Madison. With Ginny and Katy, Megan has co-authored the annual publication *CCBC Choices* since 1993. Megan compiled the bibliography *Poetry for All Seasons and Many Reasons: Selected Books for Children and Young Adults* (CCBC, 1996). She currently coordinates the CCBC's annual compilation of books by Wisconsin authors and illustrators and books about Wisconsin, and edits the bi-annual *CCBC Resource List for Appearances by Wisconsin Book Creators*. With Ginny and Katy, she co-teaches Educational Telecommunications Network (ETN) continuing education courses for librarians and teachers across the state, and she is an active member of the American Library Association. Megan has worked as a writer and editor on several publications in the Madison area and continues this work in various capacities outside the CCBC. Megan has a B.A. degree in English from UW–Whitewater and a Master's Degree in Library and Information Studies from the University of Wisconsin–Madison.

Tana Elias is a librarian at the Meadowridge Branch of the Madison Public Library and a freelance researcher and indexer. Tana created the index for *Multicultural Literature for Children and Young Adults, Volume Two.* Previously she created the index for *CCBC Choices* (1996, 1995 and 1994). Tana also compiled *Children's Books by Wisconsin Authors and Illustrators and Children's Books about Wisconsin: An Identification Record of Titles Published in 1992* (CCBC, 1993). Tana currently sits on the Board of Directors of the Friends of the CCBC, Inc., and she reviews books for *School Library Journal.* Tana has a B.A. in History from Hamline University and a Master's Degree in Library and Information Studies from the University of Wisconsin–Madison.

INDEX

The following index incorporates names of book creators, book titles, and partial subject access to all the titles listed in *Multicultural Literature for Children and Young Adults, Volume Two.*

Entries are arranged in alphabetical order, with initials appearing first and "Mc" or "Mac" filed before "Maa."

Book titles appear in CAPITAL LETTERS, subjects referring to book content appear in **bold type**, and page numbers referring to an annotation appear in **bold type**. Biographical and autobiographical references are listed under the individual's name. Book creators or titles mentioned more than once on a page have only one page reference listed for that page.

F

Fadden, David Kanietakeron **40**
Fadden, John Kahionhes **40**,54, **94**
FAITH RINGGOLD **73**
Fall see **Autumn**
Falwell, Cathryn **16**
FAMILIES **80**
Families see also **Divorce, Interracial Families, Stepparents** and names of family relationships
Back Home 15
Baseball Saved Us 51
Bear E. Bear 17
Big Meeting 38
Billy and Belle 9
Bineshiinh Dibaajmowin 67
Blessing in Disguise 29
Calling the Doves 11
Celebrating Kwanzaa 34
Celebrating the Hero 26
Christmas in the Big House, Christmas in the Quarters 50
Come Home with Me 61
Daddy and Me 67
Dia's Story Cloth 69
Donavan's Word Jar 19
Down in the Piney Woods 22
Families 80
Fast Talk on a Slow Track 29
First Pink Light 10
Flower Garden 3
For the Life of Laetitia 26
Forever Family 59
From the Notebooks of Melanin Sun 30
Front Porch Stories at the One-Room School 23
Gingerbread Days 37
Glory Field 28
Going Home 32
Good Luck Gold and Other Poems 81
Goodbye, Vietnam 24
Grab Hands and Run 23
Hairs 8
Happy Adoption Day 35
Hard to Be Six 7
Hoang Anh 61
Home Field 17
How You Were Born 67
How My Family Lives in America 61
In for Winter, Out for Spring 75
In My Family 72
Island Like You 26
Jamal's Busy Day 12
Jesse 29
Just Like Martin 22
Kodomo 62
Kwanzaa (Walter) 37
Leaving Morning 13
Like Sisters on the Homefront 30
My Brother, My Sister, and I 29
My First Kwanzaa Book 32
Nate's Treasure 17
Night on Neighborhood Street 77
On the Day I Was Born 8
One Bird 28
One of Three 13

Other Side 61
Pablo's Tree 35
Parrot in the Oven 27
Plain City 22
Rite of Passage 30
Shizuko's Daughter 28
Slam! 28
So Loud a Silence 27
Sofie's Role 34
Starry Night 37
Stealing Home 23
Sweet Baby Coming 4
Tonight, by Sea 23
Two Lands, One Heart 63
Two Mrs. Gibsons 12
Voices from the Fields 59
Visit to Amy-Claire 13
Watsons Go to Birmingham—1963 21
Weaving a California Tradition 74
Well 23
Where Does the Trail Lead? 7
Whispering Cloth 66
Winter Poems 79
Winter Wood 37
Working Cotton 53
Year of Impossible Goodbyes 26
FAMILY PICTURES = CUADROS DE FAMILIA 72
Farming see also **Farms, Migrant Farmworkers, Sharecropping**
Bread Is for Eating 70
Drylongso 19
Sacred Harvest 63
Farms see also **Farming, Ranches**
Bigmama's 8
Home Field 17
Tanya's Reunion 9
FAST TALK ON A SLOW TRACK 29
Fathers see also **Families, Mothers, Stepparents**
Ahyoka and the Talking Leaves 52
Ajeemah and His Son 25
Carousel 9
Daddy and I... 3
Father's Rubber Shoes 11
Good Morning Baby 4
Home Field 17
How Many Stars in the Sky? 11
I Hadn't Meant to Tell You This 24
Joshua's Night Whispers 5
Nate's Treasure 17
Papa Tells Chita a Story 12
Plain City 22
Sacred Harvest 63
Save My Rainforest 66
Somewhere in the Darkness 29
Starry Night 37
Taxi! Taxi! 8
Winter Wood 37
FATHER'S RUBBER SHOES **11**
Feelings, Tom 2,**49**,65,**76**
Feelings, Tom
Talking with Artists, Volume 1 69
FELITA 56
FENCE AWAY FROM FREEDOM **49**
Field, Dorothy **69**
Fields, Julia 80,81

Fiesta de los Reyes Magos see **Three Kings Day**
FIESTA U.S.A. **31**
FINDING MY VOICE 27
FIRE IN MY HANDS **80**
FIRE ON THE MOUNTAIN **44**
FIREFLIES FOR NATHAN **14**
FIRST APPLE **19**
FIRST PINK LIGHT **10**
Fishing
Go Fish 20
Million Fish...More or Less 13
Nanabosho, Soaring Eagle, and the Great Sturgeon 45
Flagg, E. Alma 80
Fleming, Denise **3**
Flournoy, Valerie **9**,33
Flournoy, Vanessa 33
FLOWER GARDEN **3**
FOCUS **74**
Football
Red Dog, Blue Fly 78
FOR THE LIFE OF LAETITIA **26**
Ford, George **4**,12
FOREVER FAMILY **59**
Fortune, Amos 73
FOUR SEASONS OF CORN **34**
Foster, Stephen 73
Fradin, Dennis Brindell **54**
Frank, Mary
Visions 73
Frasconi, Antonio **82**
Fraunces, Phoebe
Tommy Traveler in the World of Black History 49
FREDERICK DOUGLASS **55**
FREE TO DREAM **56**
Freedman, Russell **54**
Freedom Fighters see also **United States Civil Rights Movement**
Great Women in the Struggle 55
FREEDOM SONGS **28**
FREEDOM'S CHILDREN **50**
Freeman, Linda **73**
FREIGHT TRAIN **8**
FRIDA KAHLO **73**
FRIENDS (Yumoto) **24**
FRIENDS (Guy) 30
Friends of the CCBC, Inc. 99
Friendship see also **Interracial Friendship**
Be Bop-A-Do-Walk! 10
Big Friend, Little Friend 3
Billy the Great 10
Bracelet 53
Crosby 11
Elijah's Angel 36
Friends 24
Hooray, A Piñata! 34
I Hadn't Meant to Tell You This 24
Koya Delaney and the Good Girl Blues 22
Little White Cabin 15
Maizon at Blue Hill 24
Margaret and Margarita 15
May'naise Sandwiches & Sunshine Tea 8
Meet Danitra Brown 77
My Best Friend 4
My Doll, Keisha 3
My Friend the Painter 66